"If we do not honor our past we lose our roots.

If we destroy our roots we can not grow."

— *Friedenreich Hundertwasser*

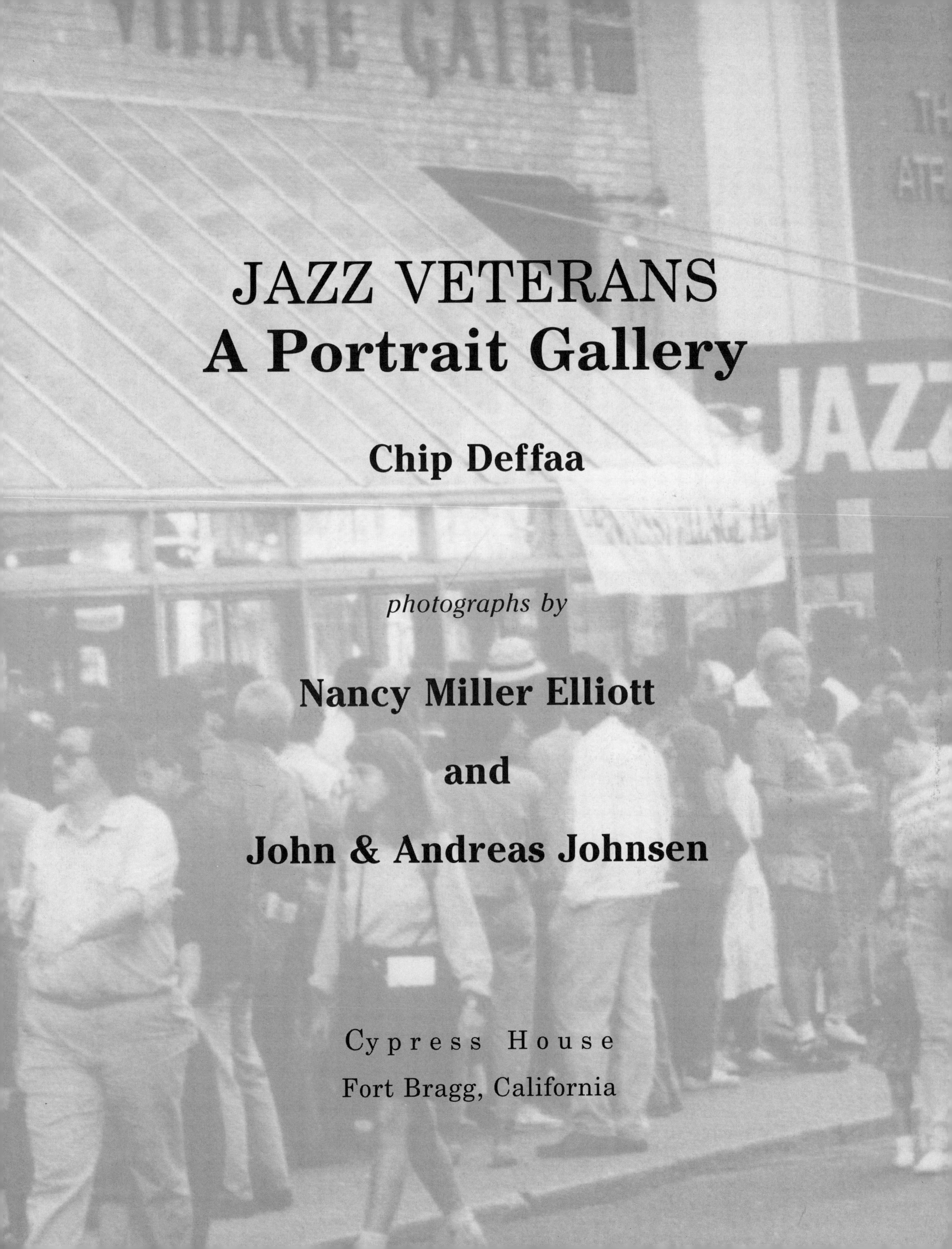

JAZZ VETERANS
A Portrait Gallery

Chip Deffaa

photographs by

Nancy Miller Elliott

and

John & Andreas Johnsen

Cypress House
Fort Bragg, California

JAZZ VETERANS: A Portrait Gallery by Chip Deffaa
Photographs by Nancy Miller Elliott and John & Andreas Johnsen

Cypress House Press
155 Cypress Street
Fort Bragg, CA 95437

cover photos

1: Illinois Jacquet, *Andreas Johnsen*

2: Billie Holiday, *Nancy Miller Elliott*

3: Chet Baker, *Andreas Johnsen*

4: Carmen McRae, *Nancy Miller Elliott*

5: Lionel Hampton, *Andreas Johnsen*

6: Doc Cheatham, *Nancy Miller Elliott*

Cover design by Mark Gatter

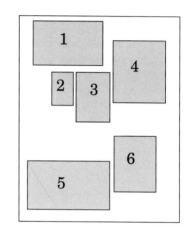

Library of Congress Cataloging-in-Publication Data

Deffaa, Chip, 1951–
    Jazz veterans : a portrait gallery / text by Chip Deffaa ;
photographs by Nancy Miller Elliott and John & Andreas Johnsen.
    p.   cm.
    Includes biographical references and index.
    LCCN: 95-83082
    ISBN: 1-879384-28-0

    1. Jazz musicians — United States — Biography.   2. Jazz musicians — United States —
Pictorial works.   I. Title.

ML385.D44 1996   781.65'092'273
                                                   QB195-20743

Printed by McNaughton & Gunn, Inc.
Saline, MI

Manufactured in the USA

First edition

9 7 5 3 1 2 4 6 8 10

This book is for

V. A. Musetto
— C. D.

Wilbur Clayton
— N. M. E.

Thelonious Monk
— J. R. J.

and Claudia
— A. J.

The Players

𝄞

INTRODUCTION .... *ix*

JABBO SMITH 3

WILLIE "THE LION" SMITH 5

WILD BILL DAVISON 7

SAMMY PRICE 8

DOC CHEATHAM & PHIL SCHAAP 9

JOHNNY LETMAN 14

BENNY GOODMAN 15

FLETCHER HENDERSON 18

COLEMAN HAWKINS 20

BENNY CARTER 22

BENNY WATERS 25

BENNY MORTON 27

SANDY WILLIAMS 29

ELLA FITZGERALD 31

FRANKIE MANNING & NORMA MILLER 36

LIONEL HAMPTON & PASTOR JOHN GARCIA GENSEL 39

GEORGE T. SIMON & FRIENDS 47

ARTIE SHAW 49

MAXINE SULLIVAN & STUFF SMITH 51

JONAH JONES 53

JOE BUSHKIN 54

SY OLIVER 56

CHARLIE SHAVERS 58

EDDIE BAREFIELD 61

COUNT BASIE 63

LESTER YOUNG 66

BILLIE HOLIDAY 67

BILLIE HOLIDAY'S TWO BEST-LOOKING MEN 69

RAM RAMIREZ 71

FREDDIE GREEN 72

JO JONES 73

CLAUDE "FIDDLER" WILLIAMS & LINDA FENNIMORE 75

BIG ED LEWIS 77

HARRY "SWEETS" EDISON 79

EARLE WARREN & BUDDY TATE 81

CHUCK WILSON WITH EARLE WARREN 85

VIC DICKENSON 87

JOE NEWMAN 88

PAUL QUINICHETTE 89

JOE WILLIAMS 90

EDDIE JONES 92

BENNY POWELL 94

NAT PIERCE 96

FRANK WESS, FRANK FOSTER 98

GROVER MITCHELL 100

BUCK CLAYTON, JOHN HAMMOND, & WILLARD ALEXANDER 101

BUCK CLAYTON'S SWING BAND AT THE CAT CLUB 103

SWING DANCING 105

ILLINOIS JACQUET 107

DUKE ELLINGTON 108

COOTIE WILLIAMS 110

BEN WEBSTER 112

PAUL GONSALVES 115

HAROLD ASHBY 116

DUKE ELLINGTON & ELLA FITZGERALD 118

LOUIE BELLSON 119

MERCER ELLINGTON 121

CLARK TERRY 124

LOUIS ARMSTRONG 126

PERCY & WILLIE HUMPHREY 128

ARVELL SHAW 131

ARCHIE JOHNSON 133

ROY ELDRIDGE 135

DIZZY GILLESPIE 136

CHARLIE PARKER 138

DORIS PARKER 140

THELONIOUS MONK 142

CHARLIE ROUSE 144

TOMMY POTTER 147

KENNY KERSEY 149

BIG NICK NICHOLAS 151

MAX ROACH 153

TAL FARLOW 156

MILES DAVIS 158

MORE MILES 163

DUKE JORDAN 167

SHEILA JORDAN 169

CARMEN MCRAE 171

SARAH VAUGHAN 174

BILLY ECKSTINE 177

ABBEY LINCOLN 179

BETTY CARTER 180

JON HENDRICKS 183

BOBBY SHORT 184

ELLIS LARKINS 187

MARIAN MCPARTLAND & JIMMY MCPARTLAND 189

JOHN BUNCH 192

ROMANO MUSSOLINI 193

JOHN LEWIS 196

RUBY BRAFF & DICK HYMAN 198

TOMMY FLANAGAN 200

MAX & LORRAINE GORDON 203

MEL LEWIS & DENNIS MACKREL 206

TOSHIKO AKIYOSHI 208

STAN GETZ 210

CHET BAKER 213

DIZZY GILLESPIE 215

ART BLAKEY 219

JEAN BACH 222

TWO BROTHERS NAMED LEE 224

JOHNNY GRIFFIN 226

ORNETTE COLEMAN 229

SONNY ROLLINS 231

BUCK CLAYTON & WYNTON MARSALIS 235

AFTERTHOUGHTS 237

BIBLIOGRAPHY 242

ACKNOWLEDGEMENTS 244

ABOUT THE COLLABORATORS 248

CREDITS 249

INDEX 251

𝄞

INTRODUCTION

This book portrays, via photographs and words, a diverse array of people in the jazz world. All were born at least 65 years ago. In most fields of endeavor today, 65 is the standard retirement age. But jazz musicians tend to keep at their craft as long as they can. Those veterans covered in this book who are still alive are (with very few exceptions) still active.

The photos are by Nancy Miller Elliott of New York City and John and Andreas Johnsen of Copenhagen — three of my favorite jazz photographers — and their work tends to be complementary. While they are all passionate jazz devotees, Elliott mostly shoots musicians offstage; the Johnsens (father and son) more often shoot them onstage.

Elliott wants to give us a feeling for overall personalities — the artists as people, not just performers. The Johnsens strive to document inspired players in action. (John Johnsen believes "you can catch the personality of a musician if you can catch the way he's doing an improvisation.")

Ideally, Elliott likes to know the musician well as a person before taking a photograph. Ideally, the Johnsens like to know the musician's work.

Besides photographing jazz musicians, Elliott has taken and exhibited highly praised, moving photos of homeless people she met through volunteer work at soup kitchens. Her shots of the homeless have been exhibited in venues ranging from commercial Soho galleries to the Cathedral of St. John the Divine. John Johnsen's other love, besides jazz photography, is dance photography, and he has captured many major dancers in action. Besides jazz, Andreas Johnsen loves covering the hip-hop scene — rap musicians and graffiti artists. He has also produced and marketed a documentary on graffiti art.

Both Elliott and the Johnsens, like so many of the jazz greats they have photographed, are essentially self-taught artists.

Elliott began checking out Harlem jazz clubs as a teenager some 40 years ago. By 1958, she was assisting with the production of "Art Ford's Jazz Party," a TV series on Channel 13, helping select musicians for the show and getting them to the Newark studio. The first two musicians she met through the show were jazz royalty: Billie Holiday and Lester Young. She took their photos — an auspicious beginning to her career — along with photos of Buck Clayton and other notables. Eventually she became Clayton's manager and intimate friend; he, in turn, encouraged her photography.

One day Clayton gave Elliott a present: a box containing a terrific assortment of cameras, lenses, and other parts, which he had bought from a man on the street in New York without asking any indelicate questions like: "Could this merchandise be hot?" Elliott quickly put the equipment to good use. She went to the homes, in Harlem and elsewhere, of musicians whose work she had admired, and asked if she could take their portraits. Over the years Elliott photographed many of the valued contributors to the jazz tradition, including some who had rarely if ever been photographed before and have since died. She has in this way made a significant contribution to documenting jazz history through photos.

Today, Elliott is a fixture in the New York jazz community (and New York is, of course, the jazz capital of the world). Because she is frequently present where musicians may be gathered — clubs and concert halls, recording studios, awards ceremonies, parties, memorial services, and so on — and because she has come to know so many so well over the years, she can take candid shots without really being noticed, without being perceived as intrusive, the way an outsider would be. Her best shots are marked by a kind of "inside" quality. And Elliott's rather accepting, tolerant personal manner encourages her subjects to drop their masks and let her catch them as they are.

Her jazz photos have been seen in *The New York Times*, *The Daily News*, and *The Village Voice*, as well as on assorted album covers — and NBC-TV's "The Cosby Mysteries." Her photos hang on the walls of the world's oldest and best-known jazz club, the Village Vanguard. Other photos are in the permanent collections at Lincoln Center and the Institute of Jazz Studies. Elliott is also a member of the National Academy of Recording Arts and Sciences (which gives out the Grammy Awards).

Although Elliott's photos have appeared in other people's books — including a few of my own — this is the first widely distributed book to really *feature* her photos. I enjoyed going through Elliott's trove of prints. Her photos provide so valuable a record of a certain scene, they must be preserved.

John Rosforth Johnsen's photos have been exhibited at the Copenhagen Museum of Decorative Art, the Stockholm Opera, the Georges Pompidou Center in Paris, and the Kennedy Center for the Performing Arts in Washington, D.C., among other venues. Several books of his photographs have been published in Denmark. Postcards bearing his jazz shots have sold for years in both the United States and Europe. His work is represented in the famed Schomburg Center for Research in Black Culture, in Harlem. He first became interested in photography as a boy of ten when he was given a basic Agfa camera. He got hooked on jazz as a teenager some 30-odd years ago, when a friend began taking him to Copenhagen jazz clubs. (And Copenhagen is, along with Paris — where Johnsen also lived for awhile — one of the two major jazz capitals of Europe.) He has photographed musicians in Europe, North America, and Japan.

Johnsen says of his jazz photography: "It's no fun for me to go someplace and take pictures right away. I like it if I know the music before-

hand. If not, I will watch two sets and only begin taking pictures in the third set. I'm not a guy who just takes pictures. I listen to the music, and see what mood that brings to me, and what I feel, and what I hear, and then I take pictures.

"Jazz is so expressive," he muses. He almost always has jazz playing while he works at home, whether he is photographing subjects or developing prints. "There are jazz records that convey every mood. People who know me well are able to tell what mood I'm in by listening to what I play."

John Johnsen's home is in the very heart of Copenhagen — so close to the important jazz clubs, in fact, that early in his career he regularly took his young sons, Andreas and Sune, to clubs with him. After a set or two, he'd walk his sons home and put them to bed, and then walk back to the club to hear more music. Not surprisingly, both of his now-grown sons share his love for jazz today.

Andreas Johnsen, who inherited his father's sensitive eye for photography, has been carrying on in his father's field — sometimes working with his father, more often these days working by himself. He got started quite young. One book on Chet Baker, published in Germany, includes a portrait of Baker which Andreas took when he was just 14 years old. Multi-lingual and widely traveled, he has shot musicians in Berlin, Paris, Geneva, Stockholm, Amsterdam, Berne, Vienna, New Orleans, New York, and, of course, Copenhagen, where he's contributed to leading newspapers and magazines. He also has the adventurous spirit, drive, and willingness to take chances that one finds in the best jazz artists. If there's someone he wants to shoot or an event he wants to cover, he'll find a way to get there even if his funds are low at the time. He thinks nothing of hitchhiking across Europe, and has a real genius for finding great, inexpensive places to stay. (Like the too-good-to-be-true mid-Manhattan apartment he sublet for months from a savvy jazz musicians' manager. He realized it *was* too good to be true the day the manager climbed the fire escape and held a sign up to his window saying: "Do not leave the apartment. There's a city inspector in the hall-way." The building was not supposed to be oc-cupied!) The main thing is, he *gets* the photos he wants; he doesn't just dream of doing so. His jazz pictures have appeared on albums and post-cards, as well as in publications ranging from *The Amsterdam News* to *The New York Post* to *JazzTimes*. His vivid "live" performance shots are regularly featured in Europe's venerable *Crescendo and Jazz Music* magazine. Johnsen also writes articles on jazz and hip-hop, and he has appeared as an actor on Danish television, although he insists he strongly prefers being be-hind the camera. In 1995 he was in Krakow, Poland, working with his father on a photo ex-hibition.

Because jazz originated in America and is generally thought of as an American art form, I suppose a few Americans might wonder if some-one from another country can properly cover jazz. The truth is, jazz long ago stopped being the exclusive property of Americans. Many American jazzmen actually find they can make better money playing abroad than at home. Good jazz recordings often have wide international appeal. (Every time I put on my CDs of *Miles Davis: A Tribute to Jack Johnson* and *Ben Webster Plays Duke Ellington* I'm mentally transported back to Copenhagen and remem-ber awakening on different mornings to the sounds of Andreas Johnsen playing his copy of that Miles Davis CD, or John Johnsen playing his copy of that Ben Webster CD.)

Many of the best known and most highly re-spected authorities on jazz actually were born in countries other than the U.S. Leading jazz historians and critics Stanley Dance, John Chilton, and the late Leonard Feather were born in England. Gene Lees was born in Canada. Dan Morgenstern was born in Germany, and resided for years in Denmark before emigrating to the U.S. Acclaimed jazz photographer Ole Brask not only lived in Denmark, but for a while lived on the very same street in Copenhagen as John and Andreas Johnsen! Brask and Morgenstern, in-cidentally, collaborated years ago to produce a masterly volume combining jazz photos and text, *Jazz People*.

We don't claim that *Jazz Veterans* covers the entire jazz world. No one book could do that, and here — with a feeling for history — the empha-sis is on older, seasoned (and in some cases over-looked) players. *Jazz Veterans* is the first jazz photo book devoted exclusively to the older art-ists. It includes a number of musicians depicted in no other book.

I enjoy telling stories about the various musi-cians I've had the pleasure to hear. As *The New York Post*'s jazz critic I think I've got one of the best jobs on earth. My supportive editors — V. A. Musetto and Matt Diebel — have given me tremendous freedom to follow my enthusiasms. Over the years, I've had the privilege to review and/or interview virtually everyone of signifi-cance active on the jazz scene. I really feel blessed: it's a terrific way to make a living.

The photos in this book would, in most cases, "work" without any text. You'd respond, I'm sure, to the memorable shots of Jabbo Smith, Duke Jordan, Miles Davis, Sandy Williams, Joe Bushkin, Duke Ellington, Harold Ashby, and Chet Baker, for example, even if you didn't know who those musicians were. But knowing a bit about who they are does help. And certainly they all deserve recognition. Rather than simply opt-ing for the kind of perfunctory text generally found in jazz photo books, we decided we wanted something a bit more substantial — so that the text and the photos would be of about equal im-portance.

The vignette format we've chosen has allowed me, as a jazz critic, to informally share some of my observations about the musicians. Writing these pieces has been a refreshing change of pace for me from the longer, more heavily researched profiles I usually do in my books. I want to make it completely clear that while Elliott, the Johnsens, and I all share an overall apprecia-tion for the talents of the various musicians in this book, we did not try to co-write the text or reach any consensus on what to say. I take sole responsibility for any and all opinions expressed. So if there are any remarks you disagree with, blame me and not my collaborators! Incidentally, if you want to drop any of us a letter (and we'd love to hear from you), you'll find our office addresses listed on the "About the Collaborators" page in the back of the book.

Virtually all of the 220-odd photographs in this book are by Nancy Miller Elliott and John and Andreas Johnsens. In a few instances (clearly identified as such), we have chosen to augment their photos with relevant archival photos. In addition, I took the shots at the Lionel Hampton Jazz Festival since my collaborators have not yet had the pleasure of attending that festival (although they're certainly looking forward to doing so). I also photographed the reclusive Artie Shaw at his home. (My collaborators have not yet had a chance to shoot him and he is too important an artist to leave out of the book altogether.) Complete photo credits will be found in the end notes.

While we haven't always been sticklers about sequencing photos chronologically, in general artists who made their marks in earlier years will be found earlier in the book, and those who made their marks in later years will be found later. Thus, if you read the book from beginning to end, you'll come away with some sense of historic progression. We start with artists whose careers began in the so-called Jazz Age of the 1920s, move on up through survivors from the subsequent big band years, the bebop era, and so on. Artists who are associated with one an-

other have been grouped together where possible. Thus, for example, Count Basie will be followed by some of his musical children, Duke Ellington by some his musical children, and Dizzy Gillespie by some of *his*. Some musicians, of course, have made important contributions over so long a span of time and have worked with so many different people, that deciding where to put them in the book is arbitrary. In most cases, an individual artist will be represented by a single photo. But a more important artist may be represented by multiple photos.

I wish there had been space for photos of younger jazz musicians as well. I would have loved to have been able to include striking photos that Elliott has taken of, say, Charles Gayle, Scott Hamilton, Randy Sandke, and Wycliffe Gordon; that John Johnsen has taken of Carla Bley, Freddie Hubbard, Keith Jarrett, and Michel Petrucciani; that Andreas Johnsen has taken of Diane Schuur, Jon Faddis, Fred Hersch, and Michael White (not to mention non-jazz notables he's photographed, such as James Brown, Little Richard, and Madonna). But those shots will have to wait for other books.

For the time being, we're simply trying to document a bit of what we've seen through the years, by offering our portraits — in photos and words — of some admirable and deserving jazz veterans.

JAZZ VETERANS
A Portrait Gallery

JABBO SMITH

What I like about the full-page photo is the eternal youthfulness of it, and the gentleness. We see legendary trumpeter Jabbo Smith (1908-1991) blowing his horn for a small child whose curiosity and delight is obvious. When this shot was taken by Nancy Miller Elliott, Smith was well up in his 70s, but you can imagine him getting along very well with his young friend. I think that's true of a lot of jazz musicians and one reason I enjoy being around them so much: they often retain positive qualities we associate with children, like spontaneity and playfulness, and a heightened sensitivity to both life's sorrows and its delights.

In this photo, Smith appears to be enjoying himself no less than the child. When I look at it, I'm reminded of comments two other distinguished jazz trumpeters made not too long before Smith's death. Don Cherry said of Smith, when we were on television's "Joe Franklin Show": "He's giving. And that's the thing about playing the music, is that it's something that you want to share and give. And Jabbo still has that quality." I think you can see that in this picture — and also a bit of what Clark Terry was talking about, when he once remarked Smith "has never lost his yen for fun and indulgence in his craft. When I grow up I want to be just like Jabbo."

Born in 1908, Smith's peak came around 1929. If you listen to the remarkable Brunswick records he made that year and to records made by other jazz trumpeters at that time, you realize he was then unsurpassed in terms of technical prowess. He had an astounding command of his horn and an unbridled gusto to go with it. The noted bass player Milt Hinton (born in 1910), one of the very few jazzmen left who remembers how Smith sounded "live" at his peak, insists that Smith was then as good as Louis Armstrong (and Armstrong was generally considered the best jazz trumpeter). Another of that dwindling number of eyewitnesses, trumpeter Jack Butler (born 1909), recalled seeing a trumpet battle between Armstrong and Smith around 1929 or '30. Armstrong, Butler insisted, "had to sing to win it." Although Smith was not as pleasingly melodic a player as Armstrong and his solos lacked Armstrong's grand sense of construction, he played with a rapidity and freedom that was ahead of its time, and that helped lay the groundwork for Roy Eldridge and Gillespie. At his zenith (when, in the words of the late drummer Tommy Bedford, he "had Chicago on its head with his trumpet playing"), he was considered a credible challenger to Armstrong. Smith's best records continue to inspire awe, while assorted less-imaginative musicians whose records significantly outsold his in 1929 have been thoroughly forgotten.

Smith, like all other black musicians of his era, faced hurdles higher than white musicians faced. Black artists' records generally weren't as widely distributed as white artists' and many performing venues were closed to them. For every Louis Armstrong and Duke Ellington who did overcome those higher hurdles and become internationally famous, there were many other highly talented black musicians who never achieved a fraction of the commercial success of numerous less talented white musicians.

Fiercely independent by temperament, Smith was unwilling to compromise in ways many black artists of his day considered necessary to get ahead. Louis Armstrong, for example, didn't question how manager Joe Glaser handled his finances; he felt he needed a tough, well-connected white manager to represent him in a white-dominated world, and Glaser was just that. If Glaser took a greater share of Armstrong's earnings than he should have (as he apparently did), Armstrong was not about to rock the boat. Smith, by contrast, told me he argued sharply with Glaser about money when Glaser managed him. He ultimately concluded he didn't want Glaser — or anybody else — running his career. He had run-ins with union leaders, too. His independence came with a price, though. He eventually drifted out of music, working for a car-rental agency in the midwest. His name was legendary to jazz record collectors, most of whom probably assumed he was long dead.

In the late '70s, Smith made a surprising comeback, playing his trumpet and singing in Vernel Bagneris' smash hit show at the Village Gate, *One Mo' Time*, projecting an irresistible winsome charm, with an undercurrent of pathos. Musicians Orange Kellin and Lars Edegran, who helped rediscover Smith, were both supportive and protective of him. Lor-

raine Gordon, who today runs the Village Vanguard founded by her late husband Max in 1934, became his manager. Thanks to the efforts of Smith (as well as those of Village Gate owner Art D'Lugoff), Smith began receiving press attention he had never achieved in the years when he was playing his best. He wound up getting bookings in clubs and at festivals. His confidence renewed (as is evident in Elliott's studio portrait of him, proudly holding his horn in his hands), he was eager to accept all offers of work. He was thrilled to see young musicians learn and perform solos that he had recorded 50 and 60 years before. He checked out the younger trumpeters, too (most of whom he thought lacked individuality). He tried to stay current on politics. (Elliott's camera caught the unlikely 1984 meeting of Smith, wearing a Mondale-Ferraro button, with one New York's most colorful and outspoken political figures, Bella Abzug.) Smith was more interested in jazz than in politics, though. He continued writing music almost until his death. There is still hope that *Fresh Air Taxi*, a musical comedy with a score by Smith and a book by Stephen Silverman (author of several fine showbiz biographies) and the multi-talented Bagneris, may someday yet be produced.

In the final weeks of Smith's life, when he was confined to a nursing home and no longer able to speak or to see, Gordon read to him a long profile of him that I'd written, and also made photocopies of it for the nursing home staff, so they'd perhaps treat him with greater respect.

During the last 12 years of his life, Jabbo Smith was one of Nancy Miller Elliott's favorite subjects — as well as a friend.

WILLIE "THE LION" SMITH

Like Jabbo Smith, Willie "The Lion" Smith (no relation) remains forever linked with the 1920s. His style of playing, as well as his style of dress, didn't change too much over the years. Although John Johnsen shot this portrait of the derby-clad, cigar-smoking Smith in the mid-1960s, it could just as easily have been taken many years before. Smith was a master of stride piano, an early, Eastern jazz style (with clear roots in ragtime) that originated around the time of World War I and flourished — particularly in Harlem — throughout the '20s.

I once made the mistake of suggesting to the pioneering jazz bandleader Sam Wooding that Duke Ellington was a great pi-ano player. "Oh no! He wasn't a piano player at all," declared Wooding, insisting that the greatest piano players he had heard in his life were the two stride giants he had so greatly admired back in Harlem in the '20s: James P. Johnson and Willie "The Lion" Smith. Young Ellington sought to emulate such men, Wooding recalled. (Ellington eventually honored Smith by composing a piece called "Portrait of the Lion"; Smith returned the compliment by composing "Portrait of the Duke.")

Tenor sax master Ben Webster recalled Count Basie telling him in Kansas City, *circa* 1927, that if he ever got to New York, he should make sure he heard Willie "The Lion" Smith. Basie gave James P. Johnson and Smith the highest rating among piano players of that era; he considered Duke Ellington, Fats Waller, and Willie Gant to be on the next rung down. (Webster related to jazz historian Stanley Dance that when he got to New York, he made a point of meeting Smith and buying him cigars and drinks, and Smith favored him with several hours of playing, giving him a day he'd never forget.)

We must accept the testimony of those who were present as to how great Smith sounded in the 1920s. There are no recordings. Had he been white, it no doubt would have been another story. But the leading record companies of the day were not always on the ball when it came to documenting the latest musical developments in Harlem. Smith's renown spread strictly by word of mouth, in jazz circles. Not until 1935, when he was 37 years old, did the first records by Willie "The Lion" Smith appear.

Born in Newark, New Jersey, Smith found the vibrant community of Harlem, where he later chose to live, inspiring. As he once put it: "I would rather be a fly on a lamppost in Harlem than a millionaire anywhere else." He was of mixed parentage. His mother was black and Christian. His father was white and Jewish. (His actual last name was Bertholoff.) He drew from both of his parents' traditions. It was his mother's church piano playing that first got him interested in playing piano. But he also learned and appreciated his father's religious music, and for a while, in fact, served as a cantor. In addition, he was well versed in classical music, influences of which were apparent in his own compositions. Until his death in 1973, it was the most natural thing in the world for him to go from a rollicking hot jazz stomp to a subtle, dreamily impressionistic original like "Echoes of Spring."

WILD BILL DAVISON

Hard-driving Chicago jazz from a hard-drinking jazzman — that's probably what most fans would associate with the name of Wild Bill Davison ("The Defiant One," as Eddie Condon called him). He long projected — both via his brashly exciting cornet playing and his wisecracks between numbers — a *life-is-one-long-party* kind of attitude that seemed a holdover from the Roaring '20s. This stark Elliott portrait, however, catches him in far from a partying mood.

A bit of background on the man, for those who have not heard any of the 800 or so sides (by his estimation) on which Davison played, from 1924 into the late 1980s. Born in Defiance, Ohio, in 1906, his first home-made instrument was simply a piece of garden hose to which he had attached a funnel. He found he could play a bugle call on it. His grandmother told him she'd provide him with a real cornet if he'd play in the Sunday school orchestra. He did, until he saved up enough money to buy his own horn. Then he gave his grandmother back the one she'd given him — and quit the church!

Davison's first musical role model was Louis Panico, whose muted sounds seemed masterly in the early 1920s. But when he heard Bix Beiderbecke blowing open horn with the Wolverines around 1924 — Bix hitting the notes with a gorgeous, bell-like purity — he set aside his mute. As he told writer Bob Byler a few years ago: "The sound of an open horn is a beautiful thing." His robust hot work may be sampled on any number of fine old Commodore sides. He was equally — and justifiably — proud of his sweet work (like *Pretty Wild*, an album he made with Percy Faith and strings).

Although he was a member of some big bands in Chicago in the late 1920s and early '30s, for most of his career Davison played in free-wheeling small groups. He turned down offers to join "name" big bands. He was happier punching out things like "That's a-Plenty" at Eddie Condon's Club.

He played with his horn cocked to one side — a position he had to adopt since his lips were badly cut when a brawl broke out in a club where he was working in the 1930s. He had been injured so severely that he could not play at all for a while. That was not the only time he had to put playing on hold. In 1984, Davison got bleeding ulcers so bad he almost died. His doctor told him if he didn't stop drinking, he'd be dead within ten days. He'd seen too many jazzmen friends die due to alcohol; he stopped, and lived five more years. It took a great deal of work for him to regain his lip after his 1984 illness, but he did.

Occasionally, in his later years, he'd perform on mandola — his insurance, he'd say, if the time ever came when he'd be forced to give up the cornet. It never came. (You can hear Davison, still vigorous at age 80, on the Atlantic album *Chicago Jazz Summit*, recorded during the 1986 JVC Jazz Festival.) He lost none of his readiness with the quip in his later years, either, as when he'd introduce a number with: "This is a lovely old piece. Of course, that's the only kind I get nowadays...."

Nancy Miller Elliott's memorable portrait of Wild Bill, quite different from the irreverent "high spirits" shots usually seen, makes me think of him telling British jazz writer Clarrie Henley a couple of years before his death in 1989: "Christ, how I hate this growin' old...."

SAMMY PRICE

If you ask an aspiring young jazz pianist today who his influences are, he's likely to give you a long list of present and past greats he's listened to — not just in person but on records and CDs, radio and TV. Chances are he'll have studied jazz in college, too; that's increasingly common.

But if you asked veteran jazz pianist Sammy Price (1908-1991) who his influences were, he'd ask you right back — sounding a tad impatient — just how many jazz pianists you imagined there *were* during his Texas boyhood. And how you were supposed to have heard them all.

When Price was very young, the term jazz hadn't even come into general use yet. The first jazz records (by the Original Dixieland Jazz Band, a white group) weren't made until 1917; several more years passed before companies began recording black jazz artists. Price took some piano lessons, and he picked up additional things both from his peers and from traveling black musicians who occasionally lodged at his family's house; but by and large, he developed his own style without past greats to lean on as models.

After working as a dancer in his mid teens with Alphonso Trent's band, playing piano professionally in Athens, Texas, and leading a big band in Dallas, Price left Texas in 1927 to tour as a pianist with traveling shows — sometimes receiving no payment other than lodging and one meal per day.

He made his first radio broadcasts in Oklahoma City around 1929 and the first of what would be hundreds of records in Dallas not long afterwards. In Kansas City, he played at the Yellow Front Cafe, where the music was a lure to get suckers to come in and gamble in the back. After working in Chicago and Detroit, he settled in New York in 1937, where he worked as a staff musician for Decca Records. He accompanied such blues and gospel art-

ists as Blue Lu Barker, Trixie Smith, Bea Booze, Sister Rosetta Tharpe, and Peetie Wheatstraw, under the general supervision of pioneering black record producer J. Mayo Williams.

Many of the blues singers played some piano themselves, but not with the polish Price could bring to recording sessions. He led his own group, too, the Texas Blusicians, which included at one time or another such notables as Lester Young, Ike Quebec, Joe Eldridge, and Sid Catlett.

As boogie woogie, always one of his strong suits, enjoyed an enormous vogue, the early 1940s found Price featured at prominent New York clubs. In 1945, he recorded a noteworthy series of boogie woogie solo piano sides (Eubie Blake, years later, declared Price "The King of Boogie Woogie"). He then went on in the next few years to record and tour with Mezz Mezzrow and Sidney Bechet.

The emergence of bebop threw Price for a bit. He wasn't into it all (although he did wind up playing with Charlie Parker on one gig, subbing for Thelonious Monk). The demand in New York for pianists playing the older styles that Price favored waned greatly. In the early 1950s, he relocated to Dallas, where he ran a couple of nightclubs and an undertaking business. Then it was back to New York (where Elliott photographed him), to continue a performing and recording career that encompassed jazz of varied styles, blues, and even some rhythm-and-blues. He worked with artists as varied as Red Allen, Jimmy Rushing, Tony Parenti, Ida Cox, Rahsaan Roland Kirk, King Curtis, Mickey Baker, and Doc Cheatham. He remained active on the club scene almost until his death, playing New York clubs including the Blue Note and Condon's — a respected jazz elder who was glad to give youngsters a reminder that there was, as he'd put it, jazz before Charlie Parker.

DOC CHEATHAM & PHIL SCHAAP

Two good reasons for a jazz buff to live in the New York area: Doc Cheatham and Phil Schaap (captured together by Nancy Miller Elliott on page 12).

Any Sunday afternoon, you can drop into the Greenwich Village club Sweet Basil for brunch and catch Doc Cheatham, trumpeting, singing in a high, somewhat quaint voice, and radiating abundant good cheer. (Cheatham's characteristic playing stance — elbows outward, horn raised skyward — is well caught in Andreas Johnsen's performance shot.) Cheatham launched the vogue for jazz brunches in New York, and always draws an enthusiastic crowd. I sometimes wonder, though, how many of the people enjoying Cheatham's bright, jaunty playing on a number such as "Struttin' With Some Barbecue," or his charming singing on a number such as "What Can I Say After I Say I'm Sorry?" realize just how much jazz history he represents.

Born June 13, 1905, Cheatham is New York's oldest regularly working jazzman, and very nearly the last link left to the Jazz Age of the 1920s. Cheatham can remember well when Red Nichols was the jazz cornetist in the spotlight, in the mid '20s, and then when Bix Beiderbecke developed a subtler, more lyrical approach that had all the jazzmen talking about him instead. He was impressed, too, by Jabbo Smith in his day. But it is Louis Armstrong he names as the greatest trumpeter he ever heard in his life. And he's heard just about all of them, as was made clear when he remarked at one 1992 concert that 18-year-old trumpeter Nicholas Payton of New Orleans reminded him, in appearance as well as sound, of King Oliver.

In the '20s, Cheatham recorded with Ma Rainey ("The Mother of the Blues"), subbed on a couple of occasions for Louis Armstrong (an impossible act to follow), and traveled to Europe with Sam Wooding's trailblazing orchestra. In the '30s, Cheatham played lead trumpet in Cab Calloway's Band, and the Calloway brass got a wonderfully tight and chewy sound. Rarely did Cheatham get to solo (one such time was when Calloway, in 1932, first recorded "I've Got

the World on a String"); his abilities as a soloist flowered late in life. He went on to work, at one time or another, with many greats — everyone from Benny Goodman and Billie Holiday to Benny Carter and Wynton Marsalis. Imbued with a gentle, kindly spirit, he's also always happy to give talented newcomers a boost if he can, recording recently, for example, with young singer Ingrid Pearlman, tap-dancing trombonist Tod Londigan, and their spirited, New Orleans Dixieland-oriented Flying Neutrinos Band.

One of Cheatham's record producers, Andrea du Plessis of New Orleans, observes that Cheatham is just about the easiest person in the world to work with — no ego problems and a disposition that seems to brighten whatever group he's in. She's extremely fond of him and is an ardent champion of his talents. He, in turn, notes that he's actually done better financially making small-label recordings for her than for industry-giant Sony.

Cheatham is unique in jazz in that he has recorded his best work after the age of 70. I hope he makes many more recordings.

Nancy Miller Elliott took both the close-up portrait of Cheatham (with the flower whimsically in his hair) and the informal shot of him seated, waiting to address attendees at the dedication of the Louis Armstrong Archives at Queens College. (Next to him in that shot — perhaps learning a bit of jazz history from the source — we see Rob Gibson, Director of Jazz at Lincoln Center.) Elliott's photo on page 13 shows alto saxist Norris Turney, Cheatham, drummer Panama Francis, and baritone saxist Joe Temperley outside of Carnegie Hall, waiting to go on at the 1994 JVC Jazz Festival.

Disc jockey/historian Phil Schaap (in Elliott's joint shot, standing behind Cheatham in the stu-

dios of WKCR 89.9 FM) has done much to educate New York jazz fans about the contributions made by the veterans covered in this book. He's a relatively young man but is, as one of my venerable musician friends likes to say, "an old soul."

On February 2, 1970, Phil Schaap began broadcasting on WKCR. Jazz has never been quite the same since.

With his encyclopedic knowledge and tireless energy — as proven in numerous unprecedented, round-the-clock marathon tribute broadcasts —Schaap has become an important part of the fabric of New York. Schaap's profound impact on the jazz scene actually extends far beyond the reaches of WKCR's transmitter. Jazz consumes his entire life, not just the many hours he's on the air.

He's won Grammy Awards for producing and annotating landmark Billie Holiday and Charlie Parker boxed sets. He's revived the careers of assorted fine older players, and given countless others their final send-offs in memorial services. As an expert audio engineer, he's restored important vintage recordings that had seemed beyond hope. He ingeniously salvaged eight hours of badly deteriorated Charlie Parker tapes, for example, by using "White-Out" as a binding backer.

If you aren't fortunate enough to be able to attend Schaap's lectures on jazz at Princeton, Rutgers, and Columbia, you'll get a rather thorough grounding in the subject listening to his broadcasts or reading his liner notes.

Schaap's extraordinary memory is legendary. You can name seemingly any musician; Schaap will tell you where and when he was born. Mention a record, he'll rattle off the personnel, the day, month, and year it was made — and much more. (The witty writer Will Friedwald coined a memorable phrase: "having a mind like a steel Schaap.") Schaap's parents became aware his memory was unusual when, as a two-year-old, he took to reciting — in proper sequence — the names and dates in office of all the U.S. Presidents. And again, when they heard the young lad singing from memory Lester Young's recorded tenor sax solos.

By age five, he was impressing legendary Basie Band drummer Jo Jones with his knowledge of obscure jazzmen like 1920s saxist Prince Robinson. By age six, he'd begun collecting records in earnest, buying from Triboro Records in Jamaica, Queens, where they sold old 78s at a price of 25¢ per pound. "I made a lot of trips with my little red wagon," Schaap told me.

He acquired such a profound knowledge of jazz that, as a sophomore at Columbia in 1970, he was hired by the university as a guest lecturer on the subject.

When he auditioned to become a disc jockey at WKCR, an older student at the station gave him a blindfold test to see if he could identify recordings by the likes of McCoy Tyner and Count Basie, which he did so quickly he was then played a recording by a far more obscure pianist.

Schaap began expounding, "That's Richard Aaron Katz, born March 13, 1924 in Baltimore, Maryland..."

"That's my father!" exclaimed the awed older student, who — unknown to Schaap — was indeed Dick Katz's son.

Within a few years, Schaap revolutionized the station's programming, making it the foremost jazz station in the area.

He instituted marathon "festival" broadcasts, in which every available recording by a given artist would be played sequentially. You'd go to sleep listening to Schaap playing his 200th recording by Louis Armstrong (or whoever). When you woke up, Schaap was still at it. He'd add interviews with musicians. If you had any resistance to acknowledging the greatness of the artists he championed — and his sincere love for them was always unmistakable — he'd eventually wear you down.

People asked: "Does Schaap ever sleep?" It was well known that he never vacationed. When it was announced he was finally taking one — for four days, in 1991 — that news was reported by *The New Yorker.* As it turned out, however, Schaap didn't actually wind up taking those four days off. Just when his vacation was set to begin, sax legend Stan Getz died. Schaap immediately headed to the studio, devoting the next 18 hours to memorializing Getz on the air. He took time off to then speak at a college, then went back on air.

He finally did get to visit relatives in Arizona — by then having gone several days with-

out sleeping — just in time to have one of them, age 91, die in his arms. "I'm hoping my next vacation will be less eventful," Schaap commented to me.

He's a positive force in the jazz community, one who has done much to see that deserving older players are shown respect. Many older jazzmen consider Schaap not just a great authority on the music but a genuine friend — a kind of honorary member of their own generation, whose ranks have thinned. I asked the late bandleader Andy Kirk, when he was 90, what he enjoyed doing, aside from listening to music. He had but one answer: "Visiting with Phil Schaap."

Doc Cheatham & Phil Schaap

JOHNNY LETMAN

"**C**hicago was *the* music city. New York was late on the jazz scene," trumpeter/vocalist Johnny Letman (1917-1992), who grew up in Chicago, told me not long before his death. "Every big musician came to Chicago. Chicago had millions of clubs."

In 1933-34, Letman played in a big band led by a contemporary of his, Nat "King" Cole. "When I was with Nat Cole, *I* was the singer. He just played the piano. He never opened his mouth back then," Letman remarked. "Later, of course, he opened his mouth and made a million dollars." Another of Letman's early gigs was in a band featuring the celebrated New Orleans trumpeter Punch Miller — a gifted improviser who couldn't read music; Letman played the written trumpet parts.

Letman's original inspiration on trumpet was Louis Armstrong.

"Louis Armstrong made everybody. First there was Louis Armstrong. Later I heard Roy Eldridge and my head came off, you know. Then I liked Charlie Shavers. And Dizzy Gillespie — who the hell can play like Dizzy?

"There are so many great trumpet players! But Louis Armstrong was the Pied Piper; he led us all, so that makes him the greatest. His influence is still here. Everything comes from Louis. I remember Roy Eldridge once trying to tell me he didn't play like Louis. I said, *'Who are you kidding?'*

"Other than Louis, I think the greatest trumpet player I ever heard was at the Panama Café in Chicago — I lived around the corner from it. The band was led by Floyd Campbell and the trumpeter was

Jabbo Smith. You ain't never heard nothing like that! This guy was the greatest. He was a bitch! And he played the trombone, too. Boy, he was something else. I never heard nobody play like Jabbo. In his right, he was every bit as good as Louis. But, you see, Jabbo had the technique — but Louis had the music. You ask anybody that heard Jabbo — they'll tell you: technically, Jabbo was better than Louis, but musically he wasn't. People don't pay for technique, though; they pay for *music*."

Letman's recollection is that he was about 14 or 15 when he first heard Smith. According to the *New Grove Dictionary of Jazz*, Smith worked at the Panama Cafe over a two year period, beginning shortly after the club's opening in 1933.

Letman's favorite trumpeter, of those still active in the early 1990s, was Clark Terry.

Through the 1940s and into the early '50s, Letman played in big bands and small groups led by Horace Henderson, John Kirby, Freddie Slack, Tommy Dorsey, Lucky Millinder, Cootie Williams, Cab Calloway, and Count Basie. In subsequent years, he found employment everywhere from Broadway pit orchestras to Latin bands, to bar mitzvahs and weddings, to the Harlem Blues and Jazz Band. In his final years, he was featured frequently in bands led by Lars Edegran and Orange Kellin, two younger Swedish traditionalists who've done much to keep older styles alive.

"You learn from everybody you hear," Letman noted. "Doc Cheatham — he's one of my advisors — tells me: 'Easy does it. You've got to remember you can't play the way you did when you were younger.' You never finish learning the instrument."

BENNY GOODMAN

It takes more than one photo to sum up the King of Swing.

What's striking about Nancy Miller Elliott's portrait of Benny Goodman on page 16 is that it shows a vulnerability I've never seen in other shots of him, and certainly few ever saw in his public appearances. This is a far cry from the usual "smile for the camera" publicity photo. Goodman did not have long to live when this shot was taken. He had achieved enormous success as an instrumentalist in his career, but had never had comparable success in forming friendships. Musicians who worked for him (and admired his abilities as a player) felt he was hard to understand as a person. Some wondered how much happiness he found in his life. Quite a few disliked him.

John Johnsen's performance shots capture well the Goodman the public saw: the consummate clarinetist, whose brilliance was as apparent in his final years as it had been in his Chicago boyhood; the concert artist whose flawlessly rising clarinet lines lifted countless audiences' spirits.

From August 21, 1935 — the night his orchestra scored a smashing success at the Palomar Ballroom, launching the big band era — until his death on June 13, 1986, Goodman was known as "the King of Swing." (Fans of his greatest rival, Artie Shaw, called Shaw "the King of the Clarinet.") When Goodman came into a room to rehearse his musicians, you could almost see an imaginary crown on his head. He acted very

much the king; the musicians were his serfs.

In his final year, Goodman enjoyed a terrific comeback. He was leading an organized big band, his concerts were all selling out, and he was recording again. The Goodman revival began on October 1, 1985 when, at New Jersey's Waterloo Village, he gave his first big-band concert in seven years. For the previous few years, he had been in and out of the hospital. Part of his intestine had been removed, and there had been other problems as well. Many had speculated he was never going to perform in public again. Some who knew him well urged him not to, for health reasons.

And yet there he was at Waterloo Village, at age 76, his total mastery of the clarinet still very much in evidence — along with his ego. I remember watching the gifted Randy Sandke rise to take an assigned trumpet solo that night; Goodman abruptly decided to solo instead, and Sandke had no choice but to awkwardly sit right back down again. Goodman had done things like that for decades.

At a rehearsal the next week, baritone saxist Danny Banks recalled for me the high turnover of personnel in Goodman's band. In the one year and nine months that he had worked for Goodman in the 1940s, he said, he had met 45 saxophone players! Banks was rehearsing regularly with Goodman now, but he predicted to me — correctly, as it turned out — that Goodman wasn't going to let him play when the band per-

formed a few days later. Banks said he'd seen it before: Goodman would rehearse with five saxes, then decide to use only four. Banks suspected Goodman privately feared five saxes might drown out his clarinet. (Goodman's own explanation was that the Fletcher Henderson charts had originally been scored for just four saxes — the fifth sax parts were later additions — and he preferred to honor the arranger's original intentions.)

During a dress rehearsal at New York's Marriott Hotel for a Goodman PBS TV special, I was struck by the manner in which Goodman addressed drum great Louie Bellson on the bandstand. Goodman spoke to him not the way you'd talk to a peer, to a gifted, important musician you'd known for 44 years; Goodman gave curt directives as if Bellson were still the green 17-year-old Goodman had originally hired in 1943. At those moments, it seemed as if Goodman had never acquired any basic social graces. On the bandstand, he appeared to be all business. And yet I was equally struck — and surprised — by the great warmth Goodman later displayed towards all of his old associates, off the stage, during breaks in the rehearsal.

When it came to music, Goodman was an absolute perfectionist. He rehearsed one brief phrase in "King Porter Stomp" over and over that afternoon. He wanted it sharper: "Bam-bam-bam!" he called out to his musicians, and they played the phrase again, punching it harder. Only when they gave him *exactly* what he wanted could they go on to rehearse the next phrase. He was in total control. He even picked what microphones were used for the TV special, supplying two oldies from his personal collection. (And that wasn't just a whim on his part. He knew that the wrong mikes could adversely affect the rich, full sound of the band that he wanted — the sound that people who remembered his hit records would want to hear again.) When the TV special aired — just three months before Goodman's death — band members voiced anger that their names had not even been listed in the closing credits. For the King of Swing, it was apparently enough to say: "Benny Goodman and his Orchestra." And yet there was

one name Goodman took great care to call attention to in all of his last public performances — that of the late Fletcher Henderson, whose arrangements had set the style for his first big band and now, 50 years later, were setting the style for his last big band. Goodman played virtually nothing but Henderson arrangements, written in the 1930s, in his last year.

Some colleagues warned Goodman he was pushing himself much too hard. They could see the effects of strain. But after several years of inactivity, he said he was glad to be back doing what he did best. He had a lot of plans for the future. And when audiences cheered him in his final public appearances, he looked — briefly — absolutely jubilant. As he'd raise his clarinet in his hand in triumph, you couldn't help sharing in his joy.

His death made front-page news. Afterwards, Goodman tributes sprung up everywhere. But no official Benny Goodman ghost band was created. For Goodman had left specific instructions that there was to be no "Benny Goodman Orchestra" without him. As he succinctly, and memorably, had put it: "I am the product."

FLETCHER HENDERSON

It is impossible to tell the story of Benny Goodman fairly without also telling a bit about Fletcher Henderson. Because Henderson died before this book's photographers began their careers, we're going to have to bend the rules a little and use archival photos of him. But I would not want to leave Henderson out. He's been too often deprived of proper recognition in the past. That Fletcher Henderson's name isn't as well known as those of many lesser white Swing Era musicians is simply a reminder of the insidious effects of racism.

As far as many Americans are concerned, the big band era started with Benny Goodman and the wonderful music his band made. But there were other excellent big bands, both black and white, before Goodman's. (Artie Shaw names the oft-overlooked Jean Goldkette as having led the first great big band he ever saw, circa 1927.) Henderson led a first-rate jazz-oriented big band that paved the way for many others. Goodman wanted — and got — a band that could swing in the Henderson style.

From 1924 to 1927, Henderson's may have been the best jazz orchestra around, featuring arrangements by Don Redman, and such major jazz soloists as (at one time or another) Louis Armstrong, Coleman Hawkins, Joe Smith, Rex Stewart, Tommy Ladnier, Charlie Green, Benny Morton, Jimmy Harrison, and Buster Bailey. In subsequent years, it was up-and-down in quality. It faced increased competition from newer bands. The loss of chief arranger Redman in 1927 was a major setback. It took several years before Henderson himself really blossomed as an arranger. By the early 1930s, however, Henderson was writing as infectious big band arrangements as anyone in the business, and his band hit new peaks of artistic, if not commercial, success. Benny Goodman then hired Henderson to arrange for his new band.

To a significant extent, Goodman rode to fame in the mid '30s on Henderson's pace-setting arrangements. They were not, by any means, all that Goodman played, but they were central to his success. How many young Goodman fans in the mid '30s had any idea that they were listening in part to black music being played by a white band? How many would have imagined that such irresistible "Goodman specialties" as "King Porter Stomp," "Down South Camp Meetin,'" and "Wrappin' It Up" were arrangements that actually had already been played — and recorded —

by Fletcher Henderson and his Orchestra? (How many Americans of a later generation would be aware that early hits by Elvis Presley and other white rockers were numbers that had previously been recorded by black performers?)

Goodman himself was certainly not a racist. In fact, he helped break down racial barriers by hiring black musicians such as Lionel Hampton and Teddy Wilson in an era when segregated bands were the norm. And he clearly merited success. He was a master clarinetist —he and Shaw were surely the two best in the nation — who ran a highly disciplined yet exciting, star-studded band. But such facts should not blind us to the reality that Goodman benefited from —and Henderson was held back by — racism in the system.

Goodman simply wouldn't have made it as big as he did without Henderson's charts. He needed their verve and their swing. He needed the call-and-response patterns Henderson and his men had honed over the years. He wouldn't have made it as big, if he had had nothing more to offer the public than the standard fare of white dance bands of the day. Goodman also wouldn't have made it as big without the national exposure of radio. Henderson had not had much luck getting the radio exposure he needed.

Goodman's big break came when he got on the "Let's Dance" radio show. It introduced his music — including some of the very same arrangements Henderson had long been playing —to youths coast-to-coast, who presumed it was new. Goodman's triumphant appearance at the Palomar Ballroom in Los Angeles was only possible because the kids in California had already been digging Goodman's music on the radio show. Goodman believed that getting the "Let's Dance" radio show was the most important break in his career.

And the fact is, in 1935, a network show like "Let's Dance" was most likely going to be offered to white bands, not to black bands. That show featured three bands in total — all white. What if Henderson's Band, not Goodman's, had been given that kind of exposure, playing many of those same numbers? Would it have become better known? Would its records have sold better? There can be little doubt. To a considerable degree, Henderson's felicitous, unforgettable, and oft-imitated arrangements — heard every time someone puts together a tribute to Goodman today — launched the Swing Era.

COLEMAN HAWKINS

From the mid-1920s until well into the '40s, Coleman Hawkins (captured here late in his career by John Johnsen) set the pace on jazz tenor sax. Whether swaggering brawnily through an uptempo number or easing lushly through a ballad, his virile, full-bodied playing influenced countless other saxists, from such stars as Ben Webster, Herschel Evans, and Don Byas down to now-forgotten players in territory bands. So extreme was Hawkins' dominance of the field — "hegemony" was the word Bud Freeman used in talking to me about Hawkins — that it is hard to think of any major tenor saxist of the 1930s, aside from such highly distinctive stylists as Freeman and Lester Young, who didn't show obvious signs of Hawkins' influence.

Gunther Schuller noted in *The Swing Era* that "Hawkins virtually invented the jazz saxophone, at least the tenor saxophone." Schuller named two jazz sax men who preceded Hawkins, "Stump" Evans and Prince Robinson — and Freeman named another, Jack Pettis (whom Freeman felt laid the groundwork for the lighter-toned sax approaches that he and Young developed). But such sax pioneers, worthy though they may have been, certainly paled in significance compared to Hawkins.

Hawkins was the pre-eminent soloist in Fletcher Henderson's Band from 1924 to 1934 (except for the period in 1924 and '25 when Louis Armstrong was featured in the band; Henderson was then second in importance to Armstrong). As a musician, his powers seemed unlimited, and he expected payment reflecting that fact. In the glory days, Hawkins liked to walk around with two or three thousand dollars in his pockets.

From 1934 to '39, Hawkins lived and worked in Europe. He continued recording, and jazz

aficionados in the U.S. struggled to monitor his progress via records — when they could get them. Fans wondered how he could thrive, so far removed from the nurturing atmosphere of

New York. Writing in the Princeton *Tiger* magazine in March 1936, an undergraduate whose byline was simply "Jazzbo" opined that Hawkins was still the greatest of all tenor players but "his recent playing appears to have suffered from Continental tastes, and he seems to show a tendency for over-rhapsodizing nowadays."

When Hawkins finally returned to New York, he had to prove in jam sessions that he hadn't lost his position in the pecking order to jazz saxists who had come up in his absence. Hawkins was quoted by Robert Reisner in *The Jazz Titans* recalling that other sax players "were laying for me. They thought I would be stale after six years in Europe. This was the real chance to catch me. They always wanted to cut me.... They had nothing new. At first I thought they were holding back, but it was not so." If there were any doubts as to his prowess, he silenced them — at least for most people — with his definitive 1939 recording of "Body and Soul."

John Williams Jr., who played bass in Hawkins' band in 1940, told me Hawkins used to routinely order and eat two dinners in restaurants. (And somehow that oversized appetite for food seems to go with the authoritative, oversized sound Hawkins got from his horn.) Cornetist Rex Stewart wrote in *Down Beat* May 19, 1966 that Hawkins amazed him "by consuming more food at one sitting than I had ever seen anybody else eat. Perhaps that's where he gets his tremendous energy." Hawkins also had an oversized appetite for alcohol. Towards the close of his life, however, debilitated by alcoholism and an apparent inability to accept his growing old, he wound up eating very little food at all.

Unlike many of his contemporaries, Hawkins was flexible enough to work with the beboppers when they came up in the mid '40s, modifying his playing to relate to what they were doing without losing his own identity. And he was self-sufficient enough to record in 1948 an original composition, "Picasso," without any accompaniment whatsoever (setting the stage for Sonny Rollins, who would later also record impressively, unaccompanied). But by that time, due to one of those periodic (and largely inexplicable) shifts in public tastes, Hawkins found most young sax players favoring the cooler, lighter, laid-back approach of Lester Young rather than his heavier one. Hawkins saw Young — who had once been fired from Fletcher Henderson's Band because fellow band members couldn't accept a sound so much lighter than Hawkins' — supplant him as the most influential of tenor saxists. Hawkins' own playing grew harder and tougher, his attack more ferocious, and his feeling for the blues deepened. He lived long enough to see John Coltrane supplant both him and Young by the early '60s as the role model for up-and-coming saxists — a somewhat demoralizing situation for him. He died in 1969.

BENNY CARTER

Most saxists *attack* their notes; Benny Carter (captured by John Johnsen in a performance with fellow sax giant Coleman Hawkins) sidles up to notes so easily they never know they've been hit. He'll ease into this one, slur into that. He can suggest a hint of a moan one moment, a laugh the next. (Like Frankie Trumbauer, whose work he appreciated when he was first starting out in the mid-1920s, he's got a playful side — although he more often shows a suave, elegant one.) And that flawless, glistening tone he has! Tone has always been of great importance to him. "I delighted in listening to Wayne King play sax — and there was not a note of jazz in what he played," Carter recalls.

Born in 1907 in New York, Carter played in such distinguished big bands of the 1920s as Charlie Johnson's and Fletcher Henderson's ("if you could make it in that band, you could make it anywhere"). He was leading big bands by the early 1930s and, along with the likes of Henderson and Don Redman, played an important role in the development of big band arranging. He had few models to draw inspiration from (he names "Don Redman, Bill Challis, people who made stock arrangements — these people were real craftsmen"). Big band arranging was in its infancy. Although he has often been hailed as a brilliant arranger, Carter insists he's not one of *his* favorite arrangers and downplays the oft-voiced notion that he had (and still has) a particular gift for writing for saxes. "It's just that when I started, I couldn't write for anything else," he says.

In 1935, when he had become, along with Johnny Hodges, one of the most influential alto sax stylists in jazz (and a highly respected "doubler" on trumpet), he left the U.S. for Europe. He was abroad the next few years, staying out of the U.S. limelight when bandleaders like Benny Goodman, the Dorseys, and Count Basie were breaking through to fame. He formed a critically acclaimed big band overseas, whose membership mixed races and nationalities (British, French, Cuban, West Indian) in a way that was unheard-of in the U.S. Was Carter trying to make a statement in pioneering the integrated band? "I'm never trying to make a statement," he replies with characteristic dignity. "I just do what comes normally and naturally to me — which is the way it would be in this country, had we not been subject to institutionalized prejudice all these years. People are people."

In 1937, Carter and Coleman Hawkins recorded together in Paris. They seemed to bring out the best in one another — something which doesn't always happen when jazz greats meet. (Carter has recorded, for example, with the two other most respected jazz alto saxists of all time, Charlie Parker and Johnny Hodges, but the results were disappointing.) Carter's and Hawkins' paths crossed on occasion through the years. (We're lucky photographer Johnsen was able to document one such concert reunion.) In 1961, they got together for a recording session with the same instrumentation as on their landmark 1937 Paris session, and chose to re-record some of the same tunes — always a risky venture. They outdid themselves! The album they produced, *Further Definitions*, is generally considered the finest in Carter's long career.

After his European sojourn of the '30s, Carter led fine big bands and small groups in the U.S. throughout the '40s without great commercial success. He didn't worry about popularity then or now. As he puts it: "I just come out and do what I do without thinking of commercialism." Johnny Hodges and Carter continued to be the style setters for jazz alto players until the emergence of Charlie Parker in the mid '40s. One anonymous wag wrote in the January 1942 issue of *Swing* magazine:

> Johnny Hodges
> Sounds gorgeous.

He knows how to jump it.
But Benny Carter
Is smarter.
He doubles on trumpet.

After the bebop revolution, nearly all aspiring jazz alto players began following Charlie Parker's lead. Dizzy Gillespie became the player to watch on trumpet.

Though he certainly never became a be-bopper — he had his own strongly defined, long-established approach to music — Carter was more open to the new sounds than many players of his generation. He and Gillespie, in particular, became life-long friends. They actually first recorded together way back in 1939, in one of Lionel Hampton's pick-up groups. Carter first hired Gillespie as a sideman for one of his own small groups, in 1941, for an extended engagement at

Kelly's Stable on 52nd Street. That was Gillespie's first regular booking on the street, where he'd previously only sat in. (Nancy Miller Elliott's camera catches one of Carter and Gillespie's reunions of later years, for a 1984 concert in New York's Washington Square Park. We see an ebullient Carter standing, getting ready to lead a band that includes Gillespie, seated at right.)

In the 1950s and '60s, Carter was scoring motion picture and television productions, much less visible on the jazz scene than in earlier years. In 1970, he was hired as a visiting professor of music at Princeton. He interjects: "The only thing I regret is that instead of going to Princeton as I did, I wish I had gone there years

before and matriculated." In concert appearances at the university, he proved a great hit with students — this author included. (Carter was actually a significant factor in my deciding to become a jazz writer.)

Carter soon found himself being "rediscovered" after being away from the public eye. For a while, he often seemed to be booked into programs designed to evoke bygone eras, such as the '20s or the '30s. But it soon became clear those were not the ideal settings for Carter. He was happy to take part in tributes to, say, Fletcher Henderson, or veteran tap dancers (as he was asked to do). But he wasn't a nostalgia piece. He could hold his own with players of widely varied styles (swing, bebop, or beyond) and generally sought to work with fine players considerably younger than himself. Major concert bookings and record dates came his way and he continued to write new works. (For those who wish to know more about his career, *Benny Carter: A Life in American Music* by Morroe Berger, Edward Berger, and James Patrick [Scarecrow Press and the Institute of Jazz Studies] is one of the most thorough of all jazz biographies.)

Carter still places high in the annual *Down Beat* critics' polls. In his 80s, he is now almost invariably introduced in his public appearances as a "living legend." He quips he'd "rather be a legend than a myth." As he looks back on a career spanning more than 60 years, I ask him if there is anything that he's particularly proud of. He answers honestly, with a gracious smile: "I can't think of anything that I'm not proud of."

BENNY WATERS

As I write this, Benny Waters (photographed by Andreas Johnsen in front of his home in Queens, New York) is the oldest internationally touring jazzman. Benny Carter, who played alongside Waters in Charlie Johnson's Band in the 1920s, commented to me at *his* home in California, shortly before Waters' 93rd birthday, how remarkable it was that Waters was still playing so well — adding he hoped he'd get a chance to play with him again sometime. (Waters returns the compliment, naming Carter as his favorite of all saxists.)

In January 1995, Waters celebrated his 93rd birthday with performances at the New York jazz club Metropolis, playing sax with confidence, sly humor, and considerable flair. If there were times when his intonation seemed less secure than it once was, that didn't matter too much. His uninhibited gusto came through with each surprising, infectious upward swoop of his horn.

Waters conjures up the reckless gaiety of the Jazz Age. And why not? He was a part of it, playing top Harlem nightspots in the 1920s and '30s — and getting into *everything* after-hours

(as he'll roguishly tell you, adding details we can't reprint here), which no doubt helped make his playing so colorful.

He went on to become an American expatriate, a favorite in Paris for four decades, before recently deciding to move back to the U.S. to spend his final years here. At the Metropolis — just the way he would have done it for continental audiences — he impishly introduced Nellie Lutcher's "Hurry On Down To My House" in four languages: French, German, English, and "American as spoken in Georgia." He sang "I Can't Give You Anything but Love" (adding an array of W.C. Fieldsian terms of endearment). He romped through "Cherokee" and "Three Little Words." On "Them There Eyes," he swung with a panache that often eludes younger musicians trying to play the music. It was good to see such compatible near-contemporaries of his sharing the stage with him as Al Casey (Fats Waller's original guitarist), pianist Red Richards, bassist Earl May, and drummer Percy Brice.

A 29-year-old Russian saxist, Dmitry Shapko, joined in, as did venerable Les Lieber. Waters' manager, Russ Dantzler, read letters of congratulations from cornetist Ruby Braff and President Clinton. And 86-year-old trumpeter Jonah Jones, one of the well-known musicians in the audience — others included Benny Powell, Charli Persip and Jimmy Owens — said he wished he'd brought his horn so he could jam with Waters. Next time, he vowed, he would.

BENNY MORTON

Just how highly Benny Morton was regarded in his prime by jazz devotees may be inferred from the fact that when the Princeton *Tiger* magazine's resident jazz authority, "Jazzbo," picked an all-star Negro swing band, he chose Benny Morton ("noted for his powerful yet sonorous attack") as the best overall trombonist. (The same undergraduate rated Coleman Hawkins tops on tenor sax, and Johnny Hodges and Benny Carter as the two best on alto.) Jazzbo rated Morton above such stalwarts as J. C. Higginbotham, Laurence Brown, and Tricky Sam Nanton, who were his next choices. This was in 1936, when Morton was still in Don Redman's Band — a year before Morton began the association with Count Basie for which he is perhaps best remembered today! Deciding who is "best" in a given field is, of course, a subjective judgment, and most later jazz commentators would not have rated Morton so highly, but he obviously impressed fans in his youth.

Morton, who lived most of his life in New York City (where Nancy Miller Elliott photographed him at his home) was born January 31, 1907 in Harlem Hospital; he died in that same hospital nearly 79 years later, on December 28, 1985. In his later years, he expressed pride that his entire career was spent in music; he had never had to take a day job.

We can understand the significance of that statement if we consider the fates that befell many of his contemporaries from the "name" black bands, after the big band era faded. During a 1969 Morton gig at the Downbeat Club, *New York Times* jazz critic John S. Wilson noted that Dickie Wells — who with Morton had made up the trombone section of the pace-setting, late '30s Basie Band — was working as a messenger on Wall Street. Wilson further noted that Russell Bowles, who spent the '30s and '40s play-

ing trombone in the Jimmie Lunceford Band, wound up as a salesman at Macy's department store. Sandy Williams, who, like Morton, had played trombone in the bands of Fletcher Henderson and Chick Webb, was then working as an elevator operator. Tommy Benford, erstwhile drummer for Jelly Roll Morton and Coleman Hawkins, had become a messenger for Merrill Lynch, Pierce, Fenner & Smith. Julian Dash, former featured saxist for Erskine Hawkins' Band, was in charge of the receptionists at that same firm's main office. Onetime Fletcher Henderson guitarist Freddie White wound up as a file clerk. And the list went on.

Morton began playing trombone professionally while in high school. In 1926, when he was just 19, he was impressive enough to succeed Charlie Green as the only trombonist in what was then surely the greatest jazz orchestra anywhere: Fletcher Henderson's, based at New York's Roseland Ballroom. Morton showed what he was made of quickly enough, with a spirited solo on "Jackass Blues" (May 14, 1926).

In December 1926, Henderson added another trombonist to the band: Jimmy Harrison (1900-1931). Harrison had played with Charlie Johnson, Fess Williams, and others; he was sometimes referred to as "the father of the swing trombone." Many musicians in the late 1920s — Morton among them — considered Harrison the number one trombonist in jazz. Others may have preferred Jack Teagarden or perhaps Miff Mole, but there was no denying Harrison's widespread influence. And Morton absorbed a good bit of Harrison's approach, playing alongside him for the next two years.

Morton went on to play in the big bands of Chick Webb (1930-31), Don Redman (1931-37), and Count Basie (1937-40), and the small groups of Joe Sullivan (1940), Teddy Wilson (1940-43),

and Edmund Hall (1944) (all at Cafe Society). In January 1946, as the Swing Era was coming to an end, he began playing in the pit orchestras of Broadway shows — a field that was then just beginning to open up for black musicians. Over the next 15 years he played shows including *St. Louis Woman, Lend an Ear, Guys and Dolls, Silk Stockings, Shinbone Alley,* and *Jamaica.* He worked, too, in the Radio City Music Hall Orchestra. And there was always time for jazz recording sessions with such artists as Charlie Shavers, Ruby Braff, Buck Clayton, Roy Eldridge, and Eddie Condon.

In his later years, Morton gigged with Henry "Red" Allen (who years before had been a sideman on a record date Morton had led), Ted Lewis, Wild Bill Davison, and Sy Oliver. In 1973, he replaced Vic Dickenson in the World's Greatest Jazz Band of Yank Lawson and Bob Haggart. In his long career, Morton didn't always get to play the jazz he liked best, but making music of any kind sure seemed to beat working — the way so many accomplished musicians he'd known had had to — as a clerk or a messenger.

SANDY WILLIAMS

I've found myself drawn again and again to the photo by Nancy Miller Elliott on the next page. There's such depth of feeling in it. The pathos in those beseeching eyes — your heart would go out to this man even if you had no idea who he was. You sense the pain he's felt.

It's sad that his name, Sandy Williams, will mean nothing to many younger jazz fans, because Williams (1906-1992) was a noteworthy contributor to many fine Swing Era recordings.

When he died, he hadn't played his trombone professionally for at least 25 years and it had been many more years than that since he had made any significant recordings. While the specific details of his life are uniquely his, in a broad sense Williams' life is representative of quite a few jazzmen's.

He worked early on with such leaders as Claude Hopkins (1929), Horace Henderson (1929-31), and Fletcher Henderson (1932-33), but really made his name during his eight-year tenure in Chick Webb's Band (1933-40). Of Webb's sidemen, he was arguably the most impressive soloist. (Some preferred dashing trumpeter Taft Jordan, but Jordan's style was derivative of Louis Armstrong's; Williams' was more original.) He may be heard on such admirable Webb sides as "Stompin' at the Savoy," "If Dreams Come True," and "Blue Minor," although records give only a suggestion of what Webb's band sounded like "live," since the standard, 10-inch 78 only contains about three minutes' worth of music. When the band was hot, playing for enthusiastic dancers at the Savoy Ballroom, it might stretch out for many more minutes, repeating riffs and letting soloists take multiple choruses.

Even with some of the big "name" bands he toured with, Williams knew hard times: dinners of bread and beans when funds were low, and the hassles all black musicians had, at times, obtaining food and lodging in the segregated South. Life was better when he was playing at the Savoy Ballroom, although the Savoy — like all Harlem nightspots — paid considerably less than downtown nightspots (which mostly booked white bands). He found solace in drinking. He felt, at first, it gave him what he needed to keep going as a musician, no matter how tired he felt.

After leaving Webb, Williams made some memorable recordings with Sidney Bechet (like "I Ain't Gonna Give Nobody None o' this Jelly Roll"), Coleman Hawkins ("Rocky Comfort"), and under his own name ("Gee Baby, Ain't I Good to You"). He worked at one time or another with Wild Bill Davison, Duke Ellington, and Rex Stewart and performed in Dixieland groups at Jimmy Ryan's Club (1949-50) and the Central Plaza (late 1950s). Dixieland was not his first choice in music, but he settled for what he could get because opportunities for swing musicians were diminishing. (Taft Jordan, for example, wound up in the 1960s as just another anonymous musician in the Broadway pit band of *Hello, Dolly* — and considered himself fortunate to get such steady, high-paying work.) By the '60s, Williams' drinking was getting the best of him (he had embouchure problems, to boot). He barely ate. By the time he finally stopped drinking, his career as a musician had died. He wasn't known to younger musicians anymore, and pride prevented him from going out and asking to be hired.

Having outlived his wife and most of his friends, he spent his final years in a nursing home. Doc Cheatham, one of the few pals from the old days who stayed in touch, told me how saddened he was to see Williams ("one of the greatest trombonists in the *world*") reduced to such a pitiful state, fruitlessly bemoaning the 45 years of his life he felt had been lost to liquor.

ELLA FITZGERALD

Ella Fitzgerald, captured on the pages that follow in performance shots by John Johnsen as a mature concert artist at the height of her powers, has been an important contributor for so long that her story might be placed almost anywhere in this book. But her deep roots in the Swing Era should not be overlooked.

Even on her very early recordings, made in the 1930s as a vocalist with Chick Webb and his Orchestra (when she was not yet out of her teens), the elements that would eventually make her the most widely-beloved of jazz singers are already present. The listener is struck by the warmth, purity and honesty of young Fitzgerald's sound. Above all, we hear the unfailing — and unsurpassed — sense of swing. On an infectious number like "A Little Bit Later On," she and the musicians get into a groove that makes you want to dance. At once a star and an ideal team player, Fitzgerald swings along with the musicians as if she were one of them.

In the 1930s, she was not scatting with the freedom, inventiveness, and masterly sense of construction she would later develop. (No one was, back then.) In her occasional early recorded forays into scat singing, she doesn't go out too far. But overall, her early records represent about as satisfying a set of debut performances I've ever heard.

Originally, Fitzgerald says she didn't want to become a singer at all, but rather a dancer. As a teenager in Yonkers, New York, she used to dance in the street for donations from passers-by. In 1934, when she was 16, she decided to enter the Apollo Theatre amateur contest as a dancer; her hope then was that if she won it, maybe she'd eventually get a job as an Apollo chorus girl. But when she got out on

stage and saw the audience, she was too nervous to dance.

Prodded by an Apollo staffer to do something, she began singing a current pop song, trying to sing like her then-idol, Connee Boswell (who was also cited as a major early influence by Maxine Sullivan). Fitzgerald's rhythmic, innocently girlish voice won her that contest, as well as a subsequent one at the Harlem Opera House.

Charles Linton, vocalist with Chick Webb's band, urged his boss to hire her. But Webb, Linton says, didn't see the need for Fitzgerald. Webb already had an excellent band, immensely popular with the dancers at Harlem's famed Savoy Ballroom, its base. Webb's records, with the likes of Linton, Taft Jordan and Sandy Williams, were doing all right. And if he were going to hire a girl singer, he added, he wanted someone who looked great. Linton insists he then went over Webb's head, urging the man who ran the Savoy Ballroom to give Fitzgerald a tryout. "And Mr. Buchanan told me he'd let her sing for two weeks: 'If the public likes her, we'll keep her. If not, out — no pay!' And in the same key as he said 'no pay,' I said, 'okay!'"

Fitzgerald was a smash with the savvy Savoy crowd. Webb began featuring her on most of his records, which meant less exposure for Linton and everyone else in the band. It was rare, in the mid '30s, for a bandleader to focus so much attention on a singer, but the crowd at the Savoy recognized her as a star. According to Linton, when the band traveled farther away from New York, Fitzgerald's jazzy vocal style initially did not go over as well. His recollection is that on one-nighters out of town, he got a better reception singing ballads in a straightforward, older style, than newcomer Fitzgerald. But in time, she far eclipsed every other member of the band in popularity. Linton (photographed by Andreas

Johnsen in 1994, wearing his usual turban — he's partly of Indian descent) still occasionally performs today. The last time Linton ran into Fitzgerald, he says, she gave no sign of recalling that he had once helped her.

Fitzgerald honed her rhythmic sense, singing frequently at the Savoy Ballroom, backed by Webb's superbly swinging band. She and the band were performing for enthusiastic fans who came to dance — not just listen — and those dancers influenced how she sang. Some of the spirit of the Savoy, which permeates her early recordings, is present wherever Fitzgerald sings today.

Among her successes with Webb's band were "Sing Me a Swing Song" in 1936, "Hallelujah" in 1937 (she stretched the word "hallelujah" at

one point, rising and falling with it the way as jazz trumpeter might have), and her blockbuster, "A-tisket A-tasket," in 1939. After Webb's death in 1939, she fronted his band for a couple of years, then went on her own with smaller groups.

Fitzgerald became a prime scat singer when bebop came up in the mid '40s (she really learned to scat from hearing Dizzy Gillespie do it in clubs, she has said). She might actually have been the first on record to use the term rebop (as bebop or bop was sometimes called early on), when she ended her 1939 recording of " 'Tain't What You Do" with that word. In the mid '50s, for producers Norman Granz and Buddy Bregman, she began recording a series of composer songbook albums (the songs of Irving Berlin, Cole Porter, the Gershwins, and so on) that have become classics. Billed as "The First Lady of Song," she attained the status of an icon.

No living female singer is more respected by other singers than Fitzgerald today. Why?

"Because what she does is impossible!" declares Annie Ross (photographed by Andreas Johnsen). Ross is one of a number of jazz singers who cite Fitzgerald as their first influence. "Like Charlie Parker, Ella can think it and execute it. Her musicality is beyond belief. That joyfulness and youthfulness in her voice will never go away. The sweetness of tone projects the sweet lady that she is today."

That assessment is echoed by Jon Hendricks (photographed by Andreas Johnsen), one of today's pre-eminent male vocalists and also, like Ross, an alumnus of the pace-setting 1950s vocal group Lambert, Hendrick, and Ross. He says of Fitzgerald: "She's the warmest soul in the world. When you put that much warmth with that beautiful an instrument, then you get an Ella Fitzgerald. A lot of female singers have beautiful instruments but don't have that warmth. It's like Toscanini said of Marian Anderson: 'A voice like that comes once in a lifetime.' Ella's a one-in-a-lifetimer."

"The first time I heard Ella, in 1937, I said, 'That is the girl. That's the champion — the Queen of Jazz,'" says Anita O'Day, herself among the all-time top song stylists. O'Day points out that Fitzgerald's exceptional vocal flights of fancy require exceptional physical attributes. "Notes and words are sung on air; you take air in and sing until you run out of air. Ella has an unusually large lung capacity." And she's made unforgettable use of her gifts, adds O'Day, who sings for me over the telephone — her voice sure and supple — the first Fitzgerald record she ever heard: "You showed me the way, when I was someone in distress...."

The mention of Fitzgerald's name prompts Ruth Brown (photographed by Andreas Johnsen) to sing samples of the first two Fitzgerald recordings she heard — "Have Mercy" and "I'm Up a Tree" — also the very first recordings ever played in Brown's Virginia home, when Brown was just 10 years old in 1938. "We didn't own a record player. My uncle bought one, and bought this record of Ella's from New York City.... Anyone who professes to be a singer has got to deal with Ella Fitzgerald." Brown explains her own reluctance to indulge in scat singing: "Once you've heard Ella, you've heard the best — why mess with the rest?"

Fitzgerald is still influencing upcoming artists. Cassandra Wilson, perhaps the brightest light among today's emerging jazz singers, notes that "the first recollection of vocal improvisation that I have is hearing the *Ella in Berlin* album when I was maybe four years old. Ella is the quintessential vocal musician. I love her!"

Fitzgerald lives quietly in retirement today. She stopped giving concerts in the early 1990s. (Nancy Miller Elliott's candid shot catches her relaxing between halves of one Carnegie Hall concert.) Her voice, in her final years as a performer, may not have had the power and flexibility it once had, but she still projected an appealing generosity of spirit, naturalness, and *joie de vivre*. She also had an unmatched gift for phrasing, and an unerring sense of construction. All of these assets were on display in a 22-song concert she gave June 25, 1988 at Carnegie Hall. When she scatted upon "Stompin' at the Savoy" — offering a fantasy upon the melody — her phrases may have appeared random to casual listeners, but they built toward climaxes, no less than Louis Armstrong's best trumpet solos did. She created the illusion of utter spontaneity, even though parts of her intricate routine — as recordings show — had been perfected and "set" 30 years ago.

She broke things up with a raspy Armstrong vocal imitation on "I Can't Give You Anything but Love." She gave " 'Tain't Nobody's Bizness" a surprising — and effective — rock touch. And she had everyone clapping on "Mack the Knife." In the 1980s, frail health limited her public appearances, and her vocal control was not always secure. But she had plenty of verve that night and seemed to grow stronger as the concert wore on.

She told the audience at the end: "You have really been medicine for me." I'm sure many were thinking, as I was, "And vice versa, Miss Fitzgerald."

Ella Fitzgerald

FRANKIE MANNING & NORMA MILLER

"This is Norma, my 50-year friend," Frankie Manning said.

"Any time you can be with a man 50 years and still be good friends...." Norma Miller interjected in wonder.

In the late 1930s and early '40s, Manning and Miller danced together as members of the famed Whitey's Lindy Hoppers, first at the Savoy Ballroom, and later in stage shows and films. They still dance together fairly often today. Miller reflected: "Ain't nobody left but us. I keep looking at him and he keeps looking at me, and we play musical chairs with life." The setting for this dialog: the apartment of Rebecca Reitz of the New York Swing Dance Society. The occasion: a private party honoring Miller's 70th birthday. (The following day, December 3, 1989 — officially proclaimed Norma Miller Day in Manhattan by Borough President Andrew Stein — would be the public birthday celebration at the Cat Club.) Reitz put on Count Basie's recording of "Shiny Stockings" and Manning beckoned Miller to dance, noting they had started the day dancing and they were going to end it dancing.

Manning (born 1916) was a key figure in the development of the Lindy Hop. According to Manning, Herbert ("Whitey") White, the one-time floor manager of the Savoy Ballroom who organized Whitey's Lindy Hoppers, wasn't so much interested in dancing as he was in making money. White was the promoter type, hustling for gigs, squelching any would-be competitors, and appropriating for himself a large cut from whatever his troupe of dancers earned. Manning, who became White's right-hand man, was interested strictly in dancing. It was Manning who originated the practice of pulling one's partner over one's shoulders — the oft-photographed aerial moves that garnered Whitey's Lindy Hoppers so much attention. And it was

Manning, beginning with an appearance by the Lindy Hoppers at the Apollo Theatre in 1936, who originated the practice of choreographing Lindy Hopping couples as an ensemble, so that instead of seeing couples all doing their own thing, you saw a theatrical form of jazz ensemble dancing. Witness the show-stealing Lindy Hopping sequence (choreographed by Manning) that Manning, Miller, and others from Whitey's company executed in the Olsen and Johnsen film *Hellzapoppin'*.

Lindy Hopping worked brilliantly with swing music. The high-flying steps created by Lindy Hoppers at the Savoy — pros and amateurs alike — seemed to mirror feelings expressed by the musicians in the great swing bands. Indeed, you'll find plenty of musicians who played the Savoy who'll tell you the reason the music swung so mightily there was that they were inspired by the dancers.

Lindy Hopping did not work well with bebop, however; the angular, unpredictable lines of Dizzy Gillespie and Charlie Parker may have fascinated many in the late '40s, but they were terrible for dancing. Manning eventually wound up taking a day job with the Postal Service, working there for several decades. But he kept his dancing skills up for his own enjoyment; Norma Miller, for one, wouldn't let him get completely away from dancing. In the 1980s, as time permitted, Manning taught dancing. And in 1989, he won a Tony Award for his choreography of Broadway's *Black and Blue*. Most Sundays in the late 1980s and early 1990s, you could spot Manning and Miller dancing together (and with others) at the New York Swing Dance Society's Savoy Sunday dances, held at the Cat Club and other locations.

Born in 1919, Miller lived from age 11 right behind the Savoy Ballroom. At age 14, she entered a dance contest there, won a prize, and was soon hired by Herbert ("Whitey") White for the troupe he managed. The best of the steps his dancers improvised were widely imitated — eventually becoming part of the regular repertoire for dancers far and near. White, she told me, was strict about his dancers' behavior: no drugs or liquor, no fooling around sexually with other members of his troupe. Miller did whatever White said, went wherever he told her to go. He soon had her (and another three of his dancers) off to England and France. She was just 15.

Her big surprise was discovering that European bands didn't swing. Until then, she had assumed that all over the world bands swung like those she'd grown up hearing in Harlem. And working with a non-swinging band was especially tough, since the Lindy Hoppers didn't carry arrangements for bands back then; they were used to dancing to whatever bands at the Savoy played.

Miller and the others went on to tour with name bands such as Cab Calloway's, Duke Ellington's, and Count Basie's, and singers such as Ethel Waters and Ella Fitzgerald; they were a part of the American jazz scene. They performed in nightclubs, in Broadway shows, in film shorts, and some full-length features. (You'll have no trouble spotting Miller Lindy Hopping, for example, the next time the Marx Brothers'

classic *A Day at the Races* turns up on TV.) In late 1941, Miller, Frankie Manning, and others of Whitey's Lindy Hoppers headed to Rio for what was supposed to be a six-week engagement. But World War II broke out and for months, as German submarines blockaded the harbor, there was no way to leave the city. Whitey's Lindy Hoppers disbanded not long afterwards as its male members were drafted into service.

Miller never left show business. When she grew too old to dance for a living, she became a comedienne. She still dances for pleasure, and has a troupe of her own, the "Norma Miller Jazz Dancers." She recently relocated from New York, home for almost all of her life, to Las Vegas.

This photo of Manning and Miller (accompanied by saxist Doug Lawrence) was taken one afternoon by Nancy Miller Elliott as they drove around Harlem looking for a setting that struck her as feeling right. Miller told Lawrence to turn the car around; she had seen some stairs she thought would work. They took this picture there. Only after the shoot did Elliott learn, from a resident who came out to see what was going on, that the site Elliott had selected had once been the studio of James Van Der Zee, the noted photographer of the Harlem Renaissance — which struck her as a most curious and pleasing coincidence.

LIONEL HAMPTON,
PASTOR JOHN GARCIA GENSEL

Some musicians want audiences to sit quietly while they perform. Not Lionel Hampton (whose zest is captured in performance shots on both vibraharp and drums — his second instrument — by Andreas Johnsen). Hampton would much rather see you dancing to his music. Or at least clapping to the beat. If he hasn't moved you in some way, he feels he hasn't succeeded.

The first — and still the most famous — of the jazz vibes players, Hampton exudes such abundant enthusiasm when he plays that even when his bands haven't been all they could have been, he leaves his audiences feeling psyched. High energy and a good beat — such qualities are more important to him than polish in a band.

Always rather religious, Hampton first became interested in music while attending the Holiness Church as a boy growing up in Birmingham, Alabama. He was so impressed by the drummer in the church band — she would beat her bass drum until the spirit seemed to possess her — he concluded that drumming provided the best means of getting close to the Lord. The day he picked up her mallet and began beat-

ing the bass drum in church was the day his musical career began.

His family eventually moved north to Chicago, where his uncle Richard (as he's recalled to me with a broad grin) worked for Al Capone. For a while, young Lionel even helped his uncle make bootleg liquor. But his interest in music was too strong for him to fall permanently into that kind of a life. In his youth, he became proficient on drums, piano, and — finally — the vibes. He made his very first recordings on vibes, with Louis Armstrong, in 1930. It was Armstrong (whose photo Hampton is holding aloft in one shot taken by Andreas Johnsen at the Armstrong Archives in Queens College) who encouraged Hampton to concentrate on vibes.

Hamp's tremendous success with Benny Goodman from 1936 to 1940, and for the following 55 years as a leader of his own bands, is well known. When I asked Hampton which of his accomplishments made him particularly happy, the first thing that came to his mind was helping to break the color barrier in jazz. It was an important advance when he and Teddy Wilson — the first black musicians to work regu-

Lionel Hampton

outspoken advocate of blacks and whites working together.*

Now in his upper 80s, Hamp continues to "make a joyful noise" with his band. And when he gets warmed up, there is no stopping him. Junior Mance, a strong, underrated pianist who in recent years has toured with Hampton's "Golden Men of Jazz" (an all-star combination Hampton uses when not fronting his own big band) told me in 1995: "Hamp loves to play. We'll be doing a set that's supposed to last no more than an hour; he'll keep us playing for 90 minutes. He wears us out!" The straw boss of Hampton's band is veteran trombonist Al Grey (caught, in Andreas Johnsen's shot, with one arm raised high to cue fellow bandmates). Like many Hampton alumni, Grey says that playing for Hampton has always been different from playing for other leaders; Hampton places more emphasis on really feeling the spirit of the music than on playing precisely or cleverly.

𝄞

---

* Six decades after Hampton and Goodman began breaking the color barrier, I'm afraid one still sees some troubling instances of racial separatism. In the pages of *The New York Post*, I've periodically registered objections when leaders (or contractors) appeared to be hiring people at least in part for reasons of race. (It's usually a case of contractors simply hiring their friends.) I expressed my objections when, for example, Mel Tormé brought into Michael's Pub a few years back a big band that was lily white (for a program whose centerpiece was a tribute to Tormé's musical idol, Duke Ellington). I objected when Frank Sinatra Jr. brought into the Tavern on the Green a 19-piece jazz-oriented orchestra (whose members, he announced, were "the finest musicians in the business") that was all-white. Such bands seem hard to defend on either musical or sociological grounds. As Ol' Blue Eyes sang memorably in "The House I Live In": "all races and religions — that's America to me...." I've also objected in print to examples of what appears to be reverse bias, such as the fact that in eight years of presenting classical jazz concerts at Lincoln Center, Wynton Marsalis has yet to salute a composer who happens to be white; I think valuable opportunities to foster racial togetherness in these oft-polarized times — as well as to present some good music —are being missed.

larly with a prominent white leader — became members of the Benny Goodman Quartet in 1936; that really helped the cause of racial integration, much as Jackie Robinson's later success in breaking the color barrier in baseball would. The jazz community has generally been ahead of society at large on racial matters.

Public acceptance of Hampton's and Wilson's work with Goodman made it much easier for other leaders to try hiring black musicians. Until then, everyone in the entertainment industry had been extremely wary of presenting blacks and whites on stage together. (Some parts of the country forbade such appearances by law.) Hampton remembers a *Down Beat* headline after one of his earliest appearances: "Predicted Race Riot Fades As Crowd Applauds Goodman Quartet." Hampton has high regard for Goodman's integrity on racial matters. In an era when many taxi drivers wouldn't take black patrons, Hampton notes that Goodman would freely invite Hampton to ride with him in his Packard. Hampton also remembers Goodman threatening to "bust the head" of one patron who directed racially abusive language towards Hampton. Hampton's own big band today, not surprisingly, is racially mixed. He's an

Hampton reads the Bible daily. A Christian Scientist today, he cherishes friendships he has with religious leaders of all faiths. One of Nancy Miller Elliott's photos of Hampton shows him, in full costume, portraying one of the three wise men in a jazz version of the Nativity. Each year at a different New York house of worship, Hampton participates in that pageant.

The photo of Hampton standing alongside Pastor John Garcia Gensel of St. Peter's Lutheran Church in New York City was taken by Elliott in 1988, when Hampton received the first annual Duke Ellington/Shepherd of the Night Flock Award from Pastor Gensel. Perhaps it's appropriate to digress for a moment to talk about the pastor, for he's long been a vital part of the scene and he deserves some recognition.

Gensel was the first (and for many years the only) cleric in the world officially charged to serve the jazz community. Born in 1917 in Puerto Rico, Gensel grew up in Catawissa, Pennsylvania.

By the late 1920s, he was listening to broadcasts of Duke Ellington's Band from the Cotton Club. When he saw the band live in 1933, he became hooked on jazz for life. By the mid 1950s, he was spending so many nights in New York clubs he sought and obtained official approval from the Lutheran Church to minister to jazz performers. He established weekly jazz vespers, which have continued to this day. (The portrait of Gensel by himself was taken by Andreas Johnsen.)

Gensel has conducted memorial services for many of the giants of jazz, including Duke Ellington, Thelonious Monk, Buddy Rich, Maxine Sullivan, Coleman Hawkins, and Gil Evans. He has counseled many more musicians of all faiths (and of no faith), as well as their wives, widows, companions, and so on. They've found him easy to talk to (and still find him easy to talk to, although he's now officially in retirement, his responsibilities recently assumed by a successor, Pastor Dale Lind).

Sitting in his office looking out on East 54th Street a few days after the picture of Hampton and him was taken, he spoke with me about his calling. He noted accurately: "Musicians don't have to preface their remarks to me, as they would in talking to most pastors, with 'First, let me tell you about the jazz world, about club owners, about life on the road....' I know what they're talking about."

Jazz Veterans

Gensel likes the remark made to him one day by a stranger on Broadway: "'Aren't you the cat that believes that jazz musicians are human beings?'" He reflected: "Jazz has been put down in our society. And if you put down what a person does, you put down the person." Gensel has no patience for those who argue jazz and religion don't mix. "Jazz is a conduit through which God expresses his love and his sorrow. It touches the deepest feelings." To which Hampton would no doubt add: "Amen!"

𝄞

For the past decade, Hampton has focused considerable energy on the Lionel Hampton Jazz Festival, held each year at the University of Idaho in Moscow, Idaho. (That's where the shots were taken showing Hampton with myself and with pianist Marian McPartland and Dr. Lynn Skinner, head of the Lionel Hampton School of Music at the university and organizer of the festival.)

What makes the Hampton Festival unique is the way it offers world-class jazz artists in both formal night-time concerts, before thousands of seated patrons, and in informal day-time clinics, in which students and adults can interact with those same artists. It may not be the biggest or the best of all jazz festivals — but I certainly don't know of another that mixes entertainment with education so effectively.

After spending six days at the 10th annual Hampton Festival, which drew 13,000 attendees in February 1995, I'm convinced some other colleges ought to copy exactly what they're doing.

Dropping in on one clinic, for example, I saw Marian McPartland demonstrate all different piano styles, then invite a volunteer up to perform an original piece which she critiqued. (The young woman later told me she found McPartland's advice concerning pedal use invaluable. What other chance would she ever have to get personal tips from McPartland?) In another clinic, master jazz singer Jon Hendricks ("the James Joyce of Jive") covered pretty much the whole history of vocal jazz, from Bessie Smith, Louis Armstrong, and Billie Holiday to the present. Hendricks, of course, has quite a way with words. (He wrote the lyrics for many of the numbers he's recorded through the years, whether on his own or earlier as a member of the famed Lambert, Hendricks and Ross vocal group of the 1950s and early '60s. He also worked as a jazz critic in San Francisco for a couple of years.) He delivered his remarks, covering the history of jazz singing, in *rhyme*! He also showed film clips from his collection of all the singers he talked about. Afterwards, he pulled students from the audience to help accompany him on an informal set.

In still another clinic, I watched Canadian jazz singer Dee Daniels, who has a four-octave range, expand some kids' vocal range within the course of an hour. Pianist Jane Jarvis, 80, won over some obviously skeptical youths. (She later received copies of reports written by some clinic students, who stressed they'd known nothing about jazz when their professor, Linda Miller, made them go. One such student, named Eric Wendt, wrote: "When I received the assignment to attend a Jazz Festival clinic I thought: 'Oh great, this is going to be stupid.' Then a very old woman hobbled into the room and I thought I was right. She then proceeded to introduce herself, with great charisma and intrigue…. She took requests and changed songs around to her own liking, which sounded very good. It was truly amazing to watch her play, her fingers just flew around the keyboard…. I am very glad I attended.")

The highlight of Jarvis' concert set was a rendition of Hoagy Carmichael's "Star Dust" that showed great respect for the melody. (And with a melody of that stature, you'd be crazy not to respect it.) Hank Jones was similarly sensitive to the composer's intentions when he offered his interpretation of Carmichael's "Georgia on my Mind." Trombonist Al Grey (whose reminiscences of touring with the Count Basie Band in the '50s I enjoyed hearing over brunch) is invariably introduced these days as "the last of the big plungers." But he brought out his son Mike for a trombone duet that made it clear his son can help carry on some of that tradition.

In the nighttime concerts, jazz stars hustled on and off stage, often doing just two or three numbers before being replaced. (Sometimes that grew frustrating for me, because I wanted to hear more from certain artists. If you stepped out of the auditorium briefly, perhaps to search for a bathroom, you might return to find you'd missed the work of, say, a George Shearing or an Art Farmer. The shows were generally very fast paced.) The audience, however, seemed highly enthusiastic throughout. Lynn Skinner has succeeded in building the festival up so that it draws fans from throughout the Northwest and points beyond.

"It's so overwhelming, no words can explain it," said Aaron Steele, 16, who rode all day by bus from Canada for the festival. "And after it's over, you want more."

"It's also a chance for kids to win instruments and scholarships," noted Gabe Angerilli, a young drummer from White Rock, Canada, expressing pride that students from his own Semiahmoo Secondary School, directed by David Proznick, won a number of Hampton Festival competitions over the years.

"It totally motivates you to pursue a career in music," declared Scott Vrecko, 17, of Surrey, British Columbia. Having been voted an outstanding young alto sax player, Vrecko was among those who got to perform on the main stage. (He played in an appealingly uncluttered, rather full-bodied mainstream style.) I don't think any of the young musicians in attendance were more thrilled, though, than Dawaylon McCoy, a spirited 11-year-old vibes player from Texas who got to jam with the indefatigable "King of the Vibes," Lionel Hampton himself. Hampton himself paid all expenses involved in bringing McCoy (whom he'd discovered on an earlier trip to Texas) and McCoy's grandmother to the festival.

It spoke volumes for Hampton's abilities that, at age 86, no musician could steal the show from him. Though such pros as trumpeters Arturo Sandoval (born in Cuba) and Claudio Roditi (born in Brazil) were young enough to be his children or grandchildren, Hampton's energy level remained remarkably high. He danced a

bit, flipped drumsticks in the air and caught them, jammed on vibes with one small group after another, and gave the concert its emotional high point when his big band roared through "Hamp's Boogie Woogie," "Flying Home," and "Sunny Side of the Street" — the last a major find, a vintage Quincy Jones arrangement that Hamp and his longtime manager, Bill Titone, had rediscovered among some old papers in storage.

Hampton talks about the festival (and its role educating youths about jazz) in all of his interviews these days. (One of Andreas Johnsen's shots shows Hampton giving an interview to a reporter from the Harlem-based *Amsterdam News*.) He says he'd really love to get something like the festival going in Harlem, too, if he could find a way to do it.

About a month after returning from the 1995 festival to his Manhattan home, Hampton suffered a mild stroke. (His publicist, Phil Leshin, said it was less serious than one he'd suffered in 1992, from which he'd made a remarkable recovery.) Among the first to send Hampton get-well greetings was former President George Bush (hardly surprising, since Hamp is an ardent Republican) and Nation of Islam leader Louis Farrakhan (which *was* a bit surprising, since Hamp had been good friends with Malcolm X). Because of the stroke, Hampton wound up having to spend his 87th birthday (April 20, 1995) in Mount Sinai Hospital. Visiting him that afternoon, I found him in good spirits. "I could walk out of here today," he insisted to me, "but

I'm going to stay a little longer until I'm sure everything is sweet. I'll be playing vibes again in a couple of weeks. We're touring Europe this summer."

Jazz royalty gathered at the hospital to wish Hampton a happy birthday. There was Max Roach, perhaps the most universally respected of drummers; Tito Puente, the king of Latin jazz (who shares a birthday with Hamp); master bassist Milt Hinton, a friend of Hampton's for more than six decades; saxist Benny Golson; and pianists Junior Mance and Kuni Mikami, among others.

"If you guys had brought your instruments, what a band we could have had," declared Hampton.

Everybody sang "Happy birthday."

"Let's have another take on that," cried one of the musicians and they repeated a chorus, as Hamp (with an assist from Titone) cut the first piece of birthday cake.

"C'mere, give me a hug," he called to his five-year-old godson, Christopher Nelson, who did just that. (I snapped a photo as they hugged. Standing in the background, from left to right, are: Milt Hinton, an unidentified woman, jazz singer Gail Wynters, Junior Mance, and Mona Hinton — Milt's wife). Someone gave Hamp a miniature set of vibes. "Oh, good — I can show this to those nurses who keep asking me what instrument I play, 'What is the vibraharp?' " he quipped, gamely signing an autograph requested by a hospital aide.

Someone else asked if Hampton was up to drumming yet. "I'm not going to drum with these guys in the room," he said, glancing toward Max Roach and Bob Litwak, a doctor who also doubles as a jazz drummer.

The party was breaking up when in strolled Clark Terry, trumpet to his lips. He blew two muted choruses, soft and swinging, of "Happy Birthday."

"My, my, my," Hampton said. "It's going to be good when I can start playing again." When he was discharged, on May 4th, he headed straight to the piano (his third instrument, after vibes and drums) and began practicing.

GEORGE T. SIMON & FRIENDS

The Big Band Era wouldn't have been quite so big without George T. Simon listening to all of the bands and sharing his boundless enthusiasms in print with the public.

No magazine in the nation was regularly reviewing big bands when Simon proposed to do just that for *Metronome* back in 1935. Hired at $25 a month as the magazine's associate editor (he became editor-in-chief four years later), he soon made *Metronome*, which had previously concerned itself with such matters as instrument manufacturing and music publishing, the primary source of information on the burgeoning big band scene.

Under his own name, Simon documented the

era in hundreds of band reviews. Under the pseudonym of Jimmy Bracken, he let readers in on goings-on at record dates, jam sessions, and informal gatherings of musicians. Under the pseudonyms of Gordon Wright and Henry S. Cummings, he alerted readers to the best records. In the early years, Simon was actually the only person at *Metronome* covering the nation's many big bands and swinging small groups. (Later, other writers such as bebop enthusiasts Barry Ulanov and Leonard Feather made important contributions to the magazine — Simon always preferred swing.) Using pseudonyms not only created the illusion of a larger staff than the magazine could afford, it also helped create the illusion of consensus among critics when "Wright" and "Bracken" seemed to agree with Simon that certain musicians were especially noteworthy. Throughout the Swing Era, Simon's influence extended far beyond *Metronome*'s readership because countless opinion-shapers, writing for other magazines and newspapers or hosting radio shows, read *Metronome* religiously, as did band bookers and record executives. If Simon said, "This is someone to watch," they watched.

It couldn't have hurt when, for example, Simon repeatedly raved about the Benny Goodman Band (beginning with Simon's very first article for *Metronome* in March 1935, five months before the band's breakthrough at the Palomar Ballroom, Simon remained a lifelong Goodman champion), or when Simon started 1936 by proclaiming that Ella Fitzgerald, "unheralded, and practically unknown right now," was already "one of the best femme hot warblers...and there's no reason why she shouldn't be just about the best in time to come...watch her!"

Simon brought little-known but talented musicians to the attention of bandleaders (getting Benny Goodman, for example, to audition Mel Powell and Louie Bellson before either had reached age 18). Simon not only helped Glenn Miller find many of the guys in his first band, he played drums on some of the Miller Band's first records (Simon had been a drumming bandleader as an undergraduate at Harvard).

After leaving *Metronome* in 1955, Simon served as, among other things, a record producer, a writer/producer/consultant on various jazz TV shows, and head of the National Academy of Recording Arts and Sciences, which gives out the Grammy Awards (one of which Simon himself won, for writing the best liner notes of 1972). He penned numerous articles on jazz and popular music, not to mention such oft-cited books as *The Big Bands* (which won him the ASCAP-Deems Taylor Award in 1968), *Simon Says: the Sights and Sounds of the Swing Era, 1935-1955*, and *Glenn Miller and His Orchestra*. In his later years, you could often find Simon drumming in and co-leading (with saxist Bill Simon — no relation) his Twilight Jazz group at New York clubs, such as Jimmy Walker's and the Red Blazer Too.

In the photo by Nancy Miller Elliott, taken at Eddie Condon's Club in New York in 1985 at the celebration of Simon's 50th year as a jazz writer, Simon (wearing the bow-tie) sits between jazz greats Gerry Mulligan (left) and Benny Goodman and Cab Calloway.

ARTIE SHAW

How often do you get to visit with someone who's done something better than anyone else alive?

In December 1994, I traveled 40 miles north of Los Angeles to spend a day at the home of the reclusive Artie Shaw, who may well have been — as Duke Ellington's star clarinetist, Barney Bigard, put it — the greatest clarinetist of all time. Benny Goodman, Shaw's only real competitor for that "best ever" title, may have swung harder. But no one surpassed Shaw's facility, harmonic sophistication, and grace. Or set higher orchestral standards.

Considered the most brilliant and volatile of all the big-band leaders, Shaw organized and broke up bands repeatedly. He had the nation's number-one band — he'd just dethroned Goodman in the *Down Beat* poll — the first time he abruptly quit music, in 1939.

Judging from recordings, he was at the very peak of his powers as a player — improvising solos of absolutely flawless construction — when he quit for good, in 1954. Playing clarinet eight or nine hours per day, which his perfectionist standards had long demanded, left little time for anything else, he said. He'd had his fill of playing "Begin the Beguine" and "Star Dust." There was simply too much else he wanted to do.

𝄞

At Shaw's gate, I press the buzzer and wait a moment, eyeing the signs warning would-be trespassers that his property is protected by a security firm. The gate opens electrically. Inside his home, I'm struck first by a portrait of him which I recognize is the work of the late Don Bachardy. The house, I see, is filled with paintings, recordings, and — above, all, seemingly everywhere — books. "I like your house," I say, taking it all in. "You're looking inside my brain," he responds.

He drives me in his maroon Lexus to a restaurant where, after bantering with the waitress, he launches into some of the most stimulating conversation I've had.

The talk, continuing almost without pause through the meal, the swift drive back home, and several hours upstairs, touches on everything from politics to art to jazz history (a good bit of which Shaw, who's 84, personally witnessed). He speaks admiringly of jazz greats ranging from Bix Beiderbecke (with whom he roomed for a week, giving up when he was unable to persuade Bix to shower regularly) to Benny Carter (*always* one of the greats, in his judgment). He makes reference to the Torah, to Blake, recommends a German novel (*Perfume* by Patrick Suskind), quotes poetry by Keats, alludes to *Fairy Mythology* by Keatley, and alerts me to passages to savor in music by Ellington and Ravel.

He's a dynamic talker who hardly requires questions. But I interject one anyway: "Forty years after you stopped playing and composing, do new melodies ever still come to you?"

"All the time. Even as we speak," he says. He begins humming — simultaneously fingering the notes in the air — an intricate musical theme he's been composing while maintaining this intense conversation. "You can't stop that," he adds. "About a month ago, I thought of a new fingering for the Mozart Concerto, which I'll never play again."

He hopes, in the next year, to get onto CD some never-before-released recordings of classical music that he made in his prime. (Among many other distinctions, Shaw was the first jazz musician to play classical music in a jazz club.)

He's just issued, on the MusicMasters label, an intriguing CD *Mixed Bag* consisting of long unavailable 1940s jazz big-band recordings he made, including the ones that launched Mel Tormé. And BMG currently offers a superb Shaw CD called *Personal Best*. But these days Shaw views himself primarily as a writer.

Shaw autographs for me a collection of short stories he's written, *The Best of Intentions*. The book's first story, he tells me — dealing with his experiences jamming in Harlem 65 years ago — will also be one of 91 chapters in a huge novel he's now completing. Most of his time is spent at the computer, writing.

In addition, he's currently spearheading a project, with the University of Arizona, to make the history of jazz available on the CD-ROM format. He's contacted jazz notables of all ages with detailed descriptions of his project, to get their endorsement and/or input.

He felt slighted when — after everyone else he'd contacted responded enthusiastically to him themselves — Branford Marsalis had a secretary write that Mr. Marsalis would need more information. Shaw, who helped break the color barrier in the 1930s and '40s by hiring such top artists as Billie Holiday and Roy Eldridge, wonders if he's being rebuffed because he's white.

He notes it is "politically correct" in some quarters to think of jazz as black music, though he finds that viewpoint parochial. He assumes such political correctness lies behind the fact that Lincoln Center has not yet dealt with his music (or Goodman's), but has honored less influential clarinetists like Johnny Dodds and Jimmie Noone. "Jimmie Noone could play," he says, "but Johnny Dodds sounded like a leaky bicycle pump."

Their music, it might be added, is also easier to re-create than Shaw's. What clarinetist could really duplicate Shaw's breathtaking closing cadenza on "These Foolish Things"?

We take time out to listen to Shaw recordings. "It's no mean feat to get 50 musicians to swing," Shaw observes correctly. He'd still have much to teach any large ensemble if he were hired as a guest conductor.

As I listen to the ease with which he carries off every passage, the freedom with which he reaches for every high C above C, I also can't help thinking of the years of eight-hour playing-days he put in to attain that seeming ease. What makes an artist push himself so hard?

"Why do we do it?" Shaw reflects. "I think it comes down to a very simple thing. In the war, everywhere you went you saw 'Kilroy Was Here.' Remember that? That's I think what we're doing. Basically, I think that's the bottom line for mankind: I was here, I left a print." Shaw's will be around for a long time.

Jazz Veterans

MAXINE SULLIVAN & STUFF SMITH

When Nancy Miller Elliott photographed Maxine Sullivan and Stuff Smith together, in 1958, they were still respected and admired by other great jazz artists, but public interest in them had ebbed. (For a clearer view of Smith's features, see the next photo — of Smith alone — taken by Elliott, and the photo of Smith with Danish violinist Svend Asmussen, taken by John Johnsen.)

Both Smith and Sullivan broke through to fame — Smith in 1936, Sullivan the following year — at the Onyx Club on New York's fabled 52nd Street. Smith was the first jazzman to score on amplified violin, and no one ever outswung him on the instrument. His recordings ("Stuff Smith and his Onyx Club Boys" — Smith, trumpeter Jonah Jones, four rhythm, plus, occasionally, a clarinet or sax) exuded an impudent, spirit-lifting energy. Often, as on "I'se a Muggin'" and "Here Comes the Man With the Jive," Smith sang. Occasionally, as on "You'se a Viper" and "Joshua," Jones sang. Some of their numbers celebrated getting high on liquor or marijuana. (And when, one night, the band showed up sober, Smith told them he wanted them high; they couldn't make the music he wanted sober.) Smith would wear a top hat, Jones a derby, to add to the liveliness.

When the band went to California to make a movie in 1937, the club brought in a replacement group (John Kirby emerged as the leader) that it hoped would maintain the exuberance of Smith's band. But Kirby's sextet developed a wholly opposite approach — cool, restrained, precisely executed — which, surprisingly, proved to be no less successful. And Maxine Sullivan, who sang with the group, soon eclipsed the group in popularity. As she told *Down Beat*, she liked hitting notes "softly and without effort; a relaxed feeling at all times...I like to take sad numbers with a simple melody, changing the notes to fit the soft, straight manner — strict tempo vocalizing and no jive."

In 1937-38, Sullivan was so popular she was considered for the Cotton Club. "But I wasn't experienced enough to do a show then," she told me. "They didn't necessarily use microphones in these shows; those singers had big voices and could project. Well, I was a microphone singer. And, then, I didn't have any stage presence." But she was developing rapidly. In the next few years, she appeared in two films (getting bigger billing in one, she told me with some satisfaction, than young Ronald Reagan), on radio, and finally played the Cotton Club and other prominent venues.

In the 1950s, American public interest in Sullivan and Smith (and many other Swing Era veterans) waned. Musicians still held them in great esteem. (Dizzy Gillespie, in fact, acknowl-

edged Smith as a significant influence upon him.) But jobs weren't always plentiful. Smith found more appreciative audiences in Europe. He died in 1967, before the revival of interest in older jazz stylists in the United States that benefited so many others of his generation. Sullivan stayed out of music from the late 1950s to the late 1960s. In fact, the kids in her daughter's school system (where she became a school board trustee) had no idea she had even been a singer until one of them spotted a photo of her with Louis Armstrong in a book about jazz. By the time she re-entered show business, things had begun turning around; she found herself appreciated more, and getting increasingly frequent recording opportunities. And her warm, no-pretense personality endeared her to many.

Although she smoked a lot (I remember well the sound of her cigarette lighter — it played "Smoke Gets In Your Eyes"), her voice retained great loveliness until the end, whether brimming with confidence or tinged with uncertainty. In her last decade, she recorded too frequently for all of her albums to be equally successful (some were hasty affairs), but her final album, *Together — Maxine Sullivan Sings the Music of Jule Styne* (1987) was first-rate, as satisfying as anything she'd ever done. She moved comfortably from vintage numbers such as a moving "I Don't Want to Walk Without You" and a zesty "Sunday" (sung with a greater jazz playfulness than she projected in her youth) to a contemporary (and no less effectively interpreted) "Killing Time."

JONAH JONES

The thing trumpeter Jonah Jones could never have anticipated, as the big band era faded, was that his greatest commercial success still lay ahead. When the bottom dropped out of the big band business in the late 1940s, some fine sidemen left music entirely; the jobs simply weren't there any longer. Others clung to whatever work was available.

Jones stayed with Cab Calloway when Calloway, in 1948, was forced to cut back from his 16-piece big band to a septet (occasionally re-forming big bands for specific dates). Jones had been featured with Calloway since 1941 — Calloway had even recorded a special number, "Jonah Joins the Cab," in honor of his arrival (after previously having played for Fletcher Henderson, Benny Carter, and Stuff Smith — with whom he had made a name for himself). Jones stayed with Calloway, too, when Calloway subsequently cut back from the septet to just a quartet. And when Calloway went into a Broadway revival of *Porgy and Bess,* Jones played for about a year (1953) in the pit orchestra.

After freelancing sporadically — and considering getting a day job, since work was not steady — Jones, backed by a rhythm section, went into the Embers on New York's East 54th Street in 1955. He scored such a hit, playing softly swinging standards and show tunes, often muted (and he'd never been much for mutes before), that his week-long engagement got held over.

And held over. He played the Embers often enough over the next decade to consider it his home. And when he wasn't there, he was working posh rooms elsewhere in the U.S., Europe, Australia, and the Far East. He recorded albums for Capitol, featuring numbers like "Baubles, Bangles, and Beads" and "On the Street Where You Live," which became hits.

Some of the music he was making now was rather bland, aimed more at the tired businessman than at the jazz aficionado. But critics who might have wondered if he was "selling out" artistically couldn't begrudge him his success; he was certainly better off working regularly as a trumpeter than being forced to find a job as a bank messenger or taxi driver, as some of his Swing Era contemporaries had been. Jones had proven himself as a jazz soloist long ago, not just in his main affiliations (with Calloway and Smith), but also on records he had made with Teddy Wilson, Billie Holiday, and Lionel Hampton.

When I went to hear him at Jimmy Weston's Club, on Manhattan's East Side, in 1987, he was still using an array of mutes and playing a lot of the "easy listening" type numbers that had sold so many albums for him in the 1950s and '60s. I must admit I was much more interested when he played pure jazz, with an Armstrong type of spirit, on numbers like "Struttin' With Some Barbecue" and "Rose Room." But if he hadn't made all those commercial albums for Capitol, he wouldn't have been working — at age 77 — at Jimmy Weston's Club at all. I'm sure some people listening to "If My Friends Could See Me Now" had no idea that a half-century before his friends had included the very greatest of jazz players.

When Jones and I chatted between sets, I was surprised to find he seemed to be as proud of the fact that he had played top hotels worldwide as of anything he had done in jazz — and particularly proud of the fact that, after he had made hit records in the 1950s, Fred Astaire (he showed me a photo) had chosen him to play on his TV specials.

JOE BUSHKIN

This playful photo by Nancy Miller Elliott (no other jazz photographer I know would take such a shot) shows jazz pianist and composer Joe Bushkin (at right) and his longtime collaborator, the late artist and lyricist John de Vries. Together they produced such hits as "Oh! Look at Me Now," which the Tommy Dorsey Band, featuring Frank Sinatra, Connie Haines, and the Pied Pipers, recorded in 1942; "A Hot Time in the Town of Berlin," which Bing Crosby and the Andrews Sisters recorded in 1944; and "Boogie Woogie Blue Plate," which Louis Jordan recorded in 1947. But since this is a jazz book, we'll focus on the irrepressible Joe Bushkin.

Are we to infer that Nancy Miller Elliott sees him as just a big kid? And that perhaps he agrees with that assessment? They ain't talking — but the picture works.

I'd often heard that Bushkin can't read music. The truth, I've since learned, is a bit more complicated: Bushkin *can* read music, but he much prefers playing freely to reading written parts. Back in the days when he was with Tommy Dorsey's Orchestra, he actually encouraged the rumors that he didn't know how to read music. He deliberately never kept piano parts in front of him. He succeeded in fooling Dorsey, a notoriously stern taskmaster, who stopped giving him written piano parts. Bushkin contin-

ued playing piano by ear — and everybody stayed happy.

Bushkin was born in 1916 in East Harlem. It was a white neighborhood but not far from the black areas, and he grew up with an exposure to — and fondness for — black music that the average white American never had. After his family heard Fats Waller one night at Harlem's Lafayette Theater, his father bought every Waller record he could find, and threw out some records by white dance bands they had listened to previously. And some of Waller's infectious lilt found its way into Bushkin's playing. Bushkin also heard records by Louis Armstrong's Hot Five before the average American knew who Armstrong was. He soaked up black entertainment — jazz, comedy, dance — at Harlem's Lafayette and Apollo theaters. He liked the whole atmosphere — the zest for enjoying life. And all of that helped make him a more swinging player. He was a natural pianist. As a novice student in his early teens, he found he could identify any notes his piano teacher struck, whether singly or in chords, and could easily play back by ear passages he heard. Just how talented he was, and how accepted he was by jazz royalty, may be inferred from the fact that when Bushkin was just 22, stride piano giant Willie "The Lion" Smith chose to record a duet with him.

Bushkin found plenty of work on 52nd Street (or "Swing Street" as it was known to fans in the '30s). He played the Famous Door — legendary in jazz lore because so many greats worked there — when it was new, and (on most nights) half empty. He worked and recorded with the likes of Billie Holiday and Bunny Berigan.

Bushkin was in Tommy Dorsey's Band around the peak of its artistic and commercial success. Bushkin played on nearly 120 Dorsey recordings between April 1940 and March 1942, and also wrote songs on the side. Later came stints with Benny Goodman, residencies at the Embers, and concerts with Bing Crosby.

Bushkin remains a marvelous pianist today. He ought to be much better known to younger listeners than he is, but he doesn't choose to work frequently. In 1988, Bushkin attended a celebration honoring Marian McPartland's 10th anniversary on public radio. The Lincoln Center Library auditorium contained many of McPartland's friends, and that means some real heavyweights of the piano world. An assortment played. When Bushkin finally loped up towards the stage with a walk that brought to mind a comedian pretending to be drunk, you couldn't help wondering if he was kidding around or too intoxicated to perform. Yet once he sat down, with an impish grin on his face, his fingers began flying over the keyboard. In terms of technical prowess, sense of swing, and *elan*, he stole the show.

I caught his opening night at New York's posh Tavern on the Green in February of 1995. His playing was notably more spirited the second set. His explanation: "It takes a couple of drinks to get into the right tempo."

In a wonderfully extravagant gesture, Bushkin brought out surprise guests, turning his quartet into an octet. Even Lenny Triola, who books the room, was surprised as the extra players (whom Bushkin announced to the audience would be joining him for the second set every night of his two-week engagement) took the bandstand. His intention, Bushkin cracked, was to outnumber the audience.

Joe Bushkin

55

SY OLIVER

The arrangers were no less important than the instrumentalists in creating the sounds of the Swing Era.

Although that era was over before I was born, some radio stations continued playing big band favorites when I was growing up. I can remember standing in the kitchen as a youth and hearing on WNEW-AM a number that just struck me — pow! — as big band perfection from beginning to end. After it was over, the announcer noted it was Tommy Dorsey's version of "Opus One" and I knew I had to have that record. I was already into the Dorseys, having discovered old 78s in the basement and having gotten a requested Tommy Dorsey album for Christmas, before I was even out of grade school. But this particular record knocked me out — and it still does — as few others had. In time I came to realize the man primarily re-

sponsible for making it so great wasn't Dorsey but the number's composer and arranger, Sy Oliver. I soon found that I recognized and dug Oliver's handiwork, whether his arrangements were being played by the bands of Dorsey or Jimmie Lunceford. By my mid-teens, Oliver was my favorite arranger.

He could take songs such as "For You" and "The One I Love Belongs to Somebody Else" and give them a curiously laidback lilt that was so naturally hip as to make other renditions of the songs that I'd previously enjoyed seem square. I loved the marvelous relaxation — no pushing now, please — he brought as arranger and vocalist to "Don't Be a Baby, Baby" by Tommy Dorsey's Clambake Seven, which had favored a kind of bright and jangly Dixieland before his arrival. I listened over and over to the Jimmie Lunceford Band playing Oliver's easy-going treatments of "Rain," "Four or Five Times," "Cheatin' on Me," and "Since My Best Girl Turned Me Down," and savored such livelier Dorsey/Oliver specialties as "Well, Git It," "Yes, Indeed," and "Deep River."

Oliver (1910-88) made his mark with Lunceford first, from 1933-39, before joining Dorsey. More than anyone else, he established the style of the Lunceford Band. And then he reshaped the Dorsey Band.

Although Dorsey paid much better than Lunceford, Oliver almost quit Dorsey soon after joining him because the men Dorsey had then couldn't swing his arrangements properly. Differences between black and white conceptions of jazz were still quite pronounced in 1939, and Dorsey sidemen who were into brisk Dixieland often had trouble with Oliver's lithe, supple brand of swing. In the next year, Dorsey made heavy personnel changes, hiring players like Joe Bushkin, Buddy Rich, and Ziggy Elman, so his band could better execute Oliver's ideas.

Oliver crafted one superb chart after another for Dorsey over the next half-dozen years. Oliver was of crucial importance to Dorsey, much as Fletcher Henderson had been to Benny Good-man a few years earlier (not that Oliver or Henderson ever earned a fraction of the money and glory that the bandleaders whose careers they so greatly helped did).

After the big band era, Oliver went on to arrange and conduct countless sides for Decca Records, working with everyone from Mae West to Louis Armstrong. Oliver played trumpet, too, in a competent, Louis Armstrong-inspired vein, but made his real contribution in life as an arranger.

In the later years of his career, he led a nine-piece band at New York's prestigious Rainbow Room, although on the evenings I caught the band it seemed to be stressing mostly bland dinner music — perhaps appropriate for the room, but disappointing nonetheless.

Oliver always spoke modestly about his own abilities, maintaining he was simply a professional who throughout his career had done what was required of him, motivated by the need to earn a living and not by a desire to create "art." Whatever his motivations may have been, he created some of the most satisfying and enduring of all big band arrangements.

CHARLIE SHAVERS

Of all the great trumpet soloists Tommy Dorsey featured over the years — an honor roll that includes Bunny Berigan, Pee Wee Erwin, Yank Lawson, and Ziggy Elman — none had a more enduring association with him than Charlie Shavers, who worked with Dorsey, off and on, from 1945 until Dorsey's death in 1956.

Although Shavers' playing was clearly rooted in the swing tradition — he was never a bebopper — he was the most modern-sounding of Dorsey's featured trumpeters. He did some high-register work, but unlike many of the high-register trumpeters who followed, he never sounded strained or screechy; his tone remained clear, rounded, and radiant. He was a bold and always original stylist.

When he soloed in the Dorsey Band on "Marie," for example, he made no reference to Bunny Berigan's famed solo on the original hit record, but squeezed off his own notes with panache. He put his mark, too, on other numbers he inherited when he joined the band, such as "Song Of India" and "Well, Git It." Before long, he also had newly-created features of his own to shine on. And shine he did, winning the *Esquire* Silver Award in 1946 and the *Down Beat* poll in 1948. Occasionally (as on "But She's My Buddy's Chick," "At the Fat Man's," and "The Hucklebuck") Shavers got to sing, too, in a loose, engaging kind of way.

Shavers first rose to prominence as trumpeter and arranger for the John Kirby Sextet from 1937 to 1944. In 1938, he scored a success as a composer with "Undecided," a number he sold outright for a low sum to music publisher Lou Levy, who was later gracious enough to give it back to him after it became a hit.

After touring with the Dorsey Band from 1945 to 1949, Shavers mixed other activities (such as starring in a sextet with Louie Bellson and Terry Gibbs in 1950, Jazz at the Philharmonic concerts in 1952 and 1953, and appearances with Benny Goodman in 1953 and 1954) with periodic returns to the Dorsey Band. He was prominently featured, on records and radio and TV broadcasts, when the Dorsey brothers reunited (1954-56). Afterwards, he led combos of his own,

mixing jazz with dinner music in an apparent attempt to duplicate the commercial success of the Jonah Jones Quintet. And through the years he found time for freelance jazz record dates with artists as varied as Sidney Bechet, Coleman Hawkins, Gene Krupa, Georgie Auld, Eddie Condon, and Steve Allen.

By the time this photo was taken, in 1958, Shavers was playing as well as ever, but tastes in jazz had changed and players such as Maynard Ferguson, Dizzy Gillespie, and Miles Davis were receiving most of the attention. In 1960, Shavers told Jack Hutton of the Toronto *Telegram* that modern trumpet players generally struck him as being "too chord-conscious without being soul-conscious.... Too many of them have to rely on technique. Man, they shouldn't have to race their solos all the time. They sound bad when they hold a note."

In 1965, Shavers toured with the Tommy Dorsey Band, led by Sam Donahue, in a package with singers Helen Forrest, Frank Sinatra Jr., and the Pied Pipers. They appeared on a TV series, "The Big Bands." I remember watching (and audio-taping) that show, and thinking of Shavers as being one of the grand old men of the trumpet, re-creating — as he soloed dramatically on "Marie" — the music of what seemed a long-ago era.

Shavers was just 53 when he died in 1971.

EDDIE BAREFIELD

Eddie Barefield (1909-1991) was not much older than the two boys with him in the photo on the following page (by Nancy Miller Elliott) when he saw a man playing a sax — an instrument he'd never seen before — and he decided he wanted one.

He begged his mother to get him one, and at Christmas he received his first sax. Barefield's mother gave him money for music lessons, too — which he spent on the movies instead. But he taught himself to play by listening to records — everyone from Rudy Wiedoeft (a technically adept non-jazz sax player who was quite popular in the 1920s) to Coleman Hawkins (the first major jazz tenor sax soloist), who became a strong influence upon him. He eventually taught himself how to arrange music, too, from listening to Fletcher Henderson records.

He got experience playing everywhere from carnivals and minstrel shows to a midwest gathering of gangsters (for whom the band opened with "Hail, Hail, The Gang's All Here"). By 1932, Barefield was in his first really famous band, Bennie Moten's — a superbly swinging unit that laid the groundwork for Count Basie's. There were plenty of times when the band was scuffling, the musicians getting by on hot dogs, beans, and booze. On one day in 1932, the band recorded its most celebrated sides, including "Moten Swing," "Prince of Wails," and Barefield's tune, "Toby," after dining on a thin stew of questionable origin. I once heard Barefield, at a party at Nancy Miller Elliott's apartment, arguing with two other veteran musicians over whether that stew had been made from a rabbit or a cat!

Barefield was an accomplished musician — not a bravura soloist who'd capture the public's attention, but a rock-solid player who'd be an asset to any band. After leaving Moten, he played with Zach Whyte (1933), McKinney's Cotton Pickers (1933), Cab Calloway (1933-36), Les Hite (1937), Fletcher Henderson (1938), Don Redman (1938), and intermittently led bands of his own.

In Elliott's portrait of Barefield on page 60, taken not far from his New York City home, Barefield is standing beneath a rather special billboard for "Wild Irish Rose" wine — you see, that's Barefield himself playing sax in the ad. Not that anyone other than a fellow jazz musician (or a friend like Elliott) would have been likely to recognize him.

Barefield never got the degree of public recognition a number of less talented players received; often his jobs simply did not have high visibility. The bandleader for whom he worked longest in the 1930s, for example, was Cab Calloway, who had a highly paid band filled with top players — but when that dynamic leader was performing, people barely noticed the musicians behind him. Barefield occasionally got to show what he was capable of; for example, at one 1934 Calloway recording session, they were a tune short and a last-minute decision was made to do an instrumental, "Moonglow," featuring Barefield, which became a surprise hit.

Barefield also served for a while as musical director for Ella Fitzgerald and her Famous Orchestra. But again, all of the attention was focused on Fitzgerald; listeners were not aware that "her famous orchestra" was being rehearsed and supervised by Barefield. He went on, later in the 1940s, to help pioneer in breaking the color barrier of radio staff orchestras (at ABC and WOR) and in Broadway pit orchestras. And during the 1950s, he periodically served as musical director for Cab Calloway.

In later years, Barefield played in the Dukes of Dixieland, the Ringling Brothers and Barnum & Bailey circus orchestra, the Harlem Blues and Jazz Band, and the Illinois Jacquet Big Band, besides leading his own groups. At Carnegie Hall in 1988, he reunited with Cab Calloway for the last time — a star-studded concert in which Barefield's old featured number, "Moonglow," was played by David Sanborn.

Jazz Veterans

his youth. He remembers having to hit the piano keys hard in protest, when first working in a little club in New York, to stop showgirls from hiding in their clothing tips that were supposed to be shared with the musicians. He reminds us how closely jazz and entertainment were linked in the early days, recalling how on one occasion he even appeared onstage in a comedy routine — donning blackface makeup as was customary in those days. And of course he tells of the great, roaring big band he put together in the 1930s. New York had never heard anything like it: Lester Young and Herschel Evans and Buck Clayton and "Sweets" Edison, and more; he'd never have quite so many great soloists in one band again. And the classic records like "Jumpin' at the Woodside" and "One O'Clock Jump" that they made for Decca for a flat fee — no royalty payments, ever, for those records (which are still being reissued today). Yeah, they were taken advantage of. There were a lot of injustices. But he won't talk much about that, either. No, sir.

As you read Basie's autobiography, you can't help wondering how much more he could have told, had he wanted to, about his experiences and, equally important, about his feelings. But he made a policy decision early on that he was safer, smarter — better off — not expressing some things too loudly. And maybe a bit of *that* is caught in Elliott's photo, too.

Basie's alumni include some of the most respected names in jazz. In the pages that follow, we'll be meeting a number of them.

LESTER YOUNG

Nearly all of the other musicians in this book look directly into our eyes. Ultra-sensitive Lester Young's gaze in this 1958 photo — the following year he would be dead — is downcast. His head is tilted at a curious angle; it makes me think of the similarly curious angle at which he always held his saxophone as he played. We see a face that is vulnerable — he's been hurt — and also a bit puzzled, as if he hasn't quite figured out how something works. When Nancy Miller Elliott recalls the day she took this picture, the first thing that comes to mind is Young not so much walking, she says, as "floating" towards her.

Young was, of course, a musical genius. You'll find plenty who would agree with the concise description of him offered by trumpeter Lee Castle (who played on some 1939 sides with Young): "The best tenor sax player in the world."

As often happens, Young's gifts were not, at first, generally recognized. When Fletcher Henderson hired Young, in March 1934, to succeed Coleman Hawkins in his band, Young's playing was not accepted by the band's other members (some of whom even cast aspersions upon his masculinity) and he did not last. Hawkins, who for the past decade had been the most influential tenor saxist in jazz, had a big, full, domineering sound. Young had a softer, gentler, subtler sound. The other band members wanted a saxist who'd emulate Hawkins as most players in those days were trying to do. No one could have guessed then that in time Young's influence upon other tenors would exceed even Hawkins'.

We listen to the marvelously relaxed sense of swing and natural gift for construction that Young exhibited on so many recordings with Count Basie's Band from 1936-1940

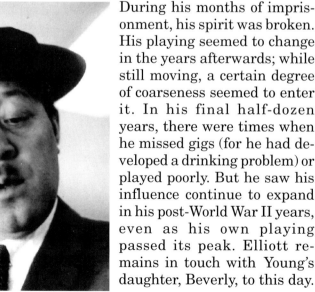

— in retrospect, he was the most impressive soloist in that star-studded outfit — and we are amazed at the mixed notices he got back then from the critics. He shone, too, on small group sides he recorded (and there were young sax players who recognized right away the perfection of his work, and learned his solos). And Young's contributions to the artistic success of many Billie Holiday records is nearly equal to her own. The records would never have worked so well without his languorous, heartfelt sax commentary. Musically, they seemed to be two people expressing the same ideas.

He was commercially unsuccessful as a small-group leader after leaving Basie. He returned to Basie in December 1943, and stayed with him for almost 10 months. In this period he really became a star, winning first place for tenor saxists in the 1944 *Down Beat* poll.

But on September 30, 1944, he was drafted into the Army, where he stayed throughout 1945. His nature was too delicate for that macho world to begin with. Add the fact that he had to deal with some authorities who were racist (and who could hardly have cared about his greatness as an artist) and you can easily predict trouble. He wound up in detention barracks on a drug charge. Reading the transcript of the proceedings against him is enough to make you weep. During his months of imprisonment, his spirit was broken. His playing seemed to change in the years afterwards; while still moving, a certain degree of coarseness seemed to enter it. In his final half-dozen years, there were times when he missed gigs (for he had developed a drinking problem) or played poorly. But he saw his influence continue to expand in his post-World War II years, even as his own playing passed its peak. Elliott remains in touch with Young's daughter, Beverly, to this day.

BILLIE HOLIDAY

Like her musical soul-mate, Lester Young, Billie Holiday avoids our gaze. She does not look downward as he did, but off into the distance. She appears guarded, almost secretive. Nancy Miller Elliott photographed Holiday (alone, and with guitarist Mary Osborne) on the same day in 1958 that she photographed Young. Holiday, like Young, would be dead the following year.

Elliott remembers Holiday as seeming "out of it" on this date. From the early 1940s onwards, Holiday had problems with drugs; as a result, in her last years her strength and the general quality of her performances (like those of Young's) deteriorated, although there were still many occasions when she could sing with devastating effect — the *feeling* she projected cut right through you. Her performance of "Fine and Mellow" on a 1957 TV special, "The Sound of Jazz," available on videotape, is a striking example. And the way she looks at Lester Young during that number is immensely touching as well.

Because of Holiday's drug arrests (the last time was on her deathbed), she became publicly associated with drugs in a way that other noted jazz artists who used drugs but never were arrested did not. The film biography *Lady Sings the Blues* ensures that even people who are unfamiliar with Holiday's actual recordings — some filled with great joy, innocence, and optimism, others with bitterness and sorrow — will know of her use of narcotics.

It's a pity that that film couldn't have included the thing for which Holiday should be best remembered: her unique voice.

The recordings she made in the 1930s and early '40s establish her as arguably the greatest of all female jazz singers. (Some will prefer Ella Fitzgerald; almost every jazz fan would rank one or the other as the greatest.) Holiday always credited Bessie Smith and Louis Armstrong as being early influences. The extent of their influence on her singing should not be exaggerated, however. Holiday created her own style and she probably had a farther-reaching influence than any other female jazz singer. If we hear other women phrasing like Holiday, we immediately recognize their indebtedness to her. Her naturalistic approach also influenced Frank Sinatra and, through him, various other pop singers.

There's a wonderful sense of ease about many of Holiday's recordings, not just in her vocals but in the exceptionally sympathetic instrumental contributions of Lester Young, Buck Clayton, Teddy Wilson, Benny Morton and the others who accompanied her. Individual players varied from session to session in the 1930s and early '40s, but the overall spirit on her recordings remained consistent. In later years, record companies often spent more money on larger orchestras and written arrangements — generally yielding results less satisfying than the early sides made with just the right jazz improvisers.

The film *Lady Sings the Blues* got so many facts wrong it should have been presented as fiction. It showed, for example, Holiday working with an exploitative white bandleader who got her onto drugs — a patent falsehood. She actually worked for only two big band leaders (neither of whom were depicted in the film), Artie Shaw and Count Basie — and she voiced high

respect for both. They treated her with great respect. The film didn't mention many musicians who were important to her. Players like Lester Young and Buck Clayton deeply inspired her.

Read Holiday's autobiography (also titled *Lady Sings the Blues*) if you want to know what she was like. Although there are inaccuracies in it, it has a general ring of truth. And she comes across as a far more interesting and complex person than the weepy, one-dimensional Billie Holiday that Diana Ross offered us on the screen. We see a mix of attitudes: gumption, testiness, generosity, suspiciousness, anger, and considerable zest, along with a masochistic streak that kept drawing her back to men who didn't treat her well. Read the book. And put on a few of her records.

BILLIE HOLIDAY'S TWO BEST-LOOKING MEN

In her autobiography, Billie Holiday referred to trumpeter Buck Clayton as "the prettiest man I'd ever seen." And then later in the book, when she met Jimmy Monroe, she noted: "He was the most beautiful man I'd laid eyes on since Buck Clayton." In this unique photograph, Nancy Miller Elliott has brought together those two men (Monroe is on the right). And even though it was taken nearly half a century after Holiday first knew Clayton and Monroe, we can see they're both strikingly good-looking men — and in a similar sort of way. We can infer her "type."

Born in 1911 in Parsons, Kansas, Buck Clayton hitched a freight train to Los Angeles at age 17. He worked his way up as a musician until, at 23, he was leading a big band in motion pictures and nightclubs on the Coast. Duke Ellington's band played at Clayton's wedding — which took place on the set of a Mae West movie, *Belle of the Nineties*! Clayton took his big band to China in 1934, where (despite a run-in with some bigoted U.S. servicemen) he lived like a king for a couple of years. Back in the United States in 1936, Clayton joined Count Basie's new band in Kansas

City. He actually took a considerable pay cut to do so but he had "never heard such swinging music." Playing and recording with Basie for the next seven years made him a jazz star.

Basie hired Holiday as a vocalist with the band in 1937. (In his autobiography, Clayton recalled how Holiday would board the bus, when they traveled together as members of the Basie Band, and say, "Buck Clayton, you MF, come over here and let me see what color your eyes are today" — she said his eyes would appear green or gray or blue depending upon the color of his suit.) Because Holiday and Basie were under exclusive contracts to different record companies, Holiday was not able to make records with the Basie Band — a real loss for jazz buffs. (For a tantalizing hint of what might have been, listen to the airchecks — recordings of "live" radio broadcast performances — of Holiday singing "Swing, Brother, Swing" and a couple of other numbers with the '37 Basie Band, which are included in the Columbia three-CD set *Billie Holiday — The Legacy*.) Clayton, however, did get to play trumpet on many of Holiday's own recordings, which were made with small pickup groups, often including Lester Young.

Holiday, Clayton, and Young liked hanging out together, as three good friends. Holiday and Young were never romantically involved. Nor were Holiday and Clayton, as far as anyone knew. Although Clayton was always quite the ladies' man, he maintained that he thought of Holiday — who swore and played craps as well as any other member of the Basie Band — as "just one of the guys." He was content to leave it at that, he insisted, especially when Holiday became romantically involved for a while with another member of the Basie Band — Clayton's good friend, guitarist Freddie Green. Anyway, that's where the story stood until Clayton's final year. In 1991, Clayton told Elliott that actually he once *had* had an affair with Holiday, but that they had chosen to keep it secret.

As for Jimmy Monroe, Holiday wrote in her autobiography that he "had taste and class." When she met him, he had already traveled extensively and had been married to singer-dancer-actress Nina Mae McKinney (who had appeared in one of the first black film musicals, *Hallelujah*). And Jimmy's brother, Clark Monroe, ran Monroe's Uptown House, a well-known Harlem jazz club where musicians often gathered to jam.

Holiday eloped with Jimmy Monroe in September 1941. The heartaches she subsequently suffered during their marriage she made use of in her art. When he came home one night with lipstick on his collar and tried to talk her out of thinking that it meant what it obviously did, she cut him off with the words: "Take a bath man, don't explain." As she put it in her autobiography: "Lying was worse to me than anything he could have done with any bitch." The words "don't explain" kept running through her head, and she drew upon the incident to write a song, "Don't Explain" (polished by songwriter Arthur Herzog), that became one of her great successes. She noted: "This is one song I couldn't sing without feeling every minute of it. I still can't. Many a bitch has told me she broke up every time she heard it. So if anybody deserves credit for that, it's Jimmy, I guess — and the others who kept coming home with lipstick on their faces."

Monroe was also involved with drugs back then. And it was during Holiday's marriage to him that she herself became hooked. She took care in her autobiography to state: "Jimmy was no more the cause of my doing what I did than my mother was. That goes for any man I ever knew. I was as strong, if not stronger, than any of them. And when it's that way, you can't blame anybody but yourself."

Monroe, who died in 1993, spent his final years quietly; he didn't seek attention as "Billie Holiday's ex" or anything else.

The photograph of two men linked by their connection with Holiday is one that only Elliott would have gotten. I'm glad she did it. It makes Monroe a real person for us, not just a name in so many books dealing with Holiday.

RAM RAMIREZ

Sometimes you'll meet someone you've previously known only by reputation and will be disappointed to find that he doesn't appear at all the way you'd secretly imagined. But the late Ram Ramirez, with his smoldering good looks and bemused, rather worldly expression, appeared exactly the way you might imagine the composer of "Lover Man" should appear.

"Lover Man" is a very grown-up song. It's hard to conceive of some of the "girl-next-door" type big band vocalists singing it. But the number was perfect for Billie Holiday, and she was perfect for it. She knew just which notes to linger over, and when she sang that line about going to bed with a prayer that her lover man would make love to her, you really felt the longing. Some may be surprised to learn that the song was actually written several years before Holiday recorded it in 1944, and she was not the first to record it. But it was her version that "made" the song, and it became her property.

Ramirez (photographed here by Nancy Miller Elliott) had no hits besides "Lover Man," nor did his collaborators on that number, Jimmy Davis and Jimmy Sherman. Although he wrote some other pieces, he was primarily a pianist, not a songwriter. Born September 15, 1913 in Puerto Rico, Ramirez grew up in New York City, where his talents manifested early. He was in the musicians' union by age 13.

He went on to work and record in the 1930s and '40s with such artists as Rex Stewart, Stew Pletcher, Willie Bryant, Putney Dandridge, Bobby Martin, Ella Fitzgerald, Frankie Newton, Charlie Barnet, John Kirby, Hot Lips Page, and Sid Catlett. From the late 1940s on, he worked mostly on his own, either as a solo pianist or as leader of a piano trio, sometimes spurring on his playing with enthusiastic grunts, or laughing in wonder after playing something that appeared to surprise him. He switched to the Hammond organ for a period, when Hammond organs came into vogue in the early and mid-1950s. He toured with bluesman T-Bone Walker in 1968, and with the Harlem Blues and Jazz Band in 1979, 1980, and 1987.

Ramirez grew fairly elusive in his later years, spotted more often in the audience at a jazz club or concert hall than on the stage. He took gigs as they came, usually not in venues offering high visibility. George T. Simon noted with some surprise in *The New York Post*, January 2, 1981, that Ramirez, "...who has been playing with the greats of jazz for almost half a century, appears with absolutely no fanfare each Friday and Saturday evening at a friendly spot called The Cockatoo" on First Avenue at 73rd Street, far from the center of the action of New York's jazz scene. Ramirez's repertoire included blues, excerpts of Gershwin's *Rhapsody in Blue*, uptown Swing Era favorites such as "Blue Lou" and "If Dreams Come True," current sambas, and even "Willow Weep for Me" done in 6/8 time — as well as, of course, "Lover Man" (which he somehow

never got around to recording himself until the 1960s). John S. Wilson reported in *The New York Times*, July 1, 1981, following a successful Kool Jazz Festival appearance by Ramirez: "He is scarcely known to most jazz followers.... But given the unaccustomed opportunity to step into a concert spotlight at Carne-gie Recital Hall, Mr. Ramirez revealed himself as a superbly swinging pianist who moves steadily between suggestions of Fats Waller's stride and the pastel melodies of Duke Ellington."

FREDDIE GREEN

The Basie Band had drawn a good, if somewhat noisy, audience to the Blue Note in New York City on this January 1985 night. As the band eased into "Good Time Blues," the chattering of a couple of women was becoming a real distraction. From the bandstand — almost as startling as if the Sphinx were to suddenly open his mouth and speak — Freddie Green ordered firmly: "Quiet!" Immediately, the house grew hushed. Never breaking the rhythm, Green continued playing his barely audible acoustic guitar.

That's the only time I've ever seen a sideman speak out like that during a band's performance.

But Green was no ordinary sideman. A key member of the Basie Band from March 1937 until his death in March 1987, he had long ago earned deep respect both from fellow musicians and from jazz fans, and he wanted the music treated with respect.

Green rarely soloed; it was enough that he was the best in the business on rhythm guitar. Longtime Basie trumpeter Sonny Cohn once noted: "The most important part of your body is your heart. It keeps everything going. That's what Freddie does." Saxist Eric Dixon said: "People could imitate Basie for a couple of seconds, but not longer. You can't imitate that unique touch. It's the same with Freddie." Green would hold his guitar, tilted diagonally, and pick the strings with his thumb and a finger rather than a plectrum, helping to propel the band.

Fellow members of the rhythm section could hear the sounds Green made better than members of the audience. I remember one time at a Basie Band recording session, the engineer remarked that he couldn't really hear Green, and he wanted to boost Green in the mix. A band member had to explain that listeners weren't *supposed* to really hear Green; his pulse would be sensed, even if it were not noticed. If the band played without Green, you'd notice his absence.

Green didn't have a great many interests outside of the music. He had a family, but the band's constant traveling meant he saw more of his fellow musicians than of his family. When he could, he liked to wake early and play golf, a rare pastime among jazzmen (Sir Charles Thompson and Sandy Williams are two other golf-playing jazzmen who come to mind). He didn't drink, didn't smoke cigarettes, and, except for some pot, which was commonplace in the early Basie Band, he never had any interest in drugs.

The only significant interruption to his association with Basie came when economics forced Basie, in 1950 and '51, to give up his big band and try working with a smaller group instead — a group that initially did not include a guitar. Green didn't accept being excluded; playing in Basie's Band was his life. One day, he simply showed up where Basie's group was booked, just as if he had been asked to report for work. Basie welcomed him; Green remained with Basie until Basie's death on April 26, 1984. Green plaintively noted then: "I've been with the band since 1937 — what am I to do now?" Green's own death, on March 1, 1987, came just three days after participating in the recording session for the GRP album *Diane Schuur and the Count Basie Orchestra*, which was then dedicated to his memory.

CLAUDE "FIDDLER" WILLIAMS
& LINDA FENNIMORE

When Nancy Miller Elliott took this chapter's final photograph in 1989, Claude "Fiddler" Williams was playing violin in the long-running Broadway revue *Black and Blue*. At 81, he was an authentic link to the era evoked by the show — and a source of inspiration for up-and-coming jazz violinist Linda Fennimore. Both of these musicians are very definitely *survivors*.

Born in Muskogee, Oklahoma (the same town as the wonderfully earthy, bluesy pianist/vocalist Jay McShann, with whom he's worked many times), Williams originally played both violin (the instrument for which he is best known today) and rhythm guitar. His early experiences included working with the likes of T. Holder, Andy Kirk, and a young and not-yet-famous Nat "King" Cole (so young, in fact, that he hadn't yet begun singing). The high point of what might be considered Williams' "first career" came in 1936, when Count Basie hired him. Williams was the original guitarist (and occasional violinist as well) in the Basie Band. He played with the band in Chicago, New York City (where the band cut its first records — he was on guitar when it recorded "Honeysuckle Rose," "Roseland

Shuffle," and "Swinging at the Daisy Chain" for Decca on January 21, 1937), and Pittsburgh (he may be heard on violin on some airchecks from Pittsburgh's William Penn Hotel, released on LP by Jazz Archives). Williams believes to this day that the very best rhythm section that Basie ever had was the one Williams was part of. In March 1937, Williams — to his disgust — was abruptly fired and replaced by guitarist Freddie Green, part of a personnel change that also included replacing the lead alto saxist and a couple of the brass men.

The changes in personnel have generally been viewed in jazz history as a strengthening of the Basie Band, then still in its formative stages. But Williams didn't see it that way. In his opinion, Green wasn't quite his equal as a player then. Williams took some consolation in the fact that *Down Beat* magazine named him the number-one rhythm guitarist that year.

Williams didn't believe his being fired reflected any failing on his part (and there isn't enough recorded evidence to fairly evaluate his work with Basie) — he thought John Hammond, who had helped get Basie to New York, had instigated the changes to throw some work to players he happened to favor. Williams returned to Kansas City, soon becoming a forgotten man for most jazz fans, nationwide.

He dramatically re-emerged in the 1970s, via some critically acclaimed recordings with Jay McShann (photographed here by Andreas Johnsen). They often performed together — a

natural, superb combination — until friction developed between their wives, leading them to decide to mostly work separately. Williams held his own in a 1979 Nice Festival appearance with Stephane Grappelli and Svend Asmussen, and won new fans via club and concert appearances. In recent years, his conscientious manager Russ Dantzler (who specializes in representing elder statesmen of jazz) has kept Williams' visibility high. (Andreas Johnsen's photo on page 75 catches Williams in action at New York's Louisiana Bar and Grill, during a 1994 CD-release party.)

As for Fennimore, her "comeback," while not so well known as Williams', is even more dramatic. Shortly after completing grad school, she was thrown through a windshield in a car accident which broke her neck; vertebrae broke outwards, severing nerves and muscles, although not the spinal cord itself. Practically paralyzed below the neck — she had some finger movement — she was not expected to walk again. Her determination was to not just walk but play the violin again — a goal she held to through eight years of operations and physical therapy, until she was able to begin practicing again, initially for only a minute a day. It took her five months before she was able to get up to five minutes a day. Today, she is a working violinist. She believes the accident left her with a deeper sensitivity to both sorrows and joys, and a deeper ability to reach people emotionally through her music.

Jazz Veterans

BIG ED LEWIS

ig Ed Lewis, shown in Nancy Miller Elliott's first shot relaxing with his dog, Bebop, in 1983, is another one of those players whose contributions have often been overlooked. He was the lead trumpeter in the Basie Band during its pace-setting years of the late 1930s and early '40s. Fans of the band understandably focused attention on its star soloists, such as Lester Young, Herschel Evans, Buck Clayton, Harry "Sweets" Edison, and Dicky Wells. But those soloists weren't playing in a vacuum. The band's impact came from the exuberant bluesy riffs of the sections, not just from the improvisations of the soloists. Indeed, the band would never have lasted long enough for the soloists to have won the public's attention had not the section-work impressed — and section leaders Lewis and Earle Warren deserve their share of recognition.

Born January 22, 1909 in Eagle City, Oklahoma, Lewis grew up in Kansas City, Missouri. In his youth, he played in a brass band along with his father. By 1926, he was a key soloist of the Bennie Moten Orchestra, then the greatest of the big jazz bands in the region. (Count Basie became a member of that band in 1929.) He

Big Ed Lewis

stayed with Moten until 1931, then played for such leaders as Thamon Hayes (1932-34), Harlan Leonard (1934-37), and Jay McShann (1937).

Meanwhile, the Basie Band left Kansas City for New York in late 1936, but it did not make an immediate hit. George T. Simon of *Metronome* noted some of the players were often out of tune. In 1937, Basie made some crucial personnel changes that set the band straight, including hiring Ed Lewis to replace Joe Keyes and alto saxist Earle Warren to replace Caughey Roberts. He soon had the crisp, jubilantly shouting brass and flowing reeds that he wanted.

Lewis was a strong, full-toned player who led the brass in precise phrases (without losing a jazz feeling — he had, after all, originally been a jazz soloist). He was a great admirer of Red Nichols, who similarly favored full, rounded tones and precise execution, and whose records had enjoyed enormous popularity when Lewis was first making his mark with Bennie Moten. Buck Clayton couldn't understand Lewis' preferring Nichols to Louis Armstrong, but he appreciated the secure lead Lewis provided. (Lewis' other early influences were Joe Smith, who in the late 1920s had starred with Fletcher Henderson, and Bix Beiderbecke, who had starred with Jean Goldkette and Paul Whiteman.) Lewis occasionally did get to solo with Basie (as on, for example, "Blue and Sentimental"), and he also contributed some compositions, such as "It's Sand, Man" (1942).

In 1948, as public interest in big bands waned, the Basie Band was no longer working as steadily as before and Basie had to ask the men to accept downward salary adjustments. That year, Jo Jones, Buddy Tate, and Lewis all quit. The following year, Basie gave up the big band; he headed a less costly small band for a couple of years.

For the next half-dozen years, Lewis left music entirely. He eventually became a motorman on New York's D Train. (Nancy Miller Elliott, who took this portrait, remembers seeing him on that subway line well before she knew who he was.) In the mid-'50s, he began doing occasional gigs again on the side, leading a band in and around the city. Eventually, though, he gave that up, too.

In 1983, Lewis came out of retirement for a three-week European tour — his first and only trip abroad — with an all-star 17-man Basie Alumni Band, which included Harry "Sweets" Edison, Joe Newman, Eddie Durham, Earle Warren, Buddy Tate, Freddie Green, and Eddie Jones. The conductor of that band was Buck Clayton, with whom Lewis is seen (in Elliott's second photo) checking out the Venus de Milo at the Louvre.

Lewis died September 18, 1985.

HARRY "SWEETS" EDISON

When he opened at Tavern on the Green in the fall of 1994, veteran trumpeter Harry "Sweets" Edison acknowledged seasoned performers in the audience, including guitarist John Collins, who graced many of Nat "King" Cole's records, and singer Kenny Coleman. I wish the room had been packed with aspiring young musicians, though, for Edison has something to teach them that they won't learn at Juilliard.

He created a kind of magic playing his original "Centerpiece," which closed the first set. By then, he was fully warmed up. (At age 79, it

takes him a while to get limber.) And the music just flowed. It rolled effortlessly, the way jazz is meant to, but all too often doesn't.

His lines — in the middle register, which he's always preferred — were utterly to the point. (Younger musicians might play faster, stronger, higher, and more complex figures, but cluttered music doesn't swing freely.) What Edison played seemed simple — but the rarity with which others achieve his propulsive lilt attests to its difficulty. The tart sound and way of shaping phrases remains unmistakably his own. Just how individual his style was had been brought home when he'd guested with Illinois Jacquet for several numbers at Carnegie Hall a month earlier; the Jacquet Band suddenly sounded remarkably like the old Basie Band, of which Edison was a key member.

Edison not only soloed on many of the famed early Basie specialties, like "Jive at Five," "Sent for You Yesterday," and "Every Tub," he helped create them. Occasionally (as on "Jive at Five") he got composer credit on the record label. Other times, he did not. Much of the music the Basie Band played evolved right on the bandstand. A band member, such as Edison, might contribute an initial melodic idea; other soloists would make their contributions. A section leader might suggest a riff. The arrangement developed organically. It was a "head arrangement" — not written out on paper — that Basie could lengthen or shorten on any given night, depending on whom he had solo, and for how long. (Eventually, Basie might have arranger Eddie Durham write the thing down; Basie and Durham might even be credited as composers, but band members knew how the numbers had developed.) If Edison composes a new tune today, he'll sometimes be told by listeners that it sounds "Basie-ish" — which is hardly surprising. In his 13 years with Basie (1937-1950), he put his stamp on many of Basie's defining recordings. The music we think of as Basie's was Basie's — but it was also Edison's, Buck Clayton's, Lester Young's, Eddie Durham's, and so on. They all contributed.

Edison often tells the story — a classic in jazz circles — of how he almost quit the Basie Band shortly after he'd joined it in late 1937. Most of what the band played was without reference to any written music. As far as Edison could tell, the musicians had been doing fine before his arrival; his role was undefined, and he doubted he'd be missed much if he left. Ed Lewis was a superb lead player. Buck Clayton was already gaining renown as a jazz soloist. But when Edison offered his resignation to Basie, Basie scoffed, saying he played very well.

Edison protested that much of the time he had no idea what notes he was supposed to be playing. Basie, who knew Edison could become as vital a contributor to the band as the others, suggested that Edison trust his own ear: "If you find a note tonight that sounds good, play the same damned note every night!"

Edison still considers the Basie Band the best he ever played with. And he became lifelong friends with those he first met in his Basie days: Freddie Green, Buck Clayton, Lester Young, Billie Holiday, Ed Lewis, Earle Warren, and of course Basie. Nancy Miller Elliott's informal photo captures Edison, at right, and his old buddy from Basie days, the late Ed Lewis, enjoying ice cream cones in Nice, France, in 1983.

Edison has now outlived most of his friends, and these days often finds himself standing alongside much younger musicians, giving them (if they're receptive) valuable lessons in musicianship. (Note the recordings of Edison as special guest in reedman Ken Peplowski's group; as fine a player and leader as Peplowski is, his group begins swinging notably more when Edison joins it.)

Edison's original trumpet inspiration, he says, was Louis Armstrong. He became aware of Armstrong well before the general public did, taking note at age ten of Armstrong's contributions backing Bessie Smith on records in 1925. But he never became an Armstrong clone; he's always valued originality and his taut, sometimes witty style reflects his own personality. (One time when Wynton Marsalis was addressing a class at the Manhattan School of Music, he demonstrated the styles of various trumpet greats. Then he mentioned that Edison, with whom he's played on a number of occasions, was one trumpeter with a style so personal he could not imitate it.)

Edison says he was drawn to the jazz world by some non-musical factors, in addition to his admiration for the work of Armstrong and others. When, as a teen in Columbus, Ohio, he saw the great luck that touring jazzmen seemed to have with the local gals, he became thoroughly convinced that jazz was the field to get into. In his youth, he says, jazz musicians seemed to be the sharpest-dressed people he encountered, and that also impressed him.

He's maintained that old-time tradition of dressing sharply. The suits he wears on the bandstand are impeccably tailored. When he steps onstage and raises his horn, his rings and cufflinks flash, along with the bold accent of cobalt edging the collar and sleeves of his crisp white shirt. His sense of style — even before he begins to play — is impressive. When he finishes, the audience applauds him vigorously, not just for his playing but for the history he embodies. Slowly, smiling sagely, he blows the house a trademark kiss.

EARLE WARREN & BUDDY TATE

In November 1989, you could have gone to the New York club Birdland and seen the two saxists in Nancy Miller Elliott's first photo, Earle Warren (at left) and Buddy Tate, playing in a group called the Countsmen. A full half-century earlier, you could have seen these two playing in Count Basie's Band. Except for a two-and-a-half year hiatus in the 1940s, Warren stayed with Basie from 1937 until 1950, leading the sax section, occasionally soloing on alto sax, and singing ballads. For a decade beginning in 1939, Tate was featured on tenor.

Tate had the more visible position; he was a star, soloing frequently, his big full tone — he had been chosen to replace the late Herschel Evans — providing a contrast with the lighter sound of Lester Young. Only once in a great while (such as on "Out the Window") was the late Warren the major soloist on a Basie record. He got

Earle Warren & Buddy Tate

to put in his two cents periodically (it's his alto, for example, calling for our attention on the famous original recording of "Jumpin' at the Woodside" and he takes a brief bridge solo on "Doggin' Around"), but mostly he led the saxes in section work — an important, if not glamorous, assignment.

Warren (known to his fellow musicians as "Smiley" — a name given him by Lester Young, who'd noted Warren appeared to be smiling when he played sax) wound up managing R&B and pop groups for a while after leaving Basie. He also periodically toured and recorded, both as a sideman in small groups and on his own. For much of the 1980s, he lived in Geneva, Switzerland. "I've always liked this city," he told me by phone from his home in 1985. By that point, he had been living in Geneva for four years and he admitted it had begun to seem less appealing to him. "When I first got here, things were sort of blooming for jazz. But then they got to playing this old-time Dixieland stuff, and I don't do that too much. I can play New Orleans jazz as it comes off of Bourbon Street, you understand, but this old kind of jazz that they're playing here now, with the washboard and the banjo and stuff, I can't make." So it didn't surprise me much when he moved back to the U.S. a couple of years later, nor that he featured plenty of Basie material in his repertoire. "Basie," he told me, "was my Czar!"

Elliott's photo on the next page (which she calls "the adoration of Earle Warren") shows Warren on the campus of Columbia University with a fellow who really appreciated his talents, disc jockey Phil Schaap, who was doing a birthday broadcast salute to Warren that day.

Buddy Tate led his own group at Harlem's Celebrity Club from the early 1950s on into the 1970s. The work was steady; he was a fixture in the community, but he was often overlooked by the jazz critics, who tended to focus on what was happening downtown. In order to please younger patrons at the club, Tate had to mix contemporary pop music in with the mainstream jazz he preferred, even adding an electric guitar to his group for a while. Eventually, though, things turned around for him, and he found renewed demand for his uncompromising jazz in concerts here and abroad. Until an auto accident a couple of years ago, his brawny, vigorous Texas tenor was as compelling as ever. He was a frail, but still game, participant in the 1992 JVC Jazz Festival.

Elliott's unusual picture on page 82 shows Tate getting his hair cut by a man who has long been a behind-the-scenes part of the jazz community: Rogers Simon. For years, Simon was Duke Ellington's own hairdresser, traveling everywhere with the Duke (Europe, the Orient, and so on), to help keep him looking sharp. At one time, he took care of Nat "King" Cole's hair, too. In more recent years, Simon has tended the locks of bandleader Illinois Jacquet, traveling with him when possible. And old friends will travel great distances to have Simon style their hair, when he's in town. Tate didn't mind the fact that he had to spend a couple of hours getting from his Long Island home to the shop in the Bronx where Tate was working as a freelance barber the morning that Elliott snapped this shot in the fall of 1994.

In 1995, Tate participated in an unusual recording session — all participants were over 65 years old (some, in fact, were a good bit older) — for Mat Domber's Arbors label. Tate was one of the "Statesmen of Jazz," along with Benny Waters, Claude "Fiddler" Williams, Milt Hinton, Panama Francis, Joe Wilder, Jane Jarvis, and Al Grey.

CHUCK WILSON with EARLE WARREN

When Nancy Miller Elliott, just for the fun of it, posed Chuck Wilson (right) and Earle Warren next to a New York subway stop several years ago, it's doubtful that any of the people passing by realized they were being serenaded by two highly distinguished alto saxists — a few even helped the musicians out with some spare change!

Warren, of course, played lead alto on most of the early Basie Band classics. And Wilson, who's enhanced the bands of such leaders as Benny Goodman, Buddy Rich, Vince Giordano, Buck Clayton, and Gerry Mulligan, among others, is as graceful a lead alto saxist as you'll find working today. To my ears, there's no one more pleasing to listen to. He's helped shape the character of bands he's been in, far more than the casual

Chuck Wilson with Earle Warren

listener might realize. (I learned just how big a role Wilson played in those bands when another player would sub for him when he couldn't make a gig — the music was always so much less lyrical without him.)

Wilson and Warren had not met prior to the hot summer day that Elliott took this picture. "She introduced us," Wilson recalls, with a bit of a Texas drawl. "I was all intimidated and a-skeered. The master of the lead alto! Nobody sings it like Smiley Warren! I said, 'How do you do?' He said, kind of gruff — and it was about a hundred degrees out — 'How come you're sweating so much? You drink too much last night?'" But once the ice was broken — for Warren soon became aware that Wilson knew the Basie things that Warren had played on, and saw himself as extending the tradition — they got along just fine. Wilson has become good friends, also, with Buddy Tate (who grew up in the same region of Texas that Wilson did), Norris Turney, and other greats who were playing well before Wilson was born in 1948. "They like me," he notes. "And boy, I sure like them!"

How did Wilson become interested in making music? "From watching *The Fabulous Dorseys* on TV," he says. He chose the alto sax in emulation of Jimmy Dorsey. He went on to become a great enthusiast of Paul Desmond, one of the more melodic of the modern alto players, and one with an unusually light and luminous tone. When Wilson finally discovered Charlie Parker (while attending North Texas State College), he set aside Desmond for awhile and became — like seemingly every other aspiring jazz alto player — a Parker admirer, before finally concluding the more lyrical Desmond was really his man. ("One of the few things where you come back and you were right the first time," Wilson says.) Among others he dug were Bud Shank, Frank Wess, and Marshall Royall (lead alto in the 1950s and '60s Basie Band "...he was the whole sound of that band"). Then once he discovered the 1940s Basie records, "there was Smiley. He was the true champ." Wilson did come to appreciate John Coltrane and other modern stylists (not to mention rock and soul artists like Jimi Hendrix and James Brown) but he didn't start out with them, and his playing connects more to an earlier tradition.

Wilson has played on the soundtrack of *The Cotton Club*, in the pit orchestra of Broadway's *Forty Second Street*, on radio and TV broadcasts with Jimmy and Marian McPartland, and in diverse other settings. His favorite gigs of recent years have been with the Alden-Barrett Quintet and Buck Clayton's Band. He sees himself as fundamentally a big band player — and only wishes there were more left.

VIC DICKENSON

When Vic Dickenson died in 1984, his trombone was mounted on the wall in Eddie Condon's Club. I liked to think that the trombone was pointing to musicians in the club — to remind them to keep their playing honest, direct, and melodic.

You see, there was a thing Dickenson used to do when he was in the house band at Condon's. If a young trumpeter, for example, played a solo that was overly complicated for Dickenson's tastes, Dickenson wouldn't dress the musician down verbally, but he'd do it musically. He'd turn, aim his trombone smack at the offender's ear, and just play the melody — flawlessly and swingingly — as if to say: *That's* the direction to take. Some young musicians took offense when Dickenson pulled that stunt on them, but the wise ones realized that the veteran (Dickenson was born in 1906) had long ago earned the right to teach them, and they profited by what he was trying to tell them. And if they adapted to the way he played, they were also more likely to musically fit in with the band. Dickenson, in his 70s, sure wasn't going to try to adapt to the way they played.

Dickenson graduated from Kansas City local bands to "name" touring bands such as Blanche Calloway's (1933-36), Claude Hopkins (1936-39), and Benny Carter (1939, 1941). It was with Count Basie (1940) that he began to emerge as a soloist, not just a section man. He worked for such leaders as Frankie Newton (1941, 1942-43) and Eddie Heywood (1943-46), while recording with others on the side (such as Sidney Bechet, "After You've Gone," 1943, and Lester Young, "D. B. Blues," 1945). He freelanced in California (1947-48), then in Boston, before finally settling for good in New York around 1958. In the 1960s, he was co-leader with Red Richards of a group called "Saints and Sinners." (In Elliott's photo, Dickenson looks to me more like he's one of the sinners.) There were tours with George Wein's All Stars and with Eddie Condon, gigs with Wild Bill Davison, Bobby Hackett (co-leading a celebrated quintet), the World's Greatest Jazz Band of Yank Lawson and Bob Haggart, and finally, the Condon's house band.

He never got so far from the melody that you'd have trouble recognizing it. Yet he was a master of countless tonal variations and effects, without ever losing his sense of relaxation, without ever seeming strained. And he knew when it was healthy to bring a touch of wit to the music, too. Listen to his memorable rendition of his own tune, "Constantly," with the World's Greatest Jazz Band on their 1970 Atlantic album (recently reissued), *Live at the Roosevelt Grill*. He's wonderfully expressive and imaginative (without ever straying too far from the theme), wisely using a felt hat as a mute to take the edge off his gruff sound.

JOE NEWMAN

orn in New Orleans, Joe Newman (1922-1992) picked up the music from some of the real pioneers, went on to become a star in the Basie Band, then played a valuable role in helping make youths aware of our jazz heritage.

His father, Dwight Newman, was a pianist in the six-man Creole Serenaders. Sometimes, as a child, Joe could hear that band rehearsing in the backyard. Other times, he'd go to see them play at a dance, or later on the radio (they were the first black band in New Orleans to have their own sustaining radio program). One member of that band, cornetist/violinist Peter Bocage, had been playing professionally since 1906. As a boy, Joe Newman once sat in with the Creole Serenaders. He was soon studying with a New Orleans pro who had worked in Fate Marable's riverboat band. Newman's main inspiration, though, was Louis Armstrong, who in the late '20s and early '30s was near his zenith as a jazz trumpeter.

Newman hit the big time professionally in 1941, when he joined Lionel Hampton's Band. In 1943, he was chosen to take Buck Clayton's chair in the Count Basie Band when Clayton was drafted, staying off-and-on for a few years, until becoming a member of Illinois Jacquet's Band (1946-50). In 1952, he once again joined the Basie Band, this time taking "Sweets" Edison's place. He stayed with Basie until 1961, providing a bit of continuity between Basie's more soloist-oriented 1940s "Old Testment" band (as some writers have termed it) and Basie's more arranger-oriented 1950s and '60s "New Testament" band. Although Newman, Clayton, and Edison were individual stylists, they were all, generally speaking, from the school of Louis Armstrong; almost all trumpeters who came after them would be from the schools of Dizzy Gillespie and his successors.

In his years after Basie, Newman founded and became president of Jazz Interactions, Inc., which worked to promote appreciation of jazz in New York public schools, and played in the New York Jazz Repertory Company — both of which helped expose new audiences to the jazz heritage.

And of course, Newman played clubs with his own groups when he could. Even in his last years, he'd kid and flirt with women in the audience between sets, coming across as considerably younger than the nearly 70-year-old man he was. You could infer he'd been around a while, of course, both from his style, which while streamlined and modernized still showed clear ties to Armstrong, and his repertoire, which included old favorites like "St. James Infirmary" that most younger jazzmen might not know.

PAUL QUINICHETTE

As a featured soloist in the early 1950s Count Basie Band, tenor saxist Paul Quinichette was nicknamed the "Vice-Prez" because his playing was so reminiscent of Lester Young, whose nickname was "Prez" (short for the President, meaning the best). A lot of leading saxists of the era — including Stan Getz, Zoot Sims, and Al Cohn — drew stylistic inspiration from Young, but Quinichette was different in that he actually was a friend of Young's, and Young showed him things on the saxophone. They first met in Denver (where Quinichette was born in 1916 to a French father and American mother) in the late 1920s, when Quinichette was around 13 and Young was around 20. When Quinichette made it to highly competitive New York years later (after playing with such bands as Nat Towles' and Jay McShann's), he was glad to have Young in his corner. It was Young who eventually suggested to Basie that Quinichette should inherit what Young still thought of as his chair in the Basie Band.

Not long after hiring Quinichette, Basie hired the heavier-sounding tenor saxist Eddie "Lockjaw" Davis to provide the kind of contrast to Quinichette that Herschel Evans (and, later, Buddy Tate) had provided to Young, back when Young was in the Basie Band. The two saxists got to follow one another, in challenge-type situations, on some numbers, as well as having features of their own. Quinichette was heard to good advantage on such Basie Band recordings as "Basie Talks" (also known simply as "Basie"), "Bootsie," "HFO," and "Cash Box," as well as on a small-group recording Basie did with pianist Oscar Peterson, "Extended Blues."

While with Basie, Quinichette also began making small-group records as a leader. Under Basie's encouragement — Basie, in fact, managed him for a bit — he left the band in 1953 to pursue a career on his own. (His place was taken in the Basie Band by Frank Wess.) He was not able to get a hit record, through. He did some gigs with Benny Goodman and Billie Holiday.

Meanwhile, rock 'n' roll was coming up big. Booking agent Moe Gale urged Quinichette to get with the times, and play in more of a rock 'n' roll vein. That may have been wise from a commercial point of view, but it had no interest for him. He loathed rock 'n' roll. (As he once told Stanley Dance: "If I had had a pistol, I would have shot Elvis Presley right in the face! That's how I felt about it.") Instead, he gradually got out of music. He studied and became an electronics technician in the '60s. In the final decade of his life, he mixed both careers (occasionally gigging with Sammy Price, Brooks Kerr, and others), although his energy was limited by health problems. Nancy Miller Elliott took this photograph of Quinichette in Harlem, where he resided, in the year that he died, 1983.

JOE WILLIAMS

On stage, Joe Williams can be a man of many moods. He can clown a bit one minute (that's the side of him Nancy Miller Elliott chose to capture in these unusual shots), project smoldering sexuality the next, then sing a tender ballad. But this Grammy-winning artist will always be best known as a singer of the blues.

If you're going to really reach people singing the blues, as Williams has, do you have to have *had* the blues? Williams certainly has. "I've been through the agony, lying awake night after night," he told me quietly one April 1987 afternoon at his New York hotel room. Off-and-on, over the course of a full year in 1947-48, he explained, he was gripped by a depression so profound, so immobilizing, that he had to be institutionalized.

"I received electric shock therapy. I received insulin therapy," he recalled. He wondered if he would ever be able to leave the hospital for good and re-enter the mainstream of life.

"I wondered, how am I going to relate to a world where I'd stopped and it had gone on?"

He had begun singing professionally in Chicago in 1937, with leaders including Jimmie Noone (1937), Coleman Hawkins (1941), Lionel Hampton (1943), and Andy Kirk (1946), but his career had never really taken off. In 1947, Kirk wanted Williams to make and promote records, but Williams' descent into depression nixed those plans. After his release from

the hospital, Williams severed some past personal ties and kept a low profile. He became a door-to-door cosmetics salesman.

But if Williams had turned his back on show business, the business hadn't fully turned its back on him. In 1949, disc jockey Daddy-O Daylie began announcing that bandleader Jay Burkhardt wanted to hire Joe Williams as a singer — if any listeners knew his whereabouts. Williams was located, sight-read the band's book, and re-entered the music world.

He worked with Red Saunders off and on from 1950 to 1953. Then in 1954, he joined the big band of Count Basie, with whom he had occasionally sat in several years before. Suddenly, everything fell into place for him. His 1955 recording of "Every Day I Have the Blues" became a great hit. The number had been in his repertoire for years — in fact, he had even recorded it. But it was only now, teamed with the Basie Band, that he began wowing audiences, nationwide.

Williams and the Basie Band were good for each other. With his resonant bass-baritone, his apparent ease on stage, and a strong sexual magnetism, he proved a great drawing card for the band; and the band, punching out pace-setting, powerhouse arrangements by Ernie Wilkins, Neal Hefti, Frank Foster, and others, helped to make him an international star. Williams sang with the Basie Band for seven years. With Basie's blessings, he struck off on his own, accompanied, initially, by the combo of another former Basie-ite, Harry "Sweets" Edison. Williams has periodically reunited with the Basie Band since then.

He has frequently won (or else placed very high in) the *Down Beat* International Critics' Poll, in the "male jazz singer" category. On stage, comes across as rather urbane, occasionally leavening his act with good-natured, earthy humor. He can croon into the microphone, perhaps a spiritual sung *a capella*, such as "Let My People Go," then, with the full band backing him, let loose his power on "Shake, Rattle, and Roll" or his infectious "Who She Do." And bring it all home with the number that has become his signature, "Everyday I Have the Blues."

EDDIE JONES

The fact that Eddie Jones grew up in Count Basie's home town of Red Bank, New Jersey — quite close, in fact, to the Basie family's house — had nothing to do with his later becoming the bassist of the Basie Band.

"Growing up in Red Bank, you didn't know much about jazz," comments Jones, who is on the right in the photo of him and Howard Alden taken by Nancy Miller Elliott. He was born March 1, 1929. His early music instruction — first on piano, then on violin — was classically oriented. He didn't take up bass until the end of his junior year in high school.

His links to Basie's world were forged largely by chance. He happened to attend Howard University at the same time that reedman Frank Wess and trombonist Bill Hughes, both later to become Basie stalwarts, were students. And one summer he lived in Atlantic City with Rodney

Richardson, who had played bass for several years in the Basie Band and had plenty of Basie records. Jones fell in love with the Basie sound.

After graduating from Howard, Jones taught school for a year and then began graduate studies. In the meantime, however, Wess joined the Basie Band and told Basie about him. One day in 1953 Jones returned to the home of his aunt, with whom he was then living, and found that "Frank had been waiting there for a couple of hours. Basie needed a bass player!"

Jones' memory of the 10 years he spent in the Basie Band are positive. "It was a fabulous time, a golden age for jazz — a good time to be in that band and a good time to be alive. Working for Basie was a pleasure: all he asked was that you show up, do your job, look good, play well. You couldn't afford to get sick in that band — if you didn't show up, you disappeared!" The Basie Band was hot in the 1950s and there were plenty of musicians eager for your job. "It was a good solid band of band players and soloists and good writing. It really was the right formula for that time," Jones says. The band worked constantly. In his free hours, Jones got to play on record dates with Ray Charles, Coleman Hawkins, Roy Eldridge, Ben Webster, Joe Newman, Thad Jones, Frank Foster, Frank Wess, and Milt Jackson.

Jones quit the band in 1962 because he did not feel Basie was paying him enough. After Basie lost a number of key members of the band, including Joe Williams and Joe Newman (both in 1961), Snooky Young (in 1962), Frank Foster and Frank Wess (both in 1964), he started paying his musicians better, Jones says.

Jones tried without success — he believes racial prejudice was a factor — to get work as a musician in television. Finally, discouraged with the music business, he went to work for IBM, starting as a trainee and eventually becoming a manager. Today, he works for an insurance company in Hartford, Connecticut, and stays active in jazz as time permits.

"I play with George Wein and the Newport Jazz Festival All-Stars a lot — a couple months' work each year. I try to take my vacation time and fit it all in. And I play three days a week up here in a duo with pianist Charlie Gigliotti," he notes. He takes other offers to play when he can.

He's worked on various occasions with Howard Alden ("really a fabulous guitarist," Jones says of that pure-toned young virtuoso); Jones doesn't remember just what gig they might have had when this particular photo was taken. As for the future, he's looking forward to retiring from work for the insurance company and being able to play more.

BENNY POWELL

luent, clear-toned trombonist Benny Powell made a name for himself as a soloist in the great Basie Band of the 1950s. Powell was so highly thought of, along with fellow Basie Band trombonist Henry Coker, that when Al Grey first joined the band in 1957 he was virtually ignored by both fellow musicians and the general public. Back then, Powell was very much the man of the hour — he was, after all, a 1956 *Down*

Beat poll-winner in demand for small-group jazz recording sessions when not busy with the Basie Band; Grey, by contrast, was just "the new boy" in the band. But Powell never tried to hog all the glory. If someone else had something to contribute, as it soon became clear Grey did, he was happy for their success, and willing to help make room for them. In the bands that he himself has led, Powell has been quite democratic about letting everyone express himself.

Born March 1, 1930 in New Orleans, Powell played with King Colax and Lionel Hampton, among others, before beginning a 12-year association with Basie in 1951. Afterwards, he played in Broadway pit bands, produced concerts, taught, did studio work, and even acted a bit (look for him in the Sammy Davis film *A Man Called Adam*), besides leading groups of his own. Whether he's sitting in someplace with a friend like Doc Cheatham (as Nancy Miller Elliott has caught in one photo), touring foreign lands with a cohort like pianist Randy Weston, leading a group of his own at a New York club like the Metropolis on Union Square or the Lenox Lounge in Harlem, or at a record date (as he was the day Elliott snapped the other shot), he projects an air of calm, unflappable good grace.

What most people don't know — and is quite amazing, considering his grueling foreign tours — is that he requires regular kidney dialysis to stay alive. Traveling from country to country means keeping careful tabs on when and where he will be able to receive the dialysis treatments. To Elliott, who says he's one of her favorite musicians, his fortitude and good cheer have been inspirational.

"He's a very spiritual type of person in the real sense, always thinking of other people. He goes three or four times a week for treatments; each session takes at least three hours, sometimes four. Sometimes he has to go at five in the morning. Sometimes I've gone with him, to help keep him company," says Elliott, adding that she always enjoys his company herself.

"You know, he even looks different from everyone else being treated. Everyone else seems to look half-dead. People are moaning. But he's positive; he's really a totally positive person. He doesn't hold onto negative feelings. He's not a complainer, no matter what he's going through.

He doesn't talk about his own problems. He's more interested in talking about how the other person is doing.

"He'll take some work with him. He'll be composing music while on dialysis. I've asked him about that. He hopes he can make use of his feelings, his experience, his suffering, in his music. Well, you know he's from New Orleans," she reflects (and indeed, he was recently honored with a day of his own at the New Orleans Jazz and Heritage Festival). She adds appreciatively: "Those New Orleans people — there's just something about them, something magical, mysterious."

NAT PIERCE

In this portrait by Nancy Miller Elliott, pianist/arranger Nat Pierce (1925-1992) offers his carefully considered judgment on contemporary popular music.

You can infer what kind of music Pierce *did* like by noting his professional associations. He had extended stints in Woody Herman's Herds in the 1950s and again in the '60s, and continued to periodically reunite with Herman until Herman's death in 1987. He played for Harry James, Charlie Barnet, and Louie Bellson. And he subbed for Stan Kenton when Kenton took ill in 1972.

For years, Pierce was *the* substitute for Count Basie — filling in when needed, perhaps a couple of days here or a week there, until Basie suf-

fered a heart attack in 1976; then Pierce toured with the Basie Band for almost four straight months while the Count recuperated. On occasion, Pierce even substituted for Basie — uncredited — on recordings. Pierce also did occasional European tours with Basie alumni all-star bands.

Pierce repeatedly led big bands of his own, too: a New England-based unit in the late '40s, a New York-based unit in the late '50s, and the star-studded southern California-based "Juggernaut" he led in his last years with drummer Frank Capp. He also wrote arrangements for greats ranging from veterans Basie and Herman to comparative newcomers Warren Vaché Jr. and Scott Hamilton.

When I asked Pierce what suggestions he had to offer younger players aspiring to make it as jazz musicians, he replied, "Well, the advice is: Work hard but don't expect too much fruit for your labor, because, you know, there's dozens of kids that come out of the schools–like Eastman and North Texas and Berklee and Boston — every day. I wouldn't recommend pursuing music as a career. There'll be a rude awakening some-where along the way, unless you're exceptionally talented. And they're also going to have to immerse themselves in the history of jazz and learn about things. Some of the younger ones don't even know Charlie Parker — forget about Fats Waller and Louis Armstrong! They're way out and their playing doesn't quite fit with what we try to do." Pierce added after a bit: "But if they want to try it, let 'em go. You can't tell anybody what to do anyway. They're going to do it themselves."

I asked him if he thought the quality of the musicians coming out of the schools was getting better. "Oh it's definitely better," he answered amiably. "But by the same token, they don't play any music. They are masters of their instruments, but they don't *play* anything. All they play is like third-hand John Coltrane solos, which is already old-fashioned — that's 20 years ago."

The young music lovers with Pierce in this photo, by the way, are two of Nancy Miller Elliott's sons: Vincent (with the guitar) and Thomas. They apparently took Pierce's advice to heart; they are not in the music business today.

FRANK WESS, FRANK FOSTER

It's good seeing Frank Wess the recipient of so much appreciation. (And how can you not share in that mega-watt smile he's got in the photo Nancy Miller Elliott has taken of him with the two gals?) If I were asked to name one jazz musician I think is often under-appreciated, Wess would come quickly to mind. He's not the only under-appreciated jazz musician, of course — far from it! — but he does so many things well, he ought to get more recognition than he does.

Actually, I suspect the fact that he *does* do so many things well may have contributed to his relatively low profile. It's harder for the public to get a handle on him than on someone who does only one thing well. Are we to think of him as an alto saxist (the instrument he took up first, as a boy of ten in Kansas City in 1932)? Or as a tenor saxist (the instrument he picked up several years later out of admiration for Lester Young)? He made his first big splash in the Basie Band (from 1953-1957) on tenor; initially Basie contrasted Wess' light, smooth tenor sound with Frank Foster's heavier, rougher one, much as Basie had once contrasted the tenor sounds of Lester Young and Herschel Evans. But in 1957, Basie had Wess switch to alto, which Wess played until he left the

band in 1964. Wess gained additional attention as a fleet and facile player of an instrument that had rarely been used in jazz: the flute (listen to his noteworthy playing on such Basie Band recordings as "The Midgets," "Perdido," and "Segue in C"). He also made important contributions to the Basie book as an arranger; he was, along with Ernie Wilkins, Neal Hefti, Frank Foster and a few others, one of the people who helped give the 1950s Basie Band (which was far more of an arranger's band than earlier Basie bands had been) its oft-imitated sound.

In the years since leaving the Basie Band, Wess has co-led a well-received small group with Frank Foster ("The Two Franks"), worked in Broadway pit orchestras and TV studio bands, played in the New York Jazz Quartet and Dameronia, and periodically led big bands of his own which carry on the Basie tradition (and sometimes include other Basie alumni).

He can carry off just about any kind of situation with aplomb. In recent years, for example, I've seen him play tenor sax in Walt Levinsky's salute to Benny Goodman, rolling so easily and admirably in his spots, you would've thought he'd spent a lifetime playing Goodman's music; I've savored him hauntingly take Johnny Hodges' place (playing an alto sax that had once belonged to Hodges) in a re-creation at Carnegie Hall, which he co-led with Maurice Peress, of Ellington's 1943 Carnegie Hall concert; and when I watched Wess lead the saxes in an American Jazz Orchestra program of Benny Carter's music (conducted by Carter) at Cooper Union, I was reminded of how he had once played lead alto on a Basie Band album of Carter's music (with Carter on second alto). Wess played a vital role in the Philip Morris Superband led by Gene Harris, helping to select and rehearse the musicians, as well as contributing arrangements.

Because of his versatility, expressiveness, and professionalism, Wess has also been sought after for studio dates of all kinds. The two women expressing their appreciation to him in the first photo are Rebecca Hardiman (on the left) and Sharon Harris of the vocal group The Ritz, with whom Wess has recorded. Wess' friends in the second shot (also taken by Elliott) are James T. Maher and Phoebe Jacobs. Maher, an erudite writer with unusually broad interests — he's written well on everything from hot jazz of the 1920s to the boisterous comedy of Jimmy Durante — is particularly knowledgeable about the development of the big bands. Jacobs has been closely associated — whether as a publicist, aide, friend, confidant and/or executor — with many of the biggest names in the field,

including Louis Armstrong, Benny Goodman, Sarah Vaughan, Ella Fitzgerald, and Duke and Mercer Ellington.

Because I've told Frank Foster's story in detail in my book *Swing Legacy*, I'll only comment briefly on him here. Foster (born September 23, 1928 in Cincinnati, Ohio) became one of the top Basie arrangers in the 1950s and '60s (consider his charts of "Down for the Count," "Blues Backstage," "Misunderstood Blues," and his best-known composition, "Shiny Stockings"). From 1986 to 1995 he did an outstanding job maintaining musicianship and morale in the Basie Orchestra. Andreas Johnsen's photo captures him deep into the blues, always the heart of the Basie repertoire.

Frank Wess, Frank Foster

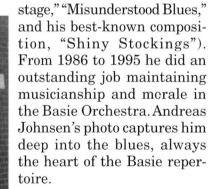

GROVER MITCHELL

Grover Mitchell, who was Count Basie's lead trombonist from 1962-70 and again from 1980-84, succeeded Frank Foster as leader of the Basie Band on July 3, 1995.

He believes in the value of musicians banding together to express themselves collectively. "It's that old thing," he says, "about the fist being stronger than the individual fingers."

Mitchell (born March 17, 1930) grew up in Pittsburgh, where his contemporaries included saxist Stanley Turrentine and singer Dakota Staton ("She was the singer in our teenage band"). He wanted to take up the trumpet in junior high, but the instructor said they were out of trumpets and suggested he try trombone instead.

Mitchell went on to a successful career in the studios, recording with the likes of Quincy Jones, Oliver Nelson, and Billy May. (If you watch carefully, you can even spot him soloing on-screen in the movie, *Lady Sings the Blues*.) He occasionally subbed in Duke Ellington's Band — not for any of the trombonists, but for lyrical alto saxist Johnny Hodges! He'd transpose Hodges' sax parts to trombone.

Mitchell, photographed by Elliott, believes strongly in the jazz big band tradition. "This way of writing and playing music is a very good way," he'll tell you simply. "It shouldn't go away."

BUCK CLAYTON, JOHN HAMMOND & WILLARD ALEXANDER

The Nancy Miller Elliott photograph on the next page captures three stalwarts of the Swing Era, who've gathered to pay their last respects at the funeral of Count Basie in 1984. From left to right we see former Basie trumpet star Buck Clayton, jazz critic/record producer John Hammond (1910-87), and band booker Willard Alexander (1908-84). Although they were unknown to most Americans, Hammond and Alexander made important contributions to shaping American musical tastes, exerting influences from the early 1930s into the 1980s.

Born into a wealthy family and educated at Yale, Hammond eschewed such standard-brand Ivy League careers as business or law. Fascinated by jazz — he could often be found checking out clubs in black neighborhoods that few from his socio-economic background might frequent — he fashioned a unique career for himself promoting the music he loved. Whether he was working (for nominal pay) as a music critic or producing records, he liked nothing better than helping bring recognition to a deserving unknown. As a talent scout, Hammond's judgment was exceptional — from the early years of his career, when he boosted such artists as Fletcher Henderson, Benny Goodman, Benny Carter, Teddy Wilson, and Billie Holiday, to his later years, when he did the same for George Benson, Aretha Franklin, Bob Dylan, and Bruce Springsteen. It was Hammond who in 1936 discovered Count Basie, then leading a nine-piece band in Kansas City, and convinced Willard Alexander that the band, if enlarged a bit and properly promoted, could be the next national sensation. Trusting Hammond's judgment, Alexander booked the band on a national tour. Hammond hyped it so strongly, some other important critics (like George T. Simon) were initially resistant, but gradually came around.

Were it not for the efforts of Hammond and Alexander, Basie might never have left the Kansas City area, might never have become internationally known.

Hammond had the finances — and the energy — to think nothing of driving from New York to check out talent in Kansas City, or wherever else he chose. Other critics, struggling to make a living in the Depression, could only look on in envy.

His enthusiasm was boundless. If he thought a performer was "swell," he'd go to seemingly any lengths to let people know about it, or to help find work for the artist. (It was Hammond, for example, who brought Charlie Christian to Benny Goodman.) That sort of thing earned Hammond the nickname, in some quarters, of "The Guardian Angel." But heaven help those whom he decided were no good. (He was known to some, back in the Swing Era, as "The Big Bringdown.")

Hammond railed tirelessly against commercialism. Fellow critic Otis Ferguson observed insightfully in 1938: "John won't compromise on anything because he never learned to and he never learned to because he never had to."

An admirable, idealistic zeal for social justice enlivened his workmanlike prose. He was ardently, outspokenly, opposed to racism. And he knew how to express his opinions, whether on music or on social issues, so persuasively and forcefully as to make others take notice — and oftentimes fall in line.

There were those who felt he could be a little absorbed in himself. Ruby Braff claimed he'd had phone conversations with Hammond along these lines: "Hello, Ruby. This is John. How are you?" "Well, I'm in bed with pneumonia and I feel awful." "Wonderful, Ruby. Now what I called

Willard Alexander led a popular dance band at the University of Pennsylvania, from which he graduated in 1929. He then tried making it professionally as a bandleader, but concluded within a few years he'd do better using his knowledge of both music and the business to promote other bands. When, in the early 1930s, he joined MCA (then the largest big band booking agency), it was primarily promoting sweet, commercial bands, along the lines of Guy Lombardo's, Eddie Duchin's, and Wayne King's. Alexander championed hotter "bands with a beat" such as Benny Goodman's, Tommy Dorsey's, and Count Basie's. In the late 1930s, he left MCA to form a big band department at the William Morris Agency. In 1947, he formed his own independent Willard Alexander Agency, which, over the next four decades, handled just about every big band of note still recording or playing one-nighters, from Buddy Rich's Band to Duke Ellington's. Alexander never lost his faith in the big bands, marketing them profitably long after they had declined in popularity. Nor did his tastes in music seem to change. He concentrated his agency's efforts on "ghost bands" bearing the names of the Dorseys, Glenn Miller, and other departed leaders from the Swing Era. His agency continued for a few years after his passing, before going bankrupt.

about...." Hammond could be effectively spoofed with a single, familiar-sounding line: "I personally was in the studio at the time...." But even those who mocked him conceded that when a lot of great records were made, Hammond *had* personally been in the studio at the time — and usually provided valuable input as to personnel or repertoire. More than a few records were (to quote the title of a memorable old Basie record) "John's Idea."

BUCK CLAYTON'S
SWING BAND at the CAT CLUB

By the early 1980s, health problems forced Buck Clayton to set aside his horn and it appeared his career in music was over.

No one could have guessed then that by the decade's end, not only would he have formed a new big band but that it would be one of the most talked-about big bands in years. What's even more unusual is that the band Clayton organized in his late 70s did not re-create hits of the past, but concentrated almost exclusively on new music written by Clayton.

The band drew widespread critical acclaim. *New York Newsday*'s critic, Stuart Troup, likened Clayton to Verdi, who did his greatest composing in his 70s. John S. Wilson noted in *The New York Times*: "Most of his compositions are developed as catchy riffs in the Basie tradition with brief solos tossed from instrument to instrument. Mr. Clayton has soloists who can make the fast impression that is essential to this kind of kaleidoscopic juggling." My colleague at *The New York Post*, Lee Jeske, observed that "Clayton's songs are so well crafted — in that old-fashioned,

Buck Clayton's Swing Band at the Cat Club

blues-based, Count Basie style — that even the new ones sound like standards; the band glided on them." Nat Hentoff reflected in *The Wall Street Journal*: "One test of whether a band is cooking, as musicians used to say, is whether the players smile a lot during a set. Some of Mr. Clayton's musicians seem to find it hard to stop grinning…. I find Buck Clayton's jazz as fresh as an April day after a cold and crabbed winter." The band's debut album, *A Swingin' Dream* (Stash Records, 1989), won the Grand Prix du Disque of the Hot Club of France — a kind of French answer to the Grammy.

Clayton credited guitarist Howard Alden and trombonist Dan Barrett with spurring his return to bandleading. In 1985, they got him to write charts for their new Alden-Barrett Quintet. That in turn led to Clayton getting requests from a variety of bandleaders for charts. Finally he decided he might as well do it for himself. "I had no intention of having a band when I first met Howard and Dan," he told me. "But it just sounded better and better every time I did something, so I went into it myself."

Barrett observed, regarding Clayton's Band: "With five brass and four reeds, you have enough to get the depth or richness of any chord, but there isn't that bombastic, heavy feel some bands get. It sounds like a big band but feels like a small group. Buck was one of *the* great trumpet players of his generation. He knows the need for soloists. He leaves room for them to play." Alden saw Clayton's music as "deceptively simple. It's unpretentious, melodic, fresh — and everybody's got a feel for the music. It's always a delight to come to work."

Clayton sought soloists who could tell their stories quickly, and sections that could play deftly and cohesively. He deliberately chose to limit the band to just 13 pieces; he felt a smaller big band could swing more freely than a larger one. And swing Clayton's band did! I've sat through sets where the band conveyed such a sense of lift and elation that it seemed on the verge of taking off from the ground.

The photo on page 103 was taken by Nancy Miller Elliott at the Cat Club in New York, where, one night in April 1989, 400 people turned out to dance and listen. (Footage of the Clayton Band's performance that night was preserved, by the way, in a British television special, "Joe Temperley's Town.") Among the musicians visible in this shot are: (in the back row) trumpeters Joe Newman and Paulie Cohen, trombonist Dan Barrett, and (in the front row) saxists Frank Wess, Chuck Wilson, Joe Temperley, and Doug Lawrence. Clayton conducts.

SWING DANCING

Dancing to jazz and big bands seems to have been growing in popularity in the last decade in New York. Robert Crease, who writes about popular dance for the *Atlantic Monthly* and is at work on a book about the subject, told me he knows of some 50 swing dance societies, most of which have sprung up, like the New York Swing Dance Society, within the last decade. The New York Swing Dance Society holds weekly Savoy Sunday dances to big bands (as well as eight or nine-piece bands playing Swing Era sounds). The popular dances were being held at the Cat Club — they have since re-located to the nearby Continental Club — when Nancy Miller

Elliott took this shot in the late 1980s. Elliott captures in mid-air Mickey Davidson, who's learned much from Norma Miller (who was doing aerial moves like this at the old Savoy Ballroom a half-century ago).

At the Savoy Sunday dances of recent years, you could spot on the dance floor anyone from East Village youths to yuppies to professional dancers to oldtime bandleaders (it was a treat to encounter the late Andy Kirk there one night), to stars of Broadway shows. One patron, E. G. Williams, told me a few years back, "This is like my second home; I live here," and added it evoked memories for him of the Savoy Ballroom, where he first began dancing in 1927 (just a year

after the Savoy opened). It's an incredible sight to see Frankie Manning — he's king at the Savoy Sunday dances — Shim-Sham-Shimmying, while behind him a couple of hundred dancers copy his moves.

Traditionally, some jazz musicians resented playing for dancers, saying they felt it put them in a category of entertainers rather than artists. When Crease told Artie Shaw he enjoyed dancing to Shaw's music, for example, Shaw bristled that he had created his music for listening, not dancing, and suggested the society use recordings for its dances rather than "demean" musicians.

Many other musicians, though, clearly enjoy playing for dancers. The late trumpeter/ bandleader Lee Castle made the astute observation to me, a few years back, that musicians often play better at dances than at concerts because they're more relaxed. Drummer/bandleader Panama Francis not only enjoys watching dancers as he plays; he's been known to step down from his drum set and join them. And alto saxist Bobby Watson has noted: "The rhythm of dancers influences me when I'm playing for them; it's a wonderful exchange."

I sometimes think a dancer who's really into the music can provide better commentary on swingin' big-band jazz than most writers. The dancer is expressing, with style, the same exuberance and elation as the musicians. The dancer is *responding*, not just passively listening, to the music. And the musicians in turn may respond to the dancers.

A lot of people viewed it as an advance when jazz moved out of the dance halls and into the concert halls, but I don't think it always was. Oh, it's good to see the music accorded the respect implicit in its being presented in concert halls, and sometimes you do want to listen attentively to every nuance. But I agree with trumpeter Don Cherry when he says it can be frustrating to have to hear a great outfit like the Basie Band or the Ellington Band play in a concert hall music that was originally created to be danced to.

Bandleader Panama Francis believes that sitting and quietly listening to music is a white European tradition. Black audiences, he feels,

generally respond more (and not just to jazz music); that's part of their cultural heritage. (Some writers have traced it back to Africa.) You see the tradition of responding in black churches, where parishoners will spontaneously call out vigorous affirmations of what the preacher is saying. You see it, too, when singers play before mostly black audiences, where people in the audience are likely to give encouraging cries ("Sing the song!"). Dancing to music, moving with it (not just passively listening) is another form of response, a way of participating in the experience.

Although the Lindy Hop became nationally (and even internationally) popular, with different regions developing different variations, it was born in — and flourished spectacularly in — New York's black community. The name "Lindy Hop," according to Crease, was first applied to the dance at the Savoy Ballroom in 1927, following aviator Charles Lindbergh's pioneering transatlantic "hop." People were Lindy-ing at the Savoy and other Harlem dance spots in the late 1920s, well before the dance swept the rest of the nation.

Why is this older style of dancing undergoing some degree of resurgence these days? You can ask around and get any number of opinions.

Crease notes that some believe the AIDS crisis is spurring a shift away from casual sex towards safer activities, including social dancing. Dance instructor Margaret Batiuchok believes the rise in popularity of older forms of dancing may relate to a general return to more traditional values in society. Dance instructor Larry Schulz, taking the long view, feels that the popularity in the 1960s, '70s, and '80s of couples dancing without any physical contact with one another was an exception to the historic norm of contact dancing — a reflection of one generation's emphasis on doing your own thing. He views a return to older types of dancing such as the Lindy Hop (which involves pulling partners close together as well as moments of separateness) as only natural. Frankie Manning seems hardly surprised to find young people in the 1990s discovering the joys of a type of dancing he became hooked on in the 1930s. As he says: "Everything that goes around comes around."

ILLINOIS JACQUET

No jazz musician projects a stronger sense of identity than tenor saxist/big band leader Illinois Jacquet, photographed here by Andreas Johnsen during a month-long 1994 engagement at New York's prestigious Tavern on the Green.

First, there's Jacquet's brawny, immediately identifiable tone — which, to my ears, is as rich, full-bodied, and satisfying as any tenor saxist's.

Then there's the oft-imitated, emotionally expressive, supercharged Jacquet style, which was almost fully developed when he recorded his classic "Flying Home" solo with Lionel Hampton's Band in 1942. A strong, highly recognizable sense of style is the one thing that's all too lacking among many of today's technically adept younger players.

Jacquet's own playing (and to some extent, that of his band as a whole) reflects his basic personality. One hears in his speech the same enormous self-confidence, sly wit, and drama that are hallmarks of his best solos. And he obviously gets such a kick out of his band, it's hard not to share in the fun. When his band (after a tension-building subdued passage) suddenly hits hard, his whole body reacts to the impact.

His current band, while not as strong as one might hope in terms of soloists (other than Jacquet) is an extraordinarily swinging one. It rolls, from first note to last. The sax section, admirably led by David Glasser, is particularly fluid.

Sometimes the band will play early Basie specialties (which is appropriate since Jacquet played with Basie in the '40s). Sometimes it'll play basic blues, or show tunes, or fresh originals with Swing Era roots. Jacquet always leaves me feeling great.

I left the Tavern on the Green the night this photo was taken feeling it had been a perfect New York evening. Even when I got to my car afterwards (parked on Central Park West at 67th Street — presumably a good location) and found that someone had smashed a window and stolen everything inside, I was glad I'd gone to see the show. For how often do you get to see a jazz legend who really created and defined a style?

DUKE ELLINGTON

When Duke Ellington had dinner one evening with New York TV talk-show host Joe Franklin, Franklin was surprised to note Ellington ordered his dessert first. Why, Franklin inquired, did Ellington do that? With complete reasonableness, Ellington explained that he planned to eat so heartily that if he didn't have his dessert first, he feared he wouldn't have room for it at the end.

One can almost hear Ellington offering that grand explanation which didn't really explain much, in that voice that seemed, at times, to be gently patronizing the whole world. He would simply have his dessert first, and then his steak. And why should anyone expect him to do things the way everyone else did?

Ellington wasn't much interested in following conventions. His longtime music copyist, Tom Whaley, told writer Stanley Dance that Ellington "goes against all rules of music. He says, if it sounds good, that's all that matters. And he's right.... The first time I was copying his music, I said, 'Duke, you got an E natural up there against an E flat.' He said, 'That's all right. Put it down.' After you hear it, it sounds great." The most important composer in jazz history, Ellington was able to imagine unorthodox combinations of sounds that others wouldn't think of using. He created big band music filled with sounds unusually lush, ripe, exotic. When I go to hear the Ellington Orchestra today, I get my biggest kicks not from the Ellington standards which I've heard many times but from pieces I've never heard before, which are obviously — because of their sensual richness — from the pen of Ellington and/or his enormously gifted musical alter-ego Billy Strayhorn. Ellington's use of tonal color was unsurpassed; the fact that he originally was interested in painting, not just making music — indeed he won a scholarship to study art at Pratt Institute — no doubt has something to do with that fact.

He was also a most observant man, forever able to make much out of something he'd seen or heard that others would have overlooked; he'd frequently take a chance phrase improvised by a sideman in his band and expand it into a song. Trombonist Britt Woodman once told me that when he joined the Ellington band, another member advised him to try and remember everything he played — because the Duke would steal phrases and make songs from them. Woodman responded that he'd be honored if Ellington would do so. It's interesting to note that none of Ellington's sidemen had careers as distinguished composers on their own.

Ellington found song inspirations in everything from billboards to old men walking. His notes on the composition of the first section of *The Queen's Suite* are typical: "While speeding across Florida from Tampa to West Palm Beach at 80 miles per hour, it was in the half-light of sunset that we passed a bird. It seemed to call to us. We would have liked to have gone back and thanked the bird, but we were too far down the road and didn't know what kind of a bird it was anyway. But the first phrase is the melody we heard."

The Queen's Suite, I might point out, is an Ellington/Strayhorn extended work that Ellington recorded for, and presented as a gift to, Queen Elizabeth of England. That is, he paid to rent a New York recording studio for three sessions, to have his musicians record the number, and then had one album made from the master tape, which he subsequently ordered destroyed: an extraordinarily extravagant gesture. So as to preserve the exclusivity of his gift to her, he never performed the suite in public. Since his death, a recording of the suite has been released and the music has been performed in concert. I think it's a pity Ellington's wishes weren't respected. As a composer, musician, and bandleader, Ellington was a major factor in jazz from the 1920s right up until his death in 1974. In a sense, he remains a major factor today. The Lincoln Center Jazz Orchestra, the Smithsonian Jazz Orchestra, the American Jazz Orchestra, and others have continued to explore the rich library of music Ellington left behind. We can expect to hear his compositions and orchestrations brought to life in concert halls for many, many years to come.

On this page and the pages that follow, we see John Johnsen's portraits of Ellington and various members of his musical world.

Duke Ellington

COOTIE WILLIAMS

When I saw Duke Ellington and his Orchestra in June of 1971, the player who held the most fascination for me was trumpeter Cootie Williams (photographed here by John Johnsen). He actually played very little that night, but what he did play had such conviction, such rugged character, I was held rapt. Most of the night, he simply sat in his chair, looking weary. He did not play any section parts; after a lifetime in the business, I figured he had earned the right to be excused from such labors if he so desired. He performed strictly as a featured soloist.

It seemed incredible to me that I should be watching a trumpeter who had been featured on Ellington records as early as 1929. Williams had been part of the Cotton Club era, which seemed almost unimaginably remote. Williams' expressive plunger-muted growl trumpet — he became known as the foremost exponent of the growl technique — was a key element in the "jungle music" Ellington played in Williams' early years with the band. And he was equally impressive playing open horn. He remained with Ellington until 1940. Then he left to join Benny Goodman — a move of such importance in the jazz world that Raymond Scott even composed a number marking the occasion: "When Cootie Left the Duke." Subsequently he led his own

bands, often working at Harlem's Savoy Ballroom until it was torn down to make way for a housing project in 1962. Then he rejoined Ellington.

To me, a college student watching him in 1971, Williams may as well have been a thousand years old — he had been part of so much jazz history. It is startling for me to look back now and realize that in June of 1971, he was actually just 59 years old.

Williams had been in Fletcher Henderson's Band before Ellington's. And while he then believed that Henderson's was the best band around, he sensed Ellington's was coming up so rapidly that switching to it would be wise.

Williams only began growling after joining Ellington. He had been called upon to replace Bubber Miley — a master of that technique — in the Ellington Band, and figured he had better try doing some growling even though it seemed funny to him at first. Eventually, of course, it came to seem quite natural to him, and he surpassed Miley in that style.

Williams remained with the Ellington Band for several years after Duke Ellington's death, providing a crucial element of continuity as Mercer Ellington struggled to keep the band going with many new members. Williams died in 1985.

BEN WEBSTER

For my money, Ben Webster (1909-1973) — captured here in photos by John Johnsen — was about as satisfying a tenor sax balladeer as has ever lived. I know of no one with a more beautiful tone. And his creativity was just as impressive.

Like Cootie Williams, he is associated readily with Ellington because he made so many superb records with Ellington. Indeed, it was during his tenure with Ellington that he seemed to reach maturity as player. And, again like Williams, he gained valuable earlier experience in Fletcher Henderson's band. (Before joining

Henderson, he had also played with such bands as Bennie Moten's and Andy Kirk's.)

It was while in Henderson's Band in the mid-'30s that Webster received an enormously useful piece of advice from Henderson's longtime lead trumpeter, Russell "Pops" Smith: "Let those other players play sixty thousand notes. You just play three with tone. That makes the difference." It *did* make the difference in Webster's career.

In his very earliest recordings, Webster's style was quite busy, and his tone had none of the lustre for which he is remembered today. Like many sax players who came up in the '20s (and, for that matter, many who are coming up today), Webster seemed to feel that the faster you could execute notes on your horn, the more impressive you were. Only gradually did he seem to realize that fewer, more carefully chosen notes, with greater attention paid to how they sounded, would touch people more deeply.

When Webster joined the Ellington Band on a permanent basis in 1940 (he had played briefly in the band on two earlier occasions), his tone continued to ripen. Playing in a section that included so sublime a player as alto saxist Johnny Hodges, he noted, couldn't help but improve his tone. In 1940 and '41, the Ellington Band reached great artistic heights. Ellington was in peak form as a composer. And the additions to the band, in 1939 and '40 respectively, of bassist Jimmy Blanton and tenor saxist Ben Webster (the first important tenor sax soloist the Ellington Band had ever had), seemed to have made an essential difference. (Indeed, the band in this period is often referred to by jazz writers as "the Blanton/Webster band.") Blanton and Webster became close friends. Blanton's death from tuberculosis in 1942, when he was just 23 years old, was a great blow to Webster.

Webster's playing grew more exquisitely sensitive. Others recognized he was reaching new depths of feeling, becoming as moving a player as could be found. His own explanation for his becoming so heartfelt and tender a player was simple — and probably as accurate as any more involved hypothesis might be: "Blanton died."

Webster left Ellington in 1943, but reunited with him on occasion in subsequent years. (Johnsen, fortunately, was able to document one such reunion in 1971, capturing him enhancing the masterly Ellington sax section once again. From left to right we see: Paul Gonsalves, Harold Ashby, Ben Webster, Harry Carney and Norris Turney.)

Unappreciated in his own country, Webster moved for good in 1964 to Denmark, where he got to record more frequently, with both big bands and small groups, and was generally treated with great respect. Like Coleman Hawkins and Lester Young, two of the other sax giants of his era, Webster drank to excess. Unlike them, however, he continued to make first-rate recordings right up until he died.

In his youth, Webster played piano, and throughout his life he was especially fond of listening to records by pianists he favored: men like Willie "The Lion" Smith, James P. Johnson, Donald Lambert, Fats Waller, and Art Tatum. Who were his favorite sax players? He once told Stanley Dance (the foremost chronicler of the Ellingtonians) that Benny Carter came first, followed by Coleman Hawkins, then Johnny Hodges ("the most feeling") and Hilton Jefferson ("the prettiest"). Webster's own earliest records show the profound influence of Hawkins. (He later, of course, developed his own unmistakable identity, playing with more grace than Hawkins. I prefer his work to Hawkins', overall.) For a while in his youth, Webster shared bandstands with Lester Young. They were both just teenagers then — traveling through the midwest in a "family band" that Young's parents had put together. (Cootie Williams was part of that band one summer, too, but not at the same time as Webster.) It's an interesting coincidence that two of the all-time great tenor saxists, who went in dramatically different stylistic directions, started out playing together. Webster recalled

little from their time together — other than, he said, that he once saved Young from drowning.

Besides countless fine recordings of Webster, there is also an intriguing video documentary, *Ben Webster, The Brute and the Beautiful,* available from Shanachie. It portrays an aging artist who's lonely, frustrated, and sometimes brutal (he was only turned on by a woman if "he could, like, force her into the action," Mercer Ellington says in the documentary) — but still capable of playing some of the tenderest tenor sax ever heard. That's preserved in the video, along with Webster's rarely heard stride piano, and his haunting words to fans at a club on what would turn out to be the very last night of his life: "You're young and growing. I'm old and going. Have your fun while you can."

PAUL GONSALVES

There is no doubt that Duke Ellington was good for Paul Gonsalves (photographed here by John Johnsen). When Ellington hired Gonsalves in 1950, $7.20 was all of the money Gonsalves had, anywhere. Although Gonsalves had previously played for Count Basie and Dizzy Gillespie, among others, it was Ellington who made him a star. Ellington provided him with employment for the rest of Gonsalves' life. (And Gonsalves died just nine days before Ellington himself did in 1974.) Ellington was willing to overlook Gonsalves' abuses of alcohol, heroin, and other drugs. (He was willing to overlook such things in any player who could make the musical contributions he needed.) Ellington kept Gonsalves on the payroll even when Gonsalves had becomeg so undependable that Ellington had to hire another tenor saxist, Percy Marion, for a late-1973 tour as "insurance," just in case Gonsalves was not able to perform some nights. (Hiring Marion turned out to be a wise decision, since Gonsalves had to be hospitalized twice during the tour due to drug-related seizures.) Ellington was never a stern taskmaster with his men, which Gonsalves appreciated. If they straggled onto the bandstand late after intermission, Ellington was tolerant, so long as they could contribute something vital musically once they got there.

And there's no doubt Gonsalves could do that. He had a gift for reaching an audience with his playing, which was good for Ellington. Ellington could have hired saxists who were better technicians than Gonsalves, and still others who were more creative. Gonsalves combined a respectable degree of technical proficiency and creativity with an energy and emotionalism that excited listeners. Gonsalves admired Ben Webster, knew all of Webster's old solos, and could bring something of Webster's sound back to the band. Initially, that's why Ellington hired him, but Ellington gradually discerned where Gonsalves' own strengths really lay.

Gonsalves was Ellington's secret weapon when Ellington got to the 1956 Newport Jazz Festival. By then, many jazz fans had written off Ellington as old hat. But when Ellington called for "Diminuendo and Crescendo in Blue," he let Gonsalves solo until Gonsalves was ready to drop — 27 choruses that roused the audience to a frenzy. The performance was the high point of the festival. Within weeks, Ellington was on the cover of *Time* magazine and his "comeback" was well underway. With a canny sense of public relations, Ellington acted as if he had been as surprised by what had happened that night as had the audience. It was, he suggested, one of those wholly spontaneous events that are the essence of jazz. They had played that number so rarely, Ellington maintained, that Gonsalves didn't even remember how it went. Before they started, Ellington simply told him it was a blues, gave him the key, and said he'd signal when Gonsalves was to start and to finish.

That made good copy, but it wasn't the whole story. Actually, Ellington had seen Gonsalves click tremendously with crowds, taking chorus after chorus on "Diminuendo and Crescendo in Blue," before. Gonsalves may well have outdone himself at Newport, but Ellington knew from past experience what Gonsalves was capable of. Musician after musician has said that Ellington knew better than any other bandleader exactly what his musicians were capable of, and how best to get them to realize their potential.

HAROLD ASHBY

John Johnsen's photographs of Harold Ashby soloing in the early '70s with Duke Ellington's Orchestra are revelatory not just of Ashby, but of Ellington. Ellington had a reputation for seeing talents in musicians they might not have seen in themselves, and of spurring them to hit new heights. In these shots, Johnsen caught Ellington coaxing Ashby to give everything he's got — and delighting when Ashby comes through. (The formal studio portrait, showing a distinguished-looking, white-haired Ashby today, was taken by Nancy Miller Elliott.)

Ashby told me that the first time Ellington telephoned, in 1960, inviting Ashby to sub in his band, Ashby hung up, sure it was someone pretending to be Ellington as a joke. When Ellington rang back, insisting, "This is *Duke*," Ashby had no choice but to agree — even though he was scared. He didn't know if he was ready for the Ellington band. Sure he had recorded with some of Ellington's sidemen, and he had jammed plenty of times with one of Ellington's most distinguished alumni (and his own idol among tenor sax players), Ben Webster — but the Ellington Band was the greatest in the world. That night, alto saxist Russell Procope assured him there'd be no problems, encouraging him: "Just blow." Ashby did, and, as he recalls: "I got across because of *my sound*, you know what I mean?"

For the next eight years, Ellington periodically called upon Ashby to sub in his band. Then in 1968, Ashby became a regular member of the band. He stayed in the band until February of 1975. Since then he has freelanced, usually working as a leader but occasionally working for others, including Benny Goodman, Buck Clayton, and George Wein (the Newport All-Stars).

Ashby's distinctive tone, which first brought him to the attention of Ellington, has only become more pleasing with time. It is full, but not hard or harsh. At times it gets wavery or watery, the edges of the sound seemingly shrouded in a mist. There's often, in his sound, the quality of a lament. There's a lot of feeling in his playing, a lot of humanity.

While Ashby occasionally (as in Johnsen's photos) featured Ashby on uptempo numbers, it is as a balladeer that I think he has done his best work. (Samples of his work may be found on such labels as Stash, Gemini, and Black and Blue.) In terms of beauty of sound, Ashby is as appealing a sax balladeer as anyone I know of who's active today.

Yearning, rapturous — coming in just a bit higher than you'd expect at the climactic moment, for added impact — Ashby gave Ellington's ballad "In a Sentimental Mood" about as satisfying an interpretation as I'd ever heard on the opening night of his week-long April 1995 engagement, dedicated to Ellington, at the Village Vanguard. There was nothing fancy about his melodic elaborations; Ashby's playing is spare and unpretentious — but it is also tender, honest, heartfelt.

He was able to maintain his concentration despite the persistent pleas of one drunken patron for "Satin Doll." He accommodated the request, but that didn't silence the drunk, who kept calling "Satin Doll" until Ashby rather patiently explained: "We just played it."

Ashby shone, too, on "In My Solitude" and "I Got it Bad and That Ain't Good." He has the ideal sound, sensitivity, and temperament for those mournful ballads. Sax immortal Ben Webster, who co-

composed "I Got It Bad" with Duke, was Ashby's mentor.

Ashby still expresses a lot of gratitude to Webster, whom he first met as a teenager in Kansas City, around 1940. When Ashby moved to New York in 1957 and was having trouble getting established, Webster used to call him up and ask if he needed any money. Sometimes Ashby did; he was absolutely broke and worried about where he would get his next meal. Webster helped out when he could, and eventually got Ashby to live at the Long Island house where he and the blues singer Big Miller were living. Webster recorded a tune dedicated to him: "Ash's Cap." Ashby, in turn, later recorded "Lullaby for Ben." He says simply of his late friend: "Ben was something else."

DUKE ELLINGTON & ELLA FITZGERALD

A meeting of jazz nobility: Duke Ellington and the First Lady of Song, Ella Fitzgerald, are caught by John Johnsen's camera. (A print of this photo was acquired by the Schomberg Center for Research in Black Culture in Harlem.)

Ellington and Fitzgerald occasionally recorded and performed in concert together — much less often than fans might have wished. That neither artist was ever given a television series (while less gifted white artists like Dinah Shore, Pat Boone, Spike Jones, and Lawrence Welk got theirs) is a reflection of institutionalized racism. In the 1950s, most TV sponsors were wary of backing black shows. Things began loosening up in the 1960s. Fitzgerald and Ellington, who had periodically made guest appearances on other people's shows, did an hour-long TV special together, and *Variety* reported that 26 episodes of a proposed, syndicated "Ella Fitzgerald Show," which would also feature Duke Ellington and his Orchestra, were being planned. A date to begin filming the shows was even announced. But nothing ever came of the proposal. For jazz fans, that was, perhaps, the ultimate "what might have been...."

LOUIE BELLSON

In early 1951, the music press wondered how Duke Ellington would survive the loss of three key sidemen. Alto saxist Johnny Hodges and drummer Sonny Greer, who had been with Ellington since the '20s, and trombonist Lawrence Brown, who had been with him since the early '30s, quit Ellington's band to become members of a small group under Hodges' leadership. While diehard Ellington fans imagined the three to be irreplaceable, Ellington serenely maintained he perceived an opportunity rather than a problem, assuring *Down Beat* (April 4, 1951): "New men mean a new sound in my band and the creation of new music."

He brought in as replacements three top players he lured from the Harry James Band: alto saxist Willie Smith, trombonist Juan Tizol, and drummer Louie Bellson. The press ran such headlines as "Ellington Raids James Band" and "Duke Robs James." In reality, the three men left the James Band to join the Ellington Band with James' blessings. James was not working steadily in that period and he knew the layoffs were hard on his sidemen financially.

Smith and Tizol were perhaps acceptable substitutes for the near-irreplaceable Hodges and Brown — about the best choices Ellington could come up with in a very tough situation. But Bellson (who had previously drummed for Benny Goodman and Tommy Dorsey besides James) proved to be an absolutely inspired choice. A superb technician, he was a stronger, more consistent drummer than Greer had ever been, and gave the band a new lift. *Down Beat* (July 7, 1951) credited Bellson — "the spark plug of the band" — with inspiring the Ellington musicians to produce "more enthusiastic blowing than they have known in years." Ellington called Bellson "the world's greatest drummer," gave him top billing among his sidemen, and

played and recorded numbers Bellson wrote and arranged. Bellson, incidentally, was the first white musician hired as a permanent member of the Ellington band (others had occasionally subbed); a prejudice-free man, Bellson was accepted readily by his fellow musicians.

Bellson stayed in the band just two years — when he married entertainer Pearl Bailey, he left Ellington to become her musical director — but he made a permanent difference in the Ellington Band. Although Ellington brought Johnny Hodges back into the band as soon as he was able to, he never brought back Greer. Instead, in subsequent years, Ellington hired other drummers who played more in the Bellson mode. (Ellington quietly — and generously — kept Greer on payroll, helping out an old friend whose freelance work didn't always bring him much income.)

In later years, Ellington periodically called upon Bellson to sub in the Ellington Band, or drum in concert performances of extended works — which Bellson was always happy to do, if he could. In 1965, for example, Bellson played Ellington's *Golden Broom and the Green Apple*, with the New York Philharmonic. Typically, Ellington had no written drum parts for Bellson; he only told Bellson that the music would start out in waltz time. For Ellington's First Sacred Concert, Ellington only explained to Bellson what he wanted from him in a drum solo: "You are the thunder and lightning." As recently as 1987, Bellson accepted an invitation from Mercer Ellington to drum on some of the tracks for the GRP album *Digital Duke*. He is happy to have been part of the Ellington musical family.

Since the death of Buddy Rich in 1987, Bellson is generally considered the best living drummer in the classic, straightforward, big band tradition. Bellson (photographed here by John Johnsen) still maintains an active schedule, leading both big bands and smaller groups, and recording for MusicMasters.

There's something so satisfyingly crisp, confident, and just plain *right* about his work, even when he's playing straight time, that you sit up and take notice. He'll beat out a tattoo on his taut snares, add color with a hit to a wonderfully resonant crash cymbal. And you feel like strutting.

He's not, fundamentally, about bombast. He gives plenty of display space to his poised and polished sidemen, staying discreetly in the background as they solo. Yet no matter how much attention he directs to them, you still find yourself periodically drawn to him. And when he finally does cut loose — those patented double bass drums of his signaling that the attack is imminent — look out!

MERCER ELLINGTON

oy, talk about having a tough act to follow! Mercer Ellington (born 1919) has spent his whole life in the unenviable position of being compared to Duke Ellington — who was, of course, a truly peerless composer/orchestrator/bandleader. Since the death in 1974 of his father, to whom he refers simply as "Ellington," Mercer has led the Duke Ellington Orchestra. And he has devoted himself to whatever unfinished business his father left behind. He completed, for example, a 17-minute composition, *Three Black Kings*, which his father had been working on, and gave it its first public performance. He brought to Broadway (and served as musical director for) a celebration of his father's legacy, *Sophisticated Ladies*, which ran for two years —far longer, incidentally, than any Ellington show produced in his father's lifetime. He oversaw the completion and first stagings

(in Washington and Philadelphia) of Ellington's opera *Queenie Pie*, which he hopes to eventually bring to New York, if a first-class production can be mounted.

Even before his father died, Mercer devoted considerable energies to helping his father look good. Beginning in 1965, for example, he served quietly as the manager of the Duke Ellington Orchestra. Duke noted with approval in his autobiography: "My son, Mercer, is dedicated to maintaining the luster of his father's image." If the son also resented on some level not being able to lead a life of his own, free from the domination of his father, he kept it to himself during his father's lifetime.

As we talked one afternoon in Mercer's New York apartment (under the watchful eyes of no less than three larger-than-life portraits of Duke Ellington), Mercer seemed to have some quite

understandable ambivalence towards his father. Beginning in the late 1930s, Mercer had tried to make it as a bandleader/composer/arranger himself. With a shy laugh, he acknowledged: "I felt that many times I might have gotten further ahead, if I hadn't had him [Duke Ellington] to fight." His father didn't really want Mercer leading an orchestra of his own — in fact, Mercer didn't really feel his father wanted him to do much of anything, other than be a dutiful son; the father didn't welcome competition.

Sometimes the father would ask his advice on something. Mercer would give it. The father would then say that he now knew what *not* to do. It didn't matter that the father said he was just kidding; Mercer always felt weakened by such digs.

He told me his life growing up as the son of someone so successful was never difficult. His father made sure he had the best clothes and went to the best schools, including Columbia and Juilliard. "The only thing I felt was a difficulty was doing something that was worthy of gaining Duke Ellington's attention," he reflected. "And I think we all go through that, growing up. You want your parents to be proud of you."

He would compose pieces of music and show them to his father, eager for the unconditional praise that was unlikely to come. His father would cross out portions of his son's compositions as being substandard. The son professed to be grateful for such help from his father. But even if, as he believed, his works were inevitably strengthened by such critiques from his father, he would have welcomed heartfelt encouragement, too. Other aspiring young composers didn't have musical-genius fathers crossing out parts as unacceptable.

He knew that some of the music that he created his father considered quite good indeed. "I used to play things around him and he used to steal 'em," Mercer told me, adding: "I used to be very happy that I had done something that was good enough for him to want to claim, or to write."

Duke Ellington couldn't always give Mercer as much time as Mercer would have liked. Submitting compositions for the Duke Ellington Orchestra to play was one way for Mercer to feel connected to his father. And his father did play many of his compositions ("Things Ain't What They Used to Be," "Blue Serge," "Jumpin' Punkins," and "Moon Mist," to name some of the more memorable ones). The father played more compositions, of course, by the eminently talented Billy Strayhorn (just three years older than Mercer), with whom he spent more time than his son. "In a sense," Mercer acknowledged to me, "I had to vie for a position along with Billy Strayhorn."

Phoebe Jacobs, who knew both Duke and Mercer well, felt Duke generally treated Mercer badly. Many times, she recalls, she saw Duke introduce every member of the band to the audience except for Mercer. When she asked Duke how he could neglect to acknowledge his own son, Duke responded lightly that if Mercer refused to dye his hair (which had turned white early), he was not about to introduce him; Mercer was making him look old. And the Duke did not want the ladies he encountered on his tours thinking of him as old.

Mercer was in something of a can't-win position. No matter how good his band was (and it was certainly far better than the typical ghost band, both in terms of personnel and repertoire), he would hear, correctly, that it wasn't the equal of the old Duke Ellington Band at its best. Of course he didn't have the same kind of budget to work with that his father had. (He couldn't command the same fees his father did, and his father was also subsidizing the orchestra with composer royalties.) And giants like Johnny Hodges and Ben Webster and Harry Carney have proven to be irreplaceable. If he introduced too much new music, he got grief from those who said he wasn't honoring his father's legacy, and who said he wasn't the equal of his father as a composer. (Who is?) If he played too much of the old tried-and-true material, critics dismissed the band as just a faint echo of what once was.

But Mercer knew his father's music well, and tried to see that it was represented respectably. He knew how his father wanted the music executed — which is something more than what may be on paper. As the band rehearsed the sensuous "Passion Flower" one afternoon while I watched, for example, Mercer stopped at one point to calmly correct the musicians' interpretation: "That is not nearly as explosive as it's supposed to be." He knew the inflections and the nuances. He was there when his father played these pieces. Duke Ellington's music was a part of his consciousness for as long as Mercer lived. As a small boy, there were nights when he went to sleep to the sound of his father working out compositions on a piano in the next room.

Watching that rehearsal of the Ellington Band, conducted by Mercer and others, I was reminded anew of just how prolific a composer Duke Ellington was, and what a wealth of different ideas he had. The band was forever switching gears that afternoon: going from "Sophisticated Lady" one minute to the evocative, rarely-heard *Harlem Suite* the next, then "Prelude to a Kiss," then the complex, rarely heard *New World a Comin'* extended work, and excerpts from *Queenie Pie*: "My Father's Island" and "Woman." Give Mercer credit for helping to keep alive not just the best-remembered Ellington hits, but an enormously broad range of intriguing compositions created over a span of nearly 50 years. Mercer remained gracious and even-tempered throughout the rehearsal. There was something almost quaint about the way he addressed the musicians: "Thank you, gentlemen."

Mercer Ellington died on February 8, 1996, as this book was being typeset.

CLARK TERRY

You're sitting in a darkened club in Greenwich Village, enjoying your dinner, when — suddenly, unexpectedly — the first, full-bodied notes from Clark Terry's open horn fill the room.

He hits the notes cleanly, strongly, authoritatively. He moves from his introduction, still unaccompanied by the other musicians, into the body of the piece. And then, as if drawn by the rhythmic pull of Terry's trumpet, the pianist, bassist, and drummer start following.

Terry eases coolly into a ballad, "My Romance." He can offer poised, extended lines (he can inhale through the nose while exhaling through the mouth, so as to be able to play without pausing to take obvious breaths). And as he goes into the final cadenza, once again the other players drop out, as if to let nothing distract from the stark purity of his sound.

Terry may be best known for his big band work — with Duke Ellington in the 1950s and then, after a stretch as an NBC staff musician in the '60s, with his own critically acclaimed band in the '70s — but he is reminding us tonight that he doesn't even need a rhythm section behind him, much less a whole band, to make an impact.

Terry alternates between the trumpet and the flugelhorn (which has a darker, more shaded sound than that of the trumpet, and seems particularly well suited for ballads). That in itself is not unusual these days, but — and this *is* unusual — Terry will sometimes switch from instrument to instrument within a single number to create a kind of dialogue with himself. (He can also suggest a dialogue by staying with one instrument and alternating between muted and unmuted passages.) In addition, when the spirit moves him, Terry scats in a unique mumbling style (hence his nickname, "Mumbles"), which got broad exposure via numerous "Tonight Show" performances. Sometimes he will even scat in what appears to be a foreign language, adopting a mock Scandinavian or Germanic accent for comic effect.

Born in St. Louis in 1920, Terry was—as he told me one afternoon at his Glen Cove, Long Island, home—initially self-taught as a musician. He and some neighborhood youths, none of whom owned real instruments, formed a band that played for spare change at a local joint. Terry played a piece of a water hose with a funnel attached to one end; others played a vacuum cleaner hose, a jug, and a bushel basket. Eventually some men in the neighborhood chipped in to buy him a real horn.

Terry notes that the aspiring musicians he grew up with shared a then widely-held belief that it was best for jazzmen to be self-taught;

the prevailing wisdom was that too much musical education would harm a jazzman. Today, he feels that that supposed wisdom was actually nonsense. He is heartily supportive of all aspiring jazzmen getting as much musical education as possible, and devotes considerable energy to giving clinics.

Terry toured with a carnival band, among others, before joining the Navy in 1942, where he played in a band that included such jazz musicians as Willie Smith, Gerald Wilson, and Ernie Wilkins. Afterwards, he played with Charlie Barnet (1947) and Count Basie (1948-51), before beginning his nine-year association with Ellington, whose music he still favors. He is proud of saying he went to the college of Duke Ellington. He is often asked to play Ellington numbers. (A New York club, Carlos 1, once billed a Terry-led group featuring several famous Ellington alumni as "Ellington's Spacemen," borrowing the name from a number Terry had composed while with Ellington. Terry was surprised and dismayed when Mercer Ellington took legal action to stop them from using the Ellington name; the group became Clark Terry's Spacemen.)

Perhaps because Terry matured as a musician in a period when swing was yielding ground to bebop, his playing today draws comfortably upon both the swing and the bebop traditions.

Although his playing can seem a bit reserved at times, he has at his disposal a wide variety of tonal effects —

squeezed notes, slurred mutters, slides, growls, and brays — to provide surprising variations in color, and occasionally (happily) even whimsy.

New York Times critic Peter Watrous summed the situation up quite well with this line (April 2, 1988): "Of all the many changes inflicted on jazz by the 1960s, perhaps the worst was the loss of a sense of play…. Clark Terry, who began his career in 1945, has that sense of play." That playful side of Terry comes through in Nancy Miller Elliott's portrait of him, taken in New York City, which he has considered home for most of his career.

The performance shot of Terry was taken by Andreas Johnsen at Ellington '92, a major celebration of the legacy of Duke Ellington, held in Copenhagen in May of 1992. Terry, whose playing has become more sensitive and moving in recent years, was the standout single artist of the many talented artists participating. One afternoon, during the week of Ellington '92, Sune and Andreas Johnsen and I were driving through Copenhagen when Sune called out: "Now there's a sight I bet you wouldn't see in New York — Clark Terry, just walking down the street like an ordinary person!" Well, you *might* spot Terry walking down the street in New York, but the fact is that these days — particularly during the summers, when so many American musicians migrate to Europe for festivals — you're almost as likely to find your favorite American musician playing to enthusiastic audiences abroad as at home.

LOUIS ARMSTRONG

Nancy Miller Elliott has been around a lot of jazz giants — everyone from Duke Ellington on down. But she speaks differently about Louis Armstrong (shown here with her in a 1959 photograph taken by Jack Bradley) than about any of the others.

"He didn't seem like a mortal person; there was something kind of other-world about him," Elliott says of Armstrong. "He was so completely sort of liberated, natural — you're not used to that. Totally free. What a blessing to be around him." When she thinks of him, she remembers his great sense of humor, and the fact that "he was just so regular; you couldn't be more regular than he was." To her — and she stresses that she doesn't generally go for such concepts — he was "a saint." When this photo was taken, Elliott adds, "originally I had my head straight. I felt this great kind of energy coming from him, like a magnet. It energized my head."

I've never met one person who had anything bad to say about Armstrong personally. Selma Heraldo, who lived next door to Armstrong in Corona, Queens, from 1941 until his death in 1971, told me, "He accepted everybody as they came along. His dressing room was open to the public. He was a loving person. And he believed

in a very simple type of living. He went to the barbershop in the neighborhood. He really enjoyed the neighborhood and the children in the neighborhood. Whenever he was here, he'd always want the children with him."

Musically, his importance cannot be overstated. "Louis Armstrong defined a style, set down a musical idiom. He was the fountainhead," former Armstrong clarinetist Joe Muranyi once told me. Armstrong (1901-1971) was far and away the most influential jazz musician of his generation — the whole Swing Era might be considered a kind of expansion upon his style — and one of the foremost artists in any field that this century has seen. He is one of the jazz musicians who played so well for so many years that his picture could justifiably be placed almost anywhere in this book. A basic jazz education begins with Armstrong.

When bebop emerged in the '40s, many younger musicians suddenly looked upon Armstrong's style as passé. Enough years have passed now, though, for astute young musicians of today to be able to speak admiringly of Armstrong as well as, of course, greats who've come after him. Wynton Marsalis has contributed to the restoration of Armstrong's image, via public pronouncements as well as concerts in which he saluted Armstrong. But Marsalis' influence barely reaches beyond the jazz community.

Most young Americans, unfortunately, are growing up today without any exposure to Armstrong's greatness. (As a society, we do not do as good a job as we should of valuing our cultural heritage.) Top-40 radio stations and MTV ensure that youths are immersed in the latest commercial pop and rock. Public school music classes may provide a modest exposure to classical music. But where is one to learn of Armstrong's majesty?

When I was a boy, Armstrong was still occasionally appearing on TV. I also found Armstrong represented among some assorted old 78s in the basement. (Of course I had no way of knowing at age nine that the side I liked, "Me and Brother Bill Went Hunting," was damned near the least impressive recording he had ever made — his best sides weren't among those to which I initially happened to be exposed.) I bought new Armstrong albums as they came out in the 1960s, and *thought* I knew what he was all about. Then when I was a student at Princeton in the early '70s, Decca released *Louis Armstrong: Rare Items (1936-1944)* and I heard for the first time Armstrong's breathtaking 1938 recording of "Struttin' With Some Barbecue." An absolute masterpiece — his clarion tone was far richer there than on his latter-day recordings, and he played with a sweeping freedom, an abandon, and a total mastery of his instrument I'd never before heard from any artist. I threw open the windows of my Campbell Hall dorm room, so people walking to lunch could share in the music. And this glorious performance — named by both Bobby Hackett and Maynard Ferguson as their favorite Armstrong recording of all time — had never before been released on any American album! I found that mind-boggling — it was as if our culture almost conspired to keep younger members ignorant of the glories of the past. I made an effort to seek out as much of Armstrong's recorded legacy as I could, from the 1920s on up. But if it was that hard for me, a self-defined jazz fan, to learn the full measure of Armstrong's genius back then, what is it like for youths growing up today?

PERCY & WILLIE HUMPHREY

ndreas Johnsen's photos capture the famed Humphrey brothers, clarinetist Willie and cornetist Percy — the last major New Orleans bandleaders of Louis Armstrong's generation — both on the bandstand and at their homes, in 1994. These pictures were taken when we visited the brothers just a few weeks before Willie's death at the age of 93.

Speaking with them, you'd feel a link to the very beginning of jazz. Percy, who passed away on July 22, 1995 at the age of 91, was probably the last musician who retained memories of Louis Armstrong as a boy in short pants. And

one of Percy's early bands included musicians who had previously worked with Buddy Bolden, the first important jazzman.

In conversations with this writer, Willie recalled being taught music by his grandfather, Professor Jim Humphrey (whom he stressed had been "born a slave"), and also playing alongside King Oliver and Freddie Keppard fully 75 years earlier. His recording career dated back to the 1920s. He worked with such famed New Orleans artists as Freddie Keppard, Kid Rena, Fate Marable, Paul Barbarin, and the Eureka Brass Band.

Willie was the last of the great New Orleans clarinetists, possessing a gnarled style that was wonderfully eccentric, dramatic, and utterly inimitable. He continued playing virtually up until the end. He and Percy were long the Hall's star attractions.

Willie graciously fulfilled every request for his old specialties that I gave him at the Hall, over the course of a couple of weeks in the spring of 1994 — even for numbers like "The Cabbage Song," which younger members of the band didn't know, and "Little Liza Jane," which he said he hadn't done for at least five years but then swung into with great vigor. A born showman, he led the band in rousing vocal calls and responses — offering an oversized performing style, rich in character, that was shaped by having witnessed long-gone tent shows and camp meetings.

Percy reigned at Preservation Hall on Wednesdays and Saturdays and could also be

Percy & Willie Humphrey

found at the Palm Court (where I also caught him, playing with a slightly more modern rhythm section than at the Hall) on other nights. He played a straight lead with a dark tone, and no wasted motions. (Even the way he acknowledged applause, with a distinctive nonchalant wave, was a model of economy.) He didn't bother announcing tunes. He simply lifted a trumpet with one hand and began playing. As soon as other members of his band recognized what tune he was playing (and in what key), they'd join in. Whatever he played, it sounded like he believed in it, like he was playing because he wanted to, not because it was a job. You don't always sense that sincerity in younger players emulating older styles.

His playing was dignified. The whimsical side of his personality emerged during the occasional vocal. His surprisingly extroverted "Tiger Rag" — replete with great growling noises and clawing motions of his hands — conjured up a long-gone vaudeville tradition. Until the death of his brother Willie, that was one of their most-requested numbers together.

While Preservation Hall frequently sends bands north for concerts, Percy Humphrey told me he was no longer up for traveling. "I'm not in good health," he acknowledged matter-of-factly. His lady friend, Evelyn Gorham, whom you see with him in one of Andreas' shots, looked after him with tender, protective solicitude.

If you're thinking of someday making a trip to New Orleans for the famed, authentic New Orleans jazz, I wouldn't put it off too long. There's still music to be heard in New Orleans that you'll hear nowhere else. There's no music more joyful than well-played New Orleans

jazz; it hits the emotions directly. But the number of musicians who can play the traditional New Orleans style well is dwindling rapidly — only a handful of players in their 80s and 90s remain active — and hardly more than a handful of younger musicians are really committed to it.

Up until just a few years ago, you could have gone to Preservation Hall almost any night of the week and caught a band led by a musician of Louis Armstrong's generation. Percy pretty much represented the end of that era. The Hall remains a must on any tourist's list — lines begin forming an hour to an hour-and-a-half before show time, nightly — but it is not the same as it was in the 1960s. The management now draws from a pool of traditional musicians one-tenth as large as existed back then. The repertoire has likewise shrunk. Too many older players have taken obscure specialties to their graves with them. In the '60s, one could attend nightly for a month without hearing a tune repeated. During one two-week visit last year, I heard several tunes repeated three and four times at the Hall.

Many nights these days, Preservation Hall bands are being led by 40-ish players like Wendell Brunious and Gregg Stafford. It is good that younger musicians are trying to sustain the tradition — Stafford plays with great conviction and drama, and Brunious possesses a quite attractive tone — but it's impossible for them to know all the tunes the older players acquired over the course of a lifetime, and their playing — shaped by different life experiences — naturally hasn't the same rugged character, nor the potent impact, as that of those who've come before them.

ARVELL SHAW

The name Arvell Shaw will have different associations for different people. A great number of jazz fans will connect the name immediately with Louis Armstrong; Shaw played bass with Armstrong for so long it once looked as if he was going to make that his entire career. A smaller number of fans will also know of Shaw's work with Benny Goodman, Teddy Wilson, and Dorothy Donegan. In addition, there are musicians and some fans who will know of his fundraising efforts on behalf of autistic children. And finally,

there is a much smaller group (including such friends of Shaw's as Clark Terry, Buddy Tate, and Hank Jones, who have assisted him in his fundraising efforts) who know why he has been so concerned about the autistic. But that is getting ahead of our story.

Louis Armstrong was always Shaw's musical hero. Many musicians of Shaw's generation (he was born in 1923) came of age thinking of Armstrong as old hat; they were more interested in the new currents developing in jazz in the 1940s. But Shaw had grown up on Armstrong's records (his father had played them frequently) and always responded to them. The first job Shaw got, in 1942, was working in the Mississippi riverboat band of piano/calliope player Fate Marable (1890-1947), in whose band, a generation before, Armstrong had likewise gained early experience. After a Navy hitch during World War II, Shaw became Armstrong's bassist.

Shaw says: "Louis Armstrong never realized how great he was or the tremendous impact he had. Well, perhaps in a way he knew, but he certainly never acted as if he did. He thought of himself as a working musician and acted that way. He was always a hard worker. We toured constantly and he was always the first on the bandstand. He expected us all to work hard. But he asked no more from us than he asked from himself.

"I went with him on at least five world tours, in the 1950s and '60s. It was like traveling with the President, the way he was received everywhere. The crowds thronged to him wherever we went. It wasn't just about the music, as great as that was. People sensed the love this man gave out. They felt it, the moment he walked onstage, and they responded to that."

Shaw also stresses that Armstrong was, "even though he had little formal education, a very brilliant man. You realized that, being around him. Really, I never met anyone else like him. I started working with him in 1947, when he still had his big band, and stayed on with him with the All-Stars small-group he led for the rest of his life. There were some interruptions, when I did things with Benny Goodman and others, but I pretty much worked with him."

After their daughter, Victoria, was born in 1958, Shaw's wife, Madeline, stayed home in Brooklyn to look after her, while Shaw continued making music. He initially believed that Victoria was an unusually gifted baby — for at the age of six months, she was humming in perfect pitch music she heard on the radio. But she was slow in taking her first steps, and she didn't speak. Shaw returned home to devote himself more to his wife and daughter. He periodically reunited with Armstrong (working steadily from 1963 to 1965, and on periodic occasions in subsequent years until Armstrong's death in 1971), but he tried to stay close to home as much as possible, working, for example, for several years with Teddy Wilson at New York clubs, occasionally leading groups of his own, and playing in the pit orchestras of the Broadway shows *Bubbling Brown Sugar*, *Guys and Dolls*, and *Ain't Misbehavin'*.

Eventually, Victoria was diagnosed as autistic. She grew to adulthood without learning to speak (although she could understand others) or to function independently in the world. Shaw got friends of his including Doc Cheatham, Roy Eldridge, Maxine Sullivan, and Vic Dickenson to help him give benefit concerts, to raise funds for group homes where autistic adults can live under supervision without having to be fully institutionalized. Having an autistic daughter, he believes, matured him, gave him something bigger to concern himself with.

Nowadays, Shaw continues to periodically appear in tributes to Armstrong organized by others, and he leads his own Armstrong Legacy Band (which plays numbers associated with Armstrong, but not in strict re-creations) at such New York venues as Michael's Pub and Fat Tuesday's. Reissues of Armstrong's recordings continue to make money for record labels worldwide, but Armstrong's former sidemen (who were paid flat fees for the dates) do not share in such profits. By his count, Shaw figures he has been heard on some 200 albums reissued in one country or another since Armstrong's death, for which he has not received any royalties. He holds no grudges about that, though. He says: "If I live to be a hundred, I'll never have another experience to equal working with Louis Armstrong."

ARCHIE JOHNSON

The quiet dignity of this subject would strike you, I think, regardless of whether or not you had any interest in jazz. In Nancy Miller Elliott's portrait of trumpeter Archie Johnson you sense a kind of brooding pride.

Drummer/bandleader Panama Francis, who played with Johnson in Lucky Millinder's Band in the early '40s, recalls: "Archie was a competitor of Roy Eldridge when they were youngsters around Pittsburgh. On 'Apollo Jump' — the Lucky Millinder record [1941] — it's Archie's solo. But later he got discouraged with music and got a day gig." Johnson didn't leave music entirely — even in the 1980s, he was still playing some dates in New York City with the band of one Bobby Booker — but there wasn't enough for him in the music business to make a living from it.

Born December 5, 1906, in Ellisville, Mississippi, Johnson was raised in Pittsburgh. Two of the hot-shot musicians in Pittsburgh when he was growing up were the Eldridge brothers: alto saxist and violinist Joe Eldridge — about a year younger than Johnson — and trumpeter Roy — about four years younger than Johnson. The three musicians' paths crossed repeatedly. Johnson gained valuable early experience in the late 1920s, both in Pittsburgh and New York, in the Elite Serenaders, a band Joe Eldridge led. From the Elite Serenaders, Johnson moved on to spend a couple of years with the Cincinnati-based band of Zack Whyte, "The Chocolate Beau Brummels" (Sy Oliver was playing trumpet and arranging for that band). Roy Eldridge also played in Whyte's band for a spell. Johnson went on to play in Speed Webb's band (both Joe and Roy Eldridge played for Webb at one time or another — Roy, in fact, later took over Webb's band). Johnson played, too, for Horace Henderson and Banjo Bernie, before joining Blanche

Calloway and her Band (sometimes billed as "Blanche Calloway and Her Joy Boys") in 1934-35. Joe Eldridge was in Blanche's band in the same period, as were trombonist Vic Dickenson and tenor saxist Prince Robinson.

In the next few years, Johnson worked in the bands of Eddie Mallory, Claude Hopkins, and Benny Carter. He stayed for several years with Lucky Millinder's Band. Johnson's last recording session with Millinder was on February 18, 1942. By the Millinder Band's next recording session, July 29, 1942, Johnson's place had been taken by an up-and-coming trumpeter named Dizzy Gillespie.

"In Drauginan, France. I've got the property, and I'd also like to acquire the adjacent lot." Gillespie, who had long lived in Englewood, New Jersey (where we were conversing that afternoon), told me he planned to then live at the school. "I'd have me a little villa. I'd have plenty of time to practice. And I really would like to teach." He would still perform when his school was not in session, he assured me, but after nearly 50 years of constant travel as a trumpeter, Gillespie was contemplating the idea of slowing down. Maybe not right away, he added — he still felt *strong*, he stressed — but eventually. That was the dream that he voiced to me — his idea of the semi-retirement he expected to someday have. It was never to be. He had less time remaining than perhaps he imagined. He maintained his usual arduous pace of international touring until he was finally forced to stop by the onset of cancer.

Once a revolutionary, controversial figure in jazz, Gillespie (shown here in a concert shot by John Johnsen) had acquired by his final years the status of a universally revered elder statesman. His influence on jazz, I mused when we talked that afternoon, was greater than that of any other musician then alive. He commented simply: "I didn't know how world-famous I was to become. I just wanted to play trumpet." When he first heard Charlie Parker, he told me, that was *it*. "I started phrasing like him. My knowledge of music and rhythm led me on. And very soon we played together. We sounded like one — every phrase was exactly alike."

One wonders how differently modern jazz would have developed, had there been no John Birks "Dizzy" Gillespie, who was born in Cheraw, South Carolina on October 21, 1917. As drummer Max Roach, another key player in bebop's formative years, once noted (in Ira Gitler's highly recommended *Swing to Bop*): "Dizzy was really the catalyst of that period. He's the man who thought about bringing in Bird [Charlie Parker] to New York and told us about Oscar Pettiford.... I think Dizzy was really the catalyst.... Not taking anything away from

people like Thelonious Monk, who was probably, along with Dizzy, with the harmonics, one of the innovators of the period. Dizzy was much more outgoing, and he organized bringing people forward. And he's a personality."

Gillespie was an engaging, gregarious bandleader. His clowning with the public helped make a complicated new music that could have been extremely off-putting, accessible to a somewhat broader range of listeners. Bebop still posed challenges, of course. Plenty of musicians — not just laymen — didn't readily grasp the logic of its structure, the strangely displaced accents, the briskly played, zig-zagging new melodies superimposed upon the foundations of older tunes. The average American would naturally prefer music that you could more easily hum or dance to than bebop. But Gillespie's sheer likability enticed more people to give the new music, which required attentive consideration, a chance. Had there been no Gillespie, the jam-session experiments of Parker and various other more introverted musicians may not have caught the attention of so many people. With his elfin humor, his memorable singing of such numbers as "Oop Pop A Da" and "I'm Be Boppin' Too," his immediately-recognizable goatee and beret, widely-puffed-out cheeks, and (eventually) his bent-upwards trumpet, Gillespie provided a focus of attention for the average Joe. The music, of course, worked without all of that, as his widely-imitated records proved. But his personal magnetism helped put it across.

When he first began recording, Gillespie was actually very much of a Roy Eldridge follower. (Check out Gillespie's solo on Teddy Hill's 1937 recording of "King Porter Stomp.") But by 1945 (when Gillespie was recording bebop classics like "Salt Peanuts" and "Groovin' High") and 1946 ("Anthropology" and "A Night in Tunisia"), his own, immediately recognizable style was firmly established. Gillespie displaced Eldridge, who had previously displaced Armstrong, as the preeminent trumpeter on the jazz scene. He and Charlie Parker emerged as far and away the most important stylists on the jazz scene.

Dizzy Gillespie

CHARLIE PARKER

"There's two of them," trombonist Bennie Green told trumpeter Johnny Carisi in the early '40s, speaking of the young musicians who, at Harlem jam sessions, were playing in a radically different, fascinating new way: Charlie Parker and Dizzy Gillespie. The two, joined by a growing cadre of fellow explorers, were the founding fathers of what would become known as bebop. News of their experimentations spread along musicians' grapevines well before any of their efforts together found their way onto records.

Because of his importance in jazz history, and because it is impossible to fully tell Gillespie's story without also telling Parker's, it seems wise to take a moment to discuss Parker's contributions, illustrated by an archival photo, since he died before Nancy Miller Elliott and John and Andreas Johnsen began their respective careers as photographers.

Jazz never changed so radically so quickly as it did during a few years in the early and mid 1940s when Parker, Gillespie, and a small group of others

brought forth that new music. Gillespie has told me it was Parker who set the pace and that all he and the others did was to copy Parker's ideas — a generous but not entirely accurate attribution of credit, since recordings establish that Gillespie was independently developing bebop ideas even before he and Parker first came together (and, of course, others had contributions to make, too). But when Parker and Gillespie did come together, they inspired each other and both contributed enduring staples to the bebop repertoire.

Parker and Gillespie became two of the most influential improvisers in the history of jazz. As pianist John Bunch told me, music "changed radically during the war — from guys playing like Benny Carter to guys playing like Charlie Parker." Benny Carter told me, "Charlie Parker was a real genius. Here we are 40 years later and everybody is still playing Charlie Parker licks." Buck Clayton was one of a number of older players who didn't care for bebop generally, yet stressed to me: "I liked the way Charlie Parker played it…. There are a million imitators and they never could do what Charlie did." Parker's genius — and influence upon younger players of many different instruments — was evident whether or not one was crazy about bebop generally. The fact that phrases Parker and Gillespie originated have become part of the common language of jazz musicians is testimony both to their commanding brilliance and to how exceptionally rare true originality is.

Born August 29, 1920 in Kansas City, Kansas, Parker honed his skills in the competitive world of Kansas City jazz and blues bands and jam sessions. He became an important soloist in Jay McShann's big band. But his mastery of his instrument did not develop overnight, nor were his strivings to find himself always appreciated. There are stories of him being thrown out of jam sessions (Jo Jones reportedly flung a cymbal at him at one session). And he was using heroin well before reaching musical (or emotional) maturity. His life became a series of episodes of pace-setting musical creativity interspersed with shat-

tering personal setbacks: a nervous breakdown in 1946, less than a year after the release of his sensational first recordings as a leader; the loss of his cabaret license, preventing him from working in New York nightclubs — a punishment for his drug problem — for two years beginning in 1951; suicide attempts in 1954; and continuing physical and psychological weakening until his death in 1955.

As revered as he was by fellow musicians, his unreliability in showing up for gigs on time (or in paying his sidemen on time) prevented him from getting much work in his last years. Others who appropriated Parker's music reaped much greater financial rewards from it than he did. Society didn't know how to make much use of what he had to offer, anyhow. (A television appearance in which he was followed by an inconsequential vocalist as if they were equally valid "entertainers" was typical.) But his legacy endures. Indeed, musicians fresh out of school today may play Parker phrases without even realizing their origins; to them, such phrases simply *are* jazz.

DORIS PARKER

"It just makes me sick to hear that heroin is now becoming the drug of choice again," says Doris Parker, widow of legendary jazzman Charlie Parker — arguably the most influential jazz stylist of all time — whose death in 1955 was due to the ravages of longtime heroin use.

"When Charlie died, the man who did the autopsy figured that he must have been about 60 years old. He was actually only 35," she recalls.

To help prevent others from suffering the fate of her late husband, she now spearheads an annual "Evening with Friends of Charlie Parker," an all-star jazz benefit, whose proceeds go to the Veritas drug-addiction treatment programs. She feels: "It's a way for Charlie to have something good come from his name."

The 1994 benefit was co-chaired by vibraphonist Milt Jackson and master drummer Max Roach. (You'll note that in the photograph Andreas Johnsen has taken of Parker being interviewed by me, she is wearing a Max Roach sweatshirt.) Among artists who donated their services: jazz singer Annie Ross, pianist Tommy Flanagan, saxists Jimmy Heath and Benny Golson, trombonist Al Grey, and trumpeter Donald Byrd, plus several complete bands: Grover Mitchell's Big Band, Nancie Banks' Jazz Orchestra, and Arthur Taylor's Wailers.

That so many greats would gladly pitch in to help out reminds her of "the camaraderie of

musicians back in the 1940s." She first met Charlie Parker in 1943, when she was a hat-check girl in a 52nd Street jazz club and he was just starting his career as a leader. "We were both Midwesterners. He was from Kansas City. I was from Illinois. I was very naive," she recalls.

He was already involved in drugs then, but she didn't recognize that the puncture marks on his arm were from hypodermic needles. "I asked him about them and he told me he'd gotten them from some barbed wire. I didn't know about heroin then. I thought smoking pot was the worst thing you could do. Little did I know."

She learned quickly enough. She was "sickened by the sight of the blood going up and down" in the needle, by the endless hours lost in quest of drugs. "He'd quit using. But wherever we went, there would always be someone willing to give him enough drugs for free to get him hooked again.

"He was actually very much against people using drugs and told me that if I ever used, he'd kill me. I was never tempted. Some musicians said they used heroin because Charlie Parker did — but that was just a cop-out. They used because they wanted to.

"I'd tell him, 'Just quit!' I didn't understand how painful it was to quit, cold turkey," she says. "It's too bad Veritas didn't exist then. The Veritas program lasts 18 months, providing counseling and support. Sometimes you'll see mothers with their babies in the program. I like to help rock the babies."

Doris Parker hated the film about her husband, *Bird*, which she calls "a fantasy." She didn't think Forrest Whittaker was right for the part of her husband, and she felt the filmmakers missed the joy that was also so much a part of the bebop scene. "Charlie had a great sense of humor. I remember him playing 'White Christmas' by letting air out of a balloon one night, on the bandstand of the Royal Roost.

"He and Dizzy Gillespie, who were like brothers, were both very funny. They had little routines they'd do. And the musicians all really loved to play. They were getting together to jam before and after gigs.

"I never dreamed, when I went to those jam sessions with Charlie, Diz, Monk, Bud Powell, Kenny Clarke, Max Roach and others that I was witnessing history. None of us did," she reflects. "We were all so young then."

THELONIOUS MONK

Thelonious Monk (1917-82), captured here in performance by John Johnsen, was — along with Charlie Parker and Dizzy Gillespie — one of the major contributors to the development of the music that became known as bebop. Exactly how much credit should be apportioned to each of those musicians is, of course, a subjective judgment, and their contemporaries offer varying opinions. Many cite Parker as a prime mover, some see Gillespie as playing a more vital role. Others say that Monk's importance has often been understated. He was certainly not as important in popularizing the new music as the others were — after all, he didn't make his first recordings under his own name until relatively late (1947) and long remained something of a musicians' musician, not widely known to the public.

In the mid-1930s, pianist Mary Lou Williams was in Kansas City with Andy Kirk's Band, when Monk, "still in his teens, came into town.... He was one of the original modernists all right, playing pretty much the same harmonies then that he's playing now. Only in those days we

called it 'Zombie music' and reserved it mostly for musicians after hours," she told Max Jones of England's *Melody Maker* magazine in 1954. She also recalled the early 1940s Harlem jam sessions at Minton's (where Monk was then house pianist), a testing ground for the new music, and maintained that "Monk, Charlie Christian, Kenny Clarke, Art Blakey, and Idries

Sulieman were the first to play bop. Next were Parker, Gillespie, and Clyde Hart...." Others, of course, had different perspectives, as Ira Gitler's *Swing to Bop* makes clear. (We'll be meeting other early beboppers in pages to come.) George T. Simon wrote in the February 1948 *Metronome* that Monk "has been credited by several leading boppists, including Charlie Parker, with having started this altered chord style of playing jazz.... Monk himself doesn't think he actually plays bop, at least not the way it's being played today. 'Mine is more original,' he says." In retrospect, Monk's quirky, highly idiosyncratic music connects as clearly to the past (you'll hear some stride piano in his playing) as

to the future. He was too unique a player to fit neatly into any one category.

And opinions as to his abilities as a player varied widely — some contemporaries thought him brilliant, others a weak player.

Lorraine Gordon has told me that when she first talked Max Gordon into booking Monk at the Village Vanguard, back in the 1940s, the booking was a flop. But Max Gordon was intrigued enough by the music to continue taking chances on him.

His influence was considerable. John Coltrane noted: "Working with Monk brought me close to a musical architect of the highest order. I felt I learned from him in every way — sensually, theoretically, technically. I would talk to Monk about musical problems, and he would show me the answers by playing them on the piano. He gave me complete freedom in my playing, and no one ever did that before." Monk believed: "Jazz and freedom go hand in hand." His sense of freedom extended to sleeping and awakening when he chose (at its most extreme that meant staying up for several days and then sleeping for several days). Ever the individualist, Monk told interviewer Grover Sales in 1959: "I say, play your own way. Don't play what the public wants — you play what *you* want and let the public pick up on what *you're* doing — even if it *does* take them fifteen, twenty years." In his case, it did take the public just that long. Such Monk compositions as "'Round Midnight" and "Well You Needn't" gradually acquired the status of jazz standards. Monk reached his greatest popularity in the 1960s (even making the cover of *Time* magazine in 1964) — recording for Columbia mostly tunes he had been playing since the 1940s and '50s, in much the same way that he had previously played them on records few people had originally bought.

CHARLIE ROUSE

Self-effacing tenor saxist Charlie Rouse (1924-88) is best remembered as a sideman of Thelonious Sphere Monk, with whom he is seen playing in this photograph by John Johnsen. Indeed, during the years of Monk's greatest public success, Rouse was — along with Monk's steadfast friend and patron, Baroness Pannonica De Koenigswarter — practically the only constant in Monk's life. Rouse played sax in Monk's group from 1958-70. During those years, no less than five different bass players and five different drummers played for extended periods in Monk's group, and a number of others filled in very briefly. Eventually, it got to the point where Monk seemed content to play with any competent local bassist and drummer he could pick up, so long as he had Rouse by his side. Rouse's slightly tart sound seemed to complement Monk's jagged piano work. And Rouse developed an exceptional musical empathy with Monk.

Rouse noted to *Coda*'s Peter Danson: "Most musicians actually play in three tempos: a slow, a medium, and a fast. Thelonious would always play somewhere in between those three steps,

always just a shade behind or ahead of the norm.... Some of the music he presented seemed impossible but he would tell us 'It's there. Play it!' Then when you'd take your time...it would just fall right in. Because everything he wrote had a meaning."

Monk largely withdrew from sight in the 1970s and early '80s (he died in 1982). He preferred living quietly at De Koenigswarter's home to performing in public. Rouse helped keep Monk's legacy alive, both as a leader of his own groups, and then as a joint leader of the cooperative group Sphere (with Kenny Barron, Ben Riley, and Buster Williams), which was organized in 1979 specifically to play Monk's music, along with some originals by its members.

Rouse became a professional while still in high school. He had a steady gig at the Crystal Cavern in his home city of Washington, D.C., in a group that included bassist Tommy Potter and pianist John Malachi. When Potter and Malachi became charter members of Billy Eckstine's progressive big band, they eventually succeeded in getting their friend Rouse into the band, which featured Charlie Parker and Dizzy Gillespie as star soloists. When Gillespie subsequently formed his own big band, he hired Rouse for it. Rouse went on to work for other notables, including Duke Ellington, Count Basie, and Oscar Pettiford, but he really seemed to find himself when he connected with Monk. (John Johnsen captures Rouse edging away from the spotlight in the photo facing the contents page of this book.)

As for the other major constant (apart from family members) in Monk's life, Baroness Pannonica de Koenigswarter was a British born member of the distinguished Rothschild family. From the early 1950s on, she was familiar presence on the New York jazz scene. Her apartment was like a salon for modern jazz greats from Monk to Charlie Parker (who actually died at her apartment in 1955). Her gray Bentley was certain to pull up to the Village Vanguard whenever Monk (or later, the group Sphere) was booked there. She liked a number of other musicians as well, of course, including Tommy Flanagan and Barry Harris, but Monk was always her favorite. She died on November 30, 1988 — the very same day that, in a curious but somehow fitting coincidence, Charlie Rouse died.

TOMMY POTTER

As a teenager, the last thing Tommy Potter could have imagined was that someday he'd be a renowned bassist.

Born September 21, 1918 in Philadelphia, he was raised by his mother and grandfather following the death of his father. He didn't take his first music lessons until he was 16, when he started on piano. That same year, however, he suffered a critical heart attack. For the next two years, he rested in bed on his back. His doctor, who doubted he'd ever be able to lead a physically active life again, said he could not risk exerting himself by playing piano.

When his condition improved, his mother and grandfather gave him a guitar; playing it, they believed, would allow him to keep up his interest in music without straining himself. By age 20, he was sufficiently recovered to join the Civilian Conservation Corps, where he played guitar in a quartet that was good enough to get some professional bookings. When the draft for the Second World War broke up the quartet, Potter took up the bass and was soon freelancing with jazz players in and around New York.

Potter reached the big time when he became the bassist in Billy Eckstine's rather progressive big band of 1944-45, which included Charlie Parker and Dizzy Gillespie. He went on to become the bassist in Parker's own group (1947-50), playing on such seminal Parker records as "Donna Lee," "Embraceable You," "The Bird Gets the Worm," "Bongo Bop," and "Don't Blame Me." After Oscar Pettiford, Potter was one of the most highly regarded bassists of bebop. Over the years, he recorded with such musicians as Bud Powell, Wardell Gray, Miles Davis, Sonny Rollins, and Gil Evans.

Unlike some other bebop notables, however, Potter was not exclusively committed to that scene. He enjoyed associations, for example, with such pre-bebop stylists as Earl Hines (1952-53) and Artie Shaw (1953-54), whom he felt had the most musical small jazz group then in existence. Potter's hobbies included fishing and baseball. He was down on the heavy drug use which he saw harming so many jazzmen of his generation.

From the mid-1950s into the '60s, he worked with artists including Bud Powell, Tyree Glenn, Harry Edison, Buck Clayton, Jimmy McPartland, and Buddy Tate. In the 1960s, he stopped playing music full time and got a job checking and tuning basses at an Ampeg factory. Ampeg gave him a few weeks off to make a 1964 European tour as part of a Charlie Parker remembrance group that George Wein organized. Potter told Max Jones of England's *Melody Maker* (October 31, 1964) that he had taken the factory job because he "wanted to be at home with my family. I have a fifteen-year-old boy, and I want to be around him while he's growing up.... So I've been working in this factory for quite a while, and playing gigs during the weekends and odd evenings.... I'd rather go back to full time playing if it would reward me sufficiently. It all comes down to finances. I'd like to play in a regular band, like I did with the Harry Edison Quintet, without touring all the time. If I can't do that, I may continue as I am. I don't want to travel too much."

He continued playing music on the side, although eventually arthritis proved a limitation. He worked for a time in the recreation department of Brooklyn Hospital, and finally wound up employed as a caretaker at Brooklyn's Orient Club, a meeting place for various fraternal organizations, which is where Nancy Miller Elliott took this picture. He died in 1988.

KENNY KERSEY

If you had passed this gentleman, sitting stiffly on a park bench in New York, would you have given him a second thought? Maybe you would have assumed he was just another retiree, taking in a bit of fresh air. Even if you'd paused to chat for a moment and he'd told you his name — Kenneth Kersey — would it have registered?

His name probably would not be recognized by most jazz fans today, but in the early 1940s, Kenny Kersey was a most promising young jazz pianist. He recorded with some of the very greatest artists — Roy Eldridge, Billie Holiday, Benny Goodman, and more — and was abreast of the latest musical developments. If you listen to a recording Kersey made with Cootie Williams' big

Kenny Kersey

149

band in 1942, "Fly Right" ("Epistrophy"), you'll note his playing initially is in a traditional, Teddy Wilson kind of vein, but at the bridge it grows notably more angular, more modern in style, giving a hint of the new direction jazz was soon to take.

Fans with even a casual knowledge of jazz history can tell you that Minton's Playhouse in Harlem was one of the places where bebop was "born," in exploratory jam sessions with the likes of Dizzy Gillespie, Thelonious Monk, Charlie Christian, and Kenny Clarke. But it wasn't always Monk who was playing piano with Gillespie, Christian, and Clarke. If you listen to recordings made at Minton's in 1941 of "Kerouac" and of "Star Dust" (reissued by Everest), the pianist you're hearing is Kersey, not Monk. He reached maturity as a player in a transitional period in jazz; he was able to work with both the innovators of his generation and the older stylists on the scene, without feeling a burning commitment to exclusively stay in either camp.

Kersey plays on "Jazz at the Philharmonic" recordings made just after the war with Charlie Parker, Lester Young, Coleman Hawkins, Buck Clayton, and Buddy Rich. In the 1950s, Kersey played in New York clubs mostly with more traditional artists such as Edmond Hall, Red Allen, Sol Yaged, and Charlie Shavers. He left the experimenting with new sounds to younger players.

Born in Harrow, Ontario, April 3, 1916, Kersey studied with his mother, who taught piano, and then at the Detroit Institute of Musical Arts, before hitting New York in 1936, where he worked prolifically until he was drafted in World War II. His most celebrated performance was his own composition, "Boogie Woogie Cocktail," which he recorded with Andy Kirk's Clouds of Joy in 1942. Kersey summed things up in one line on the questionnaire he filled out for the original (1956) edition of *The Encyclopedia of Jazz*: "never had any trouble with the piano."

Why, then, is Kersey so little known to today's jazz buffs? In the late 1950s, health problems forced him permanently out of music. "It was a terrible pity. He couldn't play anymore. And he was a beautiful person," says Nancy Miller Elliott, who became a friend of Kersey's (it's her son Thomas sharing the bench with him in one photo). According to Elliott, Kersey suffered a stroke back then. The files of the Institute of Jazz Studies indicate a bone condition forced him to stop playing.

Kersey became reclusive, staying close to home on 157th Street in Harlem, where his daughter cared for him. Elliott took these pictures at a park just a few blocks from his home, the site of a historic house; Elliott was surprised to find he had never been there before (she remembers how he enjoyed seeing an antique harpsichord there).

Some of Kersey's friends did stay in touch through the years. Elliott remembers, for example, Roy Eldridge sending a car for him, so he could hear Eldridge play at a club. Kersey died in his sleep, April 1, 1983, about a year after this photo was taken. Dan Morgenstern did a radio program in his memory.

BIG NICK NICHOLAS

ancy Miller Elliott has found a somehow perfect setting for Big Nick Nicholas. Even if you'd never seen him work, I think you might gather from the shot on the next page that you'd find him a little on the whimsical — make that outrageous — side. And that goose at the lower left seems to looking up at him with just the sort of quizzical interest you're apt to find expressed by younger jazz fans witnessing Big Nick at work for the first time.

No doubt about it, Nicholas is a trip. He'll fill a club with his sax sound — not parceling out carefully measured tidbits of music the way some players will, but exuberantly serving up great big slabs of sound, using the wide vibrato favored in the Swing Era. (He came up just as the music was beginning to change, and worked both with the older swing musicians and the younger beboppers.) Then he'll sing a number and mug outlandishly, working his eyes and mouth so vigorously that — depending upon your age and temperament — you may burst into appreciative laughter or sit in stony silence wondering what in the world he's doing. Robert Palmer commented in *The New York Times* (January 2, 1980) that Nicholas "brings to the bandstand the kind of contagious enjoyment that's been missing from too many jazz clubs for too long." Veteran critic John S. Wilson noted, in a similarly favorable *Times* review (August 29, 1981), that both Nicholas' playing and singing "are wrapped up in an ebullient attitude that leads him into shouts of enthusiasm and maniacal wiggling of his heavy eyebrows. Put it all together and he emerges as a standup Fats Waller." However, Nicholas scored a bit less favorably with younger critic Peter Keepnews, who wrote in *The New York Post* (September 7, 1984) that Nicholas "sings and mugs with unabashed energy if not incomparable artistry. Listening to him play, especially on a warm bal-lad like 'As Time Goes By,' one is apt to wish Nicholas would play the entertainer less and play the saxophone more."

To those who've grown up accustomed to the idea that a jazz musician is simply supposed to make music, some of Nicholas' routines may seem inappropriately hammy. But Nicholas is part of an older tradition — a tradition that was nearing its end as Nicholas was learning the business — in which jazz and broad, crowd-pleasing entertainment were mixed. Some of the first big band leaders Nicholas worked for in the early 1940s, like Tiny Bradshaw, felt it was as important for a leader to know how to emcee a show effectively as to know about music. Nicholas himself spent a couple of happily remembered years (1950-52) at Harlem's Paradise Club as a combination house bandleader and emcee, a type of job that no longer exists. There he did whatever it took — from booming songs joyously, to playing ballads sensuously, to kidding with the audience — to go over with a crowd that included ordinary working people looking for a little amusement, not just hardcore jazz devotees and fellow musicians. There was always a fair share of the latter, of course — people who came to seriously listen to musicians including Nicholas, Art Blakey, Thelonious Monk, and Betty Carter. And he sought to please them, as well.

Nicholas' clowning didn't blind fellow musicians to what he had to offer as a player. It is Nicholas' tenor sax you hear, soloing, for example, on Dizzy Gillespie's famed original recording of "Manteca." Charlie Parker recorded originals that he learned from Nicholas. And John Coltrane composed and recorded a number in Nicholas' honor, "Big Nick." You can get a fine sampling of Nicholas' playing and singing on an appropriately titled album he made for India Navigation Records in 1983, *Big and Warm*.

MAX ROACH

Max Roach walked into the Harlem restaurant Sylvia's and some Japanese tourists — thrilled at seeing the world's pre-eminent jazz drummer — gave him a standing ovation. One of the regulars turned to Roach and remarked in surprise: "I didn't know you were somebody!"

Sitting in his apartment near the northern end of Central Park, Roach laughs as he tells me the story. Whether or not he is always rec-ognized in his home city, jazz fans worldwide know the power of Max Roach's music.

He is a master when it comes to obtaining varied sounds from his equipment. I've seen Roach hold an audience's attention throughout a concert in which he played unaccompanied by any other musicians. There may be a few other drummers so creative — so able to vary sounds and to keep a sense of architecture in their solos — as to command an audience's attention throughout a concert. But I haven't yet encountered them.

Roach's place in jazz history has long been secure.

Like Kenny Clarke (who in the early '40s was the house drummer at Minton's Playhouse), Roach (who was the house drummer at Monroe's Uptown House, another favorite Harlem hangout for the young jazz innovators of the day) was a key figure in the development of bebop. He took part in jam sessions at Monroe's and Minton's where bebop — before it was even known as such — was taking shape.

It is fitting that in John Johnsen's portrait of Max Roach, Roach has a drumstick on the ride cymbal. For Roach, along with fellow pioneering bebop drummer Clarke, was responsible for changing the way jazz drummers played — getting them to make more prominent use of the ride cymbal and less of the bass drum, producing a lighter, more flexible overall feel, which seemed appropriate for bebop, and helped lead to greater variety in textures.

Roach drummed in groups led by Dizzy Gillespie (1944) and Charlie Parker (1945, 1947-49, and, off-and-on, 1951-53). He also recorded with such important artists as Thelonious Monk and Bud Powell. In between his bebop dates, he gained experience in seemingly every other style. He went on the road for a while with jump-blues master Louis Jordan, and played on 52nd Street with artists ranging from Coleman Hawkins (who was incorporating new developments into his classic swing style) to New Orleans-type players like Henry "Red" Allen. He took part in Miles Davis' seminal "Birth of the Cool" sessions (1948-50). But when so many other musicians got on the mellow, introspective "cool jazz" bandwagon, Roach put together a hard-hitting quintet, co-led by trumpeter Clifford Brown, that from 1954 to 1956, helped define "hard bop." After Brown was killed in a car accident, he found another promising trumpeter, Booker Little, with whom to continue in that vein.

In the 1960s, Roach became outspoken regarding the fight for civil rights, collaborating with Oscar Brown Jr. on *We Insist! Freedom Now!*, which had the singular honor of being banned by the government of South Africa. Al-

though that suite was inspired by the civil rights struggles of American blacks, its call for social justice had a universal resonance.

Roach has long voiced pride in "black creativity," noting the important roles blacks had played in American popular culture — and not just in music.

Through the years, Roach has shown an unusual degree of openness and receptivity towards different styles. He has recorded with Free Jazz experimentalists like Anthony Braxton, Archie Shepp, and Cecil Taylor. And while many musicians of his generation (Roach was born in 1924) seem oblivious to, or even hostile towards, hip-hop and other forms of today's contemporary black music, Roach is generally supportive. He drummed behind rapper Fab 5 Freddy in 1984 — which upset some jazz critics, who worried needlessly that Roach might be planning to jump aboard some commercial bandwagon. Roach was not about to turn his back on the uncompromising jazz he believes in and plays on his own gigs; he was essentially signaling his encouragement towards (and respect for) the young innovators in rap.

That doesn't mean Roach believes that every young rapper who happens to produce a hit record is making as artistically important a statement as he is. Roach knows his own worth as a committed, serious artist. (This I realized one time when I was set to interview Roach for a jazz magazine. When Roach learned that the magazine planned to have him share the cover with a rap group, he insisted — correctly — he was entitled to a cover by himself. He wouldn't budge. Eventually the magazine came around.)

But, unlike many in jazz, Roach insists that the creative spirit which in his generation manifested itself in players like Charlie Parker, Dizzy Gillespie, and himself, is just as likely to manifest itself today in a top rap group as in a top jazz group.

"Rap is part of our continuum," Roach declared to *JazzTimes'* James T. Jones IV. "With blacks, every generation comes up with some new shit. It's because we haven't really been a part of this society's mainstream, but we're always trying."

TAL FARLOW

"Can you tell me how to get to Sea Bright?"

"You're in it," answers the Jersey Shore gas-station attendant. "Home of one of the world's greatest guitarists — Tal Farlow!"

When I explain that's whom I've come to interview, the attendant not only gives me directions right to Farlow's door, he shows me a copy of *Guitar Player* magazine with Farlow's name on the cover.

A few minutes later Farlow himself is telling me that another magazine will be devoting its next issue to him. Could it be *Down Beat?* Several plaques from *Down Beat* hang on the wall; Farlow won the *Down Beat* jazz critics' "New Star" award in 1954, and continues to score well in its polls.

"It's *Sign Craft*," he says in his amiable, laconic manner. "That's the *Down Beat* magazine of the sign business." For guitar great Farlow — he even has a guitar named after him: Gibson's Tal Farlow model — has, for 45 years, chosen to double as a professional sign painter.

When Farlow (who was born in 1921) graduated from high

school at 15 in rural Greensboro, North Carolina, his father got him appreticed into a sign-making shop, because that was considered a healthier environment than working in the dust-filled textile mills nearby, where many of his peers were headed. A career in jazz seemed inconceivable.

But Farlow was impressed by the work of Charlie Christian — the first electric-guitar player he had ever heard — in Benny Goodman's 1939-40 band. And then when Farlow got to New York in the mid '40s, he heard the player who was to become his primary influence: Charlie Parker. Farlow was soon playing Parker's alto sax licks on guitar — no easy feat. But as he puts it: "It helps the development not to go for the easy stuff."

Farlow rose to prominence in the early 1950s, playing in groups led by two of the most tasteful of jazz musicians: vibraphonist Red Norvo and clarinetist Artie Shaw. (Farlow developed his brilliantly fast execution while working with the nimble Norvo.)

He began recording under his own name, for Blue Note, in 1953.

A highly influential, widely admired guitarist, Farlow was the subject of a 1981 documentary film, *Tal-*

madge Farlow. He appears periodically at major jazz festivals. And he records, from time to time, for Concord Jazz.

Farlow (photographed at home by Nancy Miller Elliott) has often seemed a rather reclusive figure. For years, he would turn up in New York only sporadically. There were younger guitarists who'd insist that was entirely Farlow's choice — that he simply preferred being somewhat of a hermit to making the scene. His apparent reclusiveness became part of his mystique.

But some veteran guitarists would tell you that the realities of the business were such that, even for a jazz player with as legendary a reputation as Farlow, there simply wasn't always as much work to be had as some might imagine.

One thing Farlow will tell you is that the idea of living in New York's never had much appeal him. He's simply never been one for big cities. He seems genuinely happy to be playing his guitar, whether it's at a seafood place not far from his home by the water in Sea Bright, New Jersey, or at an upscale Manhattan club. It's quiet in the town where Tal Farlow lives, and that suits him just fine, whether he feels like practicing his guitar — or his sign painting.

Tal Farlow

MILES DAVIS

You see more of Miles Davis in this photograph by Nancy Miller Elliott — even if his eyes are characteristically hidden by shades — than you were apt to see in an appearance by him at a club in his final years. (And I'm not alluding to the fact that this candid shot catches Davis without the hairpiece he often wore when performing.)

Let me explain. In his later years, Davis performed in clubs so rarely, and was so legendary a figure, that any appearance by him became an event. It didn't matter that his albums of recent vintage had disappointed many who'd cherished his earlier work. His albums were big commercial successes. His following was huge and fanatical, closer to that of a rock star than that of the typical jazz player. When it was announced, for example, that he would be playing for four nights at New York's Indigo Blues in September 1989, all performances almost immediately sold out. I went to Davis' opening night. Some of my friends told me how lucky I was to be seeing Miles Davis in person. I actually saw a lot less of him that night than they might have imagined. For the club was as jam-packed with people as any I can ever recall being in.

Just as there are certain sub-atomic particles that we can't quite see but that scientists infer exist by the discernible impact they have upon others, I had to assume that Davis was physically present in that absolutely mobbed room because of the way the bulky fellow blocking my view would often stand, excitedly raising his camera and snapping off shots.

Oh, occasionally, I'd catch a glimpse of Davis myself — often the back of his head. Once, he even turned face-front and briefly, unexpectedly, took off his shades; the effect was startling, like seeing the sun after an eclipse. Most of his band

was elevated on a riser behind him. But Davis, who was not a tall man to begin with, opted to stand on the floor of the club. Since he liked to play crouched over, his horn aimed downward, his head was often no higher than the heads of seated patrons. (And many patrons, like the fellow in front of me, often stood in an attempt to get a better view.)

Davis' band that night posed no threat to anyone's daydreaming. You could hear murmurings from the crowd whenever Davis would leave the room (sometimes to change outfits). It had been years since Davis had fronted a band consisting of players even approximately in his league. His band played some chugging, funky numbers; people in the audience made a half-hearted attempt to clap along, but the beat wasn't persuasive enough for that. There were a couple of interminable drum solos. Periodically, Davis himself played.

And that's what saved the night. Sometimes he wasn't saying much, just playing by the numbers for a few bars. But once in a great while, the enigmatic phrases would be so lean, so perfect in tone and execution as to make you realize you don't hear trumpeters capable of this. And the *sound* was uniquely his. It almost didn't matter what the musical background was (although I'd be a liar if I said I wouldn't have preferred the kind of real jazz heavyweights he had working with him in the '50s and '60s). He'd flare up briefly, then retreat into another long silence, or let saxist Kenny Garrett take the spotlight. Sometimes the two men would play together, their heads bowed towards one another, almost touching — as if communing with each other, aware only of each other, not the audience.

Early in the night, it seemed almost as if Davis were trying to ensure that people would see and hear as little of him as possible — which

could be construed as a hostile kind of holding back. (His well-known refusal to play his early classics anymore, which some older fans would have given anything to hear, could also be interpreted as a kind of holding back.) But his set continued, incredibly, for more than two hours — an exceptionally generous performance in a city where sets of an hour are common. By night's end, his fans — a mostly young crowd — seemed satisfied. In his own fashion, Miles Davis, 63 years old and suffering from a variety of physical ailments, was giving a lot of himself.

Perhaps even more than he could afford to. On the final night of the booking, it was announced that Davis had cracked his lip badly — and you can see even in this photo how much wear and tear his lips had endured over the years — and he could not play at all. Disappointed patrons were told they would have to wait until another occasion to see Davis.

Another look, courtesy of Nancy Miller Elliott, at Miles Davis. His expression is typically guarded, wary: we see a man who doesn't want to mess with people. This shot surely captures more of the essential Miles than the "happy face" shot adorning the back cover of *Miles, The Autobiography* (which is as intriguing — if not always accurate — a memoir as you're likely to come across). How I wish they hadn't used that forced-smile picture on the back cover. For throughout his career, Davis deliberately made a point — and for a reason that's understandable — of not smiling much in his public appearances.

Born in 1928, he grew up in an era when black performers were expected — practically required — to smile a lot, as if to imply they were amiable, simple, non-threatening individuals.

Davis didn't like the stereotype, didn't want to fit it. His frequently stern look, his practice of turning his back on audiences, his refusal to banter during performances — these were ways of demanding that he be respected as a musician. He was not there to clown for the public.

Jazz Veterans

From his first trumpet teacher in East St. Louis, Davis learned to play in a controlled, vibrato-less style. By 1944, Davis was good enough to get a chair in Billy Eckstine's progressive big band, along with Charlie Parker and Dizzy Gillespie. He went on to play in Charlie Parker small groups, both live and on record (1945-48), and to record in larger groups, with arrangements by Gil Evans that showed jazz could be cool and restrained without losing impact.

Trumpeters traditionally tried cutting one another by playing faster and higher; Davis wasn't into that game. And while some of the older players belittled what he was doing (Roy Eldridge called it "mouse music"), his stark, pure work in the 1950s — listen to "Bye, Bye Blackbird," "The Man I Love," and "'Round Midnight" — won him a growing following. The emotion was concentrated. When I listen to Davis' master performances, I think of what Okey Chenoweth, a fine acting teacher, used to say, that you convey more of an emotion to an audience if they sense you've more in reserve than if you let it all out. Miles always had more in reserve.

A triumph at the 1955 Newport Jazz Festival focused public attention on Davis. John Coltrane and Cannonball Adderley were among his sidemen when he recorded the album *Kind of Blue*. In the 1960s, he scored further successes, peaking again with an outstanding group that included Tony Williams, Herbie Hancock, Ron Carter, and Wayne Shorter. (Listen to their "live" 1965 recordings at Chicago's Plugged Nickel club.) But in any context, Miles Davis was always — unmistakably — Miles Davis. Whether harsh, rasping with suppressed rage, or sighing with an ache of unfathomable longing, his trumpet sound was as personal, immediately recognizable, and compelling as anyone's in jazz.

Starting in 1969, with albums like *In a Silent Way* and *Bitches Brew*, Davis increasingly leaned towards rock and pop. He lost a number of jazz purists, the farther into electronic pop sounds he went. But he picked up plenty of new fans — more of a rock crowd — and scored major concert successes.

As far as Davis' place in jazz history is concerned, it wouldn't have mattered if he had retired in the mid '60s; his reputation was secure quite early in his career. Such 1950s and '60s albums as *Sketches of Spain*, *Porgy and Bess*, *My Funny Valentine*, and *'Four' and More* form an extraordinary body of work.

$$\oint$$

We'll digress for a moment, before getting to other shots of Miles Davis, to include a never-before-published photo of Buck Clayton "doing" Miles Davis. This gag shot (which you'll find on the following page) was not intended for publication — Clayton simply decided to give Nancy Miller Elliott his version of Davis' renowned "angry at the world" attitude.

All kidding aside, though, Clayton actually had great respect for Davis' accomplishments as a giant of modern jazz. Clayton noted, too, that, unlike some less-talented modern players, Davis never looked down on the older jazz players who came before him. Maybe that was due to the basic values that Davis' father, a dentist and a pillar of the East St. Louis black community, had instilled in him. (In his last years, Davis was shocked at the disrespect — from his point of view — that the outspoken Wynton Marsalis showed him; Davis believed that as an elder he was entitled to a certain amount of deference.) Clayton thought there was another reason Davis treated him so respectfully. When Davis first arrived in New York some of the seasoned musicians tried to keep him out of the jam sessions at Clark Monroe's Uptown House in Harlem; Clayton, however, welcomed Davis — a fact, Clayton noted, that Davis never forgot.

Newman, and so on — and Miles, one tough fellow, had survived more bouts of ill health than anyone else I'd known in the business. The general public hadn't been aware of all of the health problems he'd endured over the years — sickle-cell anemia, heart palpitations, a liver ailment, ulcers, a stroke, gallstones, arthritis, diabetes, drug problems that exacerbated everything else, and more. He channeled the pain into that famed, far-off cry of his trumpet.

I had turned off the ringer of the telephone that day to avoid distraction, and wrote through lunch. Then I drove to the post office, mailed the completed liner notes to Sony Music, and turned on the car radio. Nat Hentoff — a welcome voice on the radio — was offering impressions of Miles Davis. And he was speaking in the past tense. I was caught short; while I'd been

Miles Davis

writing notes for a Miles Davis CD, I realized, Davis had died.

Back at my apartment, there were messages on the answering machine waiting for me: a musician friend wondering if I'd heard the news about Miles, an editor asking if I wanted to write an obituary. And on the TV news broadcasts that night, there were remembrances of Davis, illustrated by footage of 1980s appearances. It bothered me that they chose shots from those later years to represent Davis. For while his tone was as haunting as ever, his phrases had grown curt, and his brilliant originality was often obscured by busy, unfocused, jazz/rock fusion accompaniment. By and large, I think Davis' most important contributions, those for which history will accord him highest honors, were recorded in the 1950s and '60s. Davis was capable of moving listeners at almost any stage of his career. But in his later years, Davis too often let commercial considerations — what would make him more money — influence his decisions.

Davis (captured by John Johnsen in performances at various stages in his career) was unquestionably a "star" until the end, and his recordings could be found in the dorm rooms of countless college kids who would never have called themselves jazz fans. But artistically, Davis had copped out. Wynton Marsalis gave him grief for that. If Davis had not been so exceptionally talented to begin with, neither Marsalis nor any other jazz fan would have much cared whether, in his later years, Davis squandered the gift he'd been given.

DUKE JORDAN

"If there is any truth in it when they say that each human has a soul, and if it is true, when they say that when a human dies, the soul lives on..." Duke Jordan began, weighing each word carefully, when Andreas Johnsen and I met him in Copenhagen, "— then I hope with all my heart that the virus that inflicts the most pain connected with AIDS finds Miles Davis' soul, and has a feast on his soul — a slow feast that I hope will last a hundred years."

"That's pretty strong," I interjected. Johnsen and I were both startled by his sentiments. When Jordan had begun speaking, we had thought he was heading in a spiritual direction.

"I mean it to be strong," Jordan responded. "You see, what Miles Davis did to me.... When he wrote that autobiography, he put down a lot of musicians. And of course he really put me down. Now the problem with that is, that the book is translated into a whole lot of different languages, all around the world. And a lot of club owners are businessmen; they don't know a damned thing about music — who's good and who's not. So,

when they read something like that, they get a fixation in there, 'This guy can't be too good — maybe I better not get him.' Or if somebody else reads it and tells them what they read — it's the same result. So what Miles did to me, it has affected me in getting gigs I used to get."

Davis made it clear in his book that he didn't think too much of Jordan's playing, and that when they were both in Charlie Parker's group he repeatedly urged Parker to get rid of Jordan, but Parker refused to take his advice.

Parker, who had offered Jordan a job the first time he heard him, genuinely appreciated Jordan's playing. Jordan played with Parker regularly from 1946 to '48, and occasionally afterwards, and may be heard on many celebrated Parker recordings.

Because Davis was so rough on Jordan in his autobiography, it seems only fair to cite here a few contrasting assessments of Jordan's talents.

In reviewing a recording Jordan made in 1961 after a period of relatively low visibility, John

S. Wilson noted: "Jordan is one of the most inexplicably neglected musicians of the postwar jazz world. He was a striking figure in the mid-'40s bop movement, striking not because of flamboyance but because he always moved calmly, cleanly ahead amidst a sea of turbulence. He and Al Haig were possibly the most fitting of the pianists with whom Charlie Parker worked."

To jazz piano great Randy Weston, "Duke sounds like raindrops right after a sunshower when the sun breaks through the clouds and the birds begin to sing." And Dan Morgenstern,

one of the most universally respected writers on jazz, described Jordan in a review on July 20, 1972: "He's one of those rare musical beings who brings beauty to everything he touches."

Charlie Parker was far from the only noted musician who wanted Duke Jordan in his group. Jordan enhanced the work of Stan Getz, Sonny Stitt, Gene Ammons, Cecil Payne, and others. His composition "Jordu" became well-known in the jazz world, and his score for the 1960 Roger Vadim film *Les Liasons Dangereuses* was much admired. He spoke of these and other matters (including a narcotics addiction problem, which

took him many years to overcome), while Andreas Johnsen unobtrusively shot photos. (And having worked with some newspaper and magazine photographers who seriously distracted my interview subjects, I have great admiration for Johnsen's sense of how to stay out of the way.)

Now in his early 70s (he was born in New York in 1922), Duke Jordan is taking life easily, working carefully selected engagements in his adopted home of Denmark, and in other countries. There is much more to Jordan's story than his disagreement with Miles Davis, of course, and I hope I have a chance to tell his story in fuller detail elsewhere. But he was so hurt by what Davis wrote, he insisted he wanted his feelings in print.

SHEILA JORDAN

"I sing out of the need to sing, to share my experience, strength and hope. I don't do it because I want to make money. Music saved my life," declares jazz singer Sheila Jordan, former wife of Duke Jordan.

"One of the reasons I stopped drinking and drugging was because I had an awakening that said, 'If you don't stop, you're going to lose the music. You have a gift. It was given to you. And if you don't stop abusing it, I'm going to take it away.' It was a real voice that came to me, in my head and in my heart. I truly believe that."

Sheila Jordan (photographed by Andreas Johnsen at the Greenwich Village club Visiones, alone and with bassist Harvie Swartz) speaks with the same sort of quiet conviction that marks her singing. She doesn't need to go into great detail about her life in our conversation, for it's all in her songs. When she put the drinking and drugs behind her in the '80s, she wrote "The Crossing" about it; it's one of her most powerful and haunting numbers.

She tells much of her history in her oft-requested "Sheila's Blues." Her hard-scrabble childhood in Pennsylvania coal-mining country,

her discovery of bebop as a teen in Detroit — it's all in there.

She never sings that song exactly the same way, though. The first four bars are always the same, but whatever's happened to her in more recent times — perhaps the home in upstate New York that burned to the ground, or the fractured kneecap — seems to become part of the song for that night, often told with humor. Self-pity is not her thing. There's much hope in her voice, which is higher pitched and more innocent-sounding than that of other major jazz singers.

You'd know of her admiration for the late jazz legend Charlie Parker not just from the words she'll sing in a number dedicated to him, but from the way she'll choose the same ballad tempo he favored and slip easily into his distinctive way of phrasing. Parker invited her up to sing at a number of his gigs, and he also played many times at her loft, which was a gathering place for musicians.

"I always sang," she recalls. "I mean, I had such an unhappy childhood, I needed singing as an outlet, and sang from the time I got out of bed in the morning until I went to sleep at night — but it wasn't until I heard Bird that I knew what kind of music I really wanted to sing."

CARMEN McRAE

"Jazz singers are an endangered species," declared the late Carmen McRae, when I caught up with her one March 1987 afternoon at an Upper East Side New York hotel room. She pointed out: "I turn 67 next month."

McRae noted she was two years younger than Ella Fitzgerald, four years older than Sarah Vaughan, adding: "I hope there's some young ones coming along to take our places after we've gone — but I haven't heard 'em!" McRae dismissed one young singer I suggested, who'd been receiving lots of press attention and enjoying great record sales, with three words: "She doesn't swing."

Was McRae feeling her age, I wondered? "Since reaching 50," she said, "age has affected every part of me — from my big toe on up — except for my throat. And I don't gargle or take any special precautions. I'm probably doing everything wrong. I just sing."

McRae told me she liked to conserve her energy for her work. She rarely gave interviews anymore. When she was not on stage, she felt, that was her private time. Some writers inferred that her personality, from the way she put across key songs, was "bitter" or "cold." McRae scoffed at such write-ups. "If you're singing about a man who's walked out on you, of course you're going to sound bitter! How else should you sound? It's acting. Good singers are good actresses. You try to put into reality what the lyricist had in mind."

And that she certainly did. She could take a song I'd long liked, such as "For All We Know (We May Never Meet Again)," and make me hear it as if I'd never heard it before. One night she prefaced it effectively with words about how the death of a friend had made the song mean more to her, and urged us to tell those we love how we felt while the chance existed. By the time she was into the song itself, talk-singing how tomorrow was "meant for some," she had me shivering. She was brooding about mortality — hers and ours — making the song's suggestion that we may never meet again seem a personal message from her. The intensity of McRae's performance style is well caught in Nancy Miller Elliott's photos, taken in France in 1988.

McRae's original inspiration and song model was the late Billie Holiday, whom she first came to know while a teen. McRae wrote a song,

"Dream of Life," which Holiday recorded in 1938. (McRae stopped writing songs many years ago, she said that afternoon; the motivation simply vanished.) She helped keep alive the Holiday repertoire, including some of the little-known songs, not just the heavyweight numbers many singers have done.

McRae gained early experience with Benny Carter and his Orchestra (1944), and Mercer Ellington and his Orchestra (1946-47). Subsequently — and more importantly for her development — she sang and played piano at Minton's Playhouse and other New York clubs featuring the leading younger (bebop-oriented) jazz musicians, whose phrasings influenced her own.

She was thus a highly seasoned performer, with more than a decade's experience on the scene, by the time she was named "best new female singer" by *Down Beat* in 1954. But she was "new" to many Americans in the mid '50s, since for the first time in her career she was recording for a major label, Decca, which gave her much greater exposure than she'd ever had before.

Singing was always hard work, McRae stressed to me, adding that she also found the demands of traveling — the hours of sitting around in airports, taking taxis to hotel rooms, and so on — increasingly harder to accept. But she insisted that even when she was singing something sorrowful in her act, essentially she was enjoying herself. "If I didn't like what I did, I wouldn't be there. I'm having fun on stage."

McRae was ranked, for many years, as one of the greatest of living jazz singers, along with Ella Fitzgerald, Sarah Vaughan, Anita O'Day, and Betty Carter. She authorized Leslie Gourse to write a book about her; unfortunately, no buyer for the proposed book could be found, with one young editor "explaining" that no one knew who McRae was — a reminder that you can be a giant in the jazz world and still be outside the awareness of many Americans.

McRae continued to record and tour, worldwide, up until 1990, when — suffering from emphysema and other problems — she collapsed during an engagement at the Blue Note. She died in 1994.

SARAH VAUGHAN

If you were lucky enough to get a ticket to see the late Sarah Vaughan at Carnegie Hall, you could have expected to spend the first half of the night restlessly sitting through a performance by somebody else's trio or quartet. After intermission, your anticipation mounting — you'd be sure that by *now* she was about to appear — she'd again keep you waiting, frustrated, while her trio (good, but certainly not one you'd pay this kind of money to see) would play a number, or maybe two numbers, or even three numbers, before *finally*, to

deafening, pent-up applause, she'd make her entrance. We accept — even expect — such treatment from our reigning divas.

In Vaughan's June 1989 Carnegie Hall concert, when she finally strode onstage, regal in dress and bearing, she spotted on the stage a table not to her liking. She gave it a dirty look — and then dragged it off to one side, muttering "I should be getting paid for this." (Never mind that she was one of the highest paid — if not *the* highest paid — jazz singers around.) And then, as if

nothing had happened, she proceeded to sing, in that rich, vivid, ever-unruffled contralto of hers — there was no more glorious voice in jazz — "On a Clear Day."

Or consider her opening night at the Blue Note in September 1986. After she reached the bandstand, her expression one of complete perturbment, she started telling us how annoyed she was at her hotel, which had lost her luggage. People in the audience were not only paying dearly to listen to her *kvetch* about how bad she had it, they were audibly sympathetic to her. They knew that, any moment, the magic was about to happen. And it did. When she finally sang, the weariness vanished from her face, a vibrant, forceful personality emerged, and by turns — depending on the songs — she radiated sorrow or *joie de vivre*, projecting emotions no less vividly when she was scatting than when she was singing the lyrics as written. Blessed with a voice of exceptional clarity, power, and range, she exploited it fully, the audience frequently interrupting her work with deserved applause, whistles, and cheers.

As she neared the end of one number, she faded down gradually until she was no longer singing at all, but then continued to pantomime singing while her trio vamped, finally reaching a climactic (with all the gestures) — but silent — "big ending," which drew tumultuous applause. "See all the applause I get for doing nothing!" she exclaimed in childlike wonder — and then took another totally silent chorus for a well-received encore. She was having such a good time that when the managers of the club tried to wheel out a giant cake, she ordered them to return to the kitchen! She sang an encore. Afterwards, in her dressing room, I told her how superb she had sounded that night; she moaned she was miserable with a bad cold.

Vaughan could, at times, appear a bit disinterested in her work. And she was not the greatest singer for every type of song. Some singers (such as Ella Fitzgerald and Anita O'Day) could outswing her. Some (such as Ruth Brown) could pack more of a spirit-rousing wallop. Some (such as Billie Holiday) dealt with deeper emotional truths. But on certain melodically and harmonically rich slower songs, like "Someone to Watch Over Me" and "Send in the Clowns," no singer in the world could touch Vaughan. She was a virtuoso. And when, at Carnegie Hall, she approached climactic passages to those songs, her trio would stop playing, letting her moving voice fill the hall unaccompanied: absolute perfection. And you remember that, far more than the waiting.

No one in jazz has filled the place of "the divine Sarah," who died of lung cancer on April 4, 1990. (She was actually ill at the time of that magnificent June 1989 Carnegie Hall concert — which turned out to be her last New York concert appearance — although the public did not know it.) If you would like more information on Vaughan, may I recommend Leslie Gourse's *Sassy, The Life of Sarah Vaughan*?

Vaughan's essence is caught well by John Johnsen on page 175.

BILLY ECKSTINE

John Johnsen's camera caught, on page174 and (joined by bandleader Mercer Ellington) below, an early 1980s reunion of the late Billy Eckstine with Sarah Vaughan. They had originally worked together back in the '40s — first when they were both vocalists in Earl Hines' Band, and then when Vaughan was a vocalist in Eckstine's own band. Their voices always sounded good together, and they got together from time to time through the years —even making *Billboard*'s pop charts briefly in 1957 with their Mercury record "Passing Strangers."

When I went to see Eckstine (then 75) at New York's Blue Note in 1989, I was initially taken aback by how he'd aged in recent years. When he walked to the stage, I noted how thin he was underneath the immaculate outfit. On his first song, I heard the wobble in his voice when he tried to sustain a note too long.

But his *savoir-faire*, bantering between num-

bers, was winning. His still surprisingly rich-toned, deep resonant voice — you could never mistake it for anyone else's — was warming to listen to. He took "All of Me," wisely, at quite a bright tempo; so long as he didn't have to hold notes too long, he knew he'd be fine. He offered brief, confident samplings of past hits in a sure-fire medley — just enough of each song to trigger memories and bursts of applause, before moving on to the next one. Looking around the room, noticing how his old fans packing the room were gazing at him, I suspected they were seeing him just as he was back in the '40s or the '50s.

One matron near the stage held up an album of his and sighed: "I first saw you 38 years ago." Fixing her with a smoldering smile, he commanded, "Steady now!" — and the audience laughed. Eyeing an old man sitting with a very young, sexy woman, he quipped approvingly that you can't jump-start a car using two dead batteries. I was charmed by him, too, by the time he began singing again. As he eased sultrily into his famed "Jelly, Jelly," it seemed to me almost as if I were hearing the 1940 record brought to life. That was the illusion this savvy show-biz veteran somehow managed to create.

Visiting him in his dressing room upstairs after the show, the illusion vanished once again. I found him coughing deeply — he downed cough syrup right from the bottle — and looking quite fatigued. The night before, he offered by way of explanation, he'd been in London; between the jet lag and a bronchial cold, he was worn out. To me, he didn't look well at all. (He was in, fact, going into his final decline.) I felt even more impressed by the gallant professionalism he'd displayed downstairs. Sipping Chinese soup, his dinner, he reminisced with me.

He wrote "Jelly Jelly," when he was singing in Earl Hines' big band, in just 15 minutes, he told me. They needed a tune for a recording session. He knew blues would sell in the South. So he set to music a line he had heard a black comedian, whose name he couldn't recall that night, use on stage: "jelly roll killed my pappy, ran my mama stone blind." Another time, in 1942, he recalled, the band had an arrangement of "I'm Gonna Move to The Outskirts of Town" that was popular with everyone on their one-nighters, but they couldn't record the number because Louis Jordan had already made a hit record of it. So Eckstine took their arrangement — the trumpeter even got to play the very same solo — and fitted a new song to it: "Stormy Monday Blues." That number, still part of his repertoire today, unexpectedly became a hit record. And no one, he added, seemed to notice its melodic similarities to "I'm Gonna Move to the Outskirts of Town."

From 1943-47, Eckstine led his own progressive big band, which helped bring attention to such new forces in music as Dizzy Gillespie, Charlie Parker, and Sarah Vaughan, although a recording strike prevented it from being recorded at its peak. Some critics, he noted, thought the band was out of tune simply because it was playing ahead-of-its-time harmonies.

Eckstine's record of "Skylark" outsold Bing Crosby's, he told me, and there was a period when his records were outselling Frank Sinatra's. Back then, he imagined he'd soon get major motion picture offers, just as Sinatra and Crosby did. When, due to racial prejudice, he didn't, he got angry. The injustice of it still rankled him. He stuck to his singing, always trying, he told me, to think like a jazz musician, not "commercially," the way he felt many singers did. If you think commercially, he said before excusing himself to rest for a bit, you'll make records that will come back to haunt you.

ABBEY LINCOLN

"I think some of the young performers have a hard time understanding this form," says jazz singer Abbey Lincoln. "But it developed in a time when there wasn't any talk about money; it had nothing to do with being rich in money. But being rich in spirit. And I think it still is that — a music of the spirit. It's about the life that you live, you know. All the songs that I write are about the life that I live."

In her mid-60s, singing a mix of curious originals and romantic standards, Lincoln is at the zenith of her career. In the last few years, recording such striking CDs for Verve as *You Gotta Pay the Band*, *Devil's Got Your Tongue* and *When There is Love*, she seems to have reached a new level, both in terms of her abilities and in public and critical acceptance.

"Since signing with Verve — this has been the best time in my whole career," she acknowledges. "My producer, Jean-Philippe Allard, came over from France to get me to record. He's also been producing such jazz artists as J. J. Johnson and Randy Weston. He gathers up all the stuff that's been laying around that's really valuable, you know — that other people were looking away from. Maybe we're more appreciated abroad. Maybe in France they can stand off and look at our art more objectively. We in America kind of take for granted what we have."

Although Lincoln has occasionally tried acting as well as singing (co-starring in such films as *Nothing But a Man* with Ivan Dixon and *For the Love of Ivy* with Sidney Poitier), she much prefers singing. "When you are acting, you don't have as much control. You work with scripts that people

bring you, playing characters someone else has created. But as a singer, I create my own character. I write the script. I bring to the stage a woman that pleases me. And it makes me feel powerful that I can come to the stage and communicate with people who I've never seen before. And they like what I'm saying."

How does she write her songs, which have been also been recorded by other singers ranging from Dianne Reeves to Baby Jane Dexter? "I've discovered that if I write a song about something that bothers me, I can put it away. Like 'When I'm Called Home' — there was something I was grieving about. And I wrote it. So for me it's therapeutic. And since we all live similar lives — it's like an affirmation of our humanity. When people tell me, 'Yes, I understand that,' it makes me really feel thankful.

"I've learned about the music from musicians — not from other singers. I've had a chance to work with some of the very finest musicians. Max Roach was a great influence and one of my greatest teachers. It was through him that I learned this form, and approach to practicing excellence," she says, praising the master drummer to whom she was married from 1962-70. She cites Thelonious Monk and John Coltrane as others from whom she gained much.

"I've been doing this for 40 years. And it's actually easier now. What I'm doing now is a culmination of all those years of practice. Looking at the things that I'm able to do today, I feel really accomplished," she says, tempering her words with a self-effacing — and musical — laugh. "I finally learned some things. You know?"

Abbey Lincoln

BETTY CARTER

For many years, Betty Carter (photographed in performance, close-up, by John Johnsen) has been ranked by most critics as being one of our greatest jazz singers. But Carter hasn't always had the general public support one might have expected to go with the critical acclaim. That developed in the mid-1980s. Winning a Grammy and getting a major-label record contract have helped, as has a general resurgence of interest in real jazz (as opposed to jazz/rock fusion) which began in the early 1980s and has continued into the present.

By 7:30 on this December 1988 night, it's already standing-room-only at Fat Tuesday's jazz club in New York for Carter's first show, which is scheduled to begin at 8 p.m. Seeing the enthusiastic crowd — some patrons have been here since seven — beckoning waitresses to order dinner and drinks, I'm thinking: Betty Carter has finally and fully "arrived."

Well, maybe in a figurative sense she has. But on a more mundane level, she hasn't. At 8 p.m., we're awaiting her arrival and a nervous club manager is calling her Brooklyn home and getting no answer. At 8:30, her bassist Ira Coleman, drummer Troy Davis, and pianist Darrell Grant — a fine, fleet trio — begin playing. A little after 9, Carter herself finally walks in, *singing* to us as she makes her way to the stage that she's sorry she's late. She adds, with characteristic independence, that she had decided to start later so people wouldn't be eating while she worked.

No doubt most who are present tonight forgive Carter — one of the most beguiling jazz singers — as soon as they hear that clear, firm, engaging (and sometimes sardonic) voice of hers. No matter how stylized her work gets — as she stretches out quite unexpectedly on notes here,

runs words together there, reshapes melodies to suit her needs, and scats whenever the mood strikes her — coming from her, it somehow sounds natural; you sense great integrity in her work.

Born in Flint, Michigan, in 1930 and raised in Detroit, Carter (real name — Lillie Mae Jones) got hooked on bebop when it emerged. It didn't strike her as at all strange or hard to understand (as it did so many elders), she told me one afternoon at her Brooklyn townhouse. All of her friends were really into that music. As a 16 year old, she was soon sitting in with the likes of Dizzy Gillespie and Charlie Parker, and learning to use her voice as another horn.

Singing with Lionel Hampton — her first big time professional gig — from 1948-51, she was somewhat frustrated because he showcased only her scat singing rather than let her also do romantic ballads "straight." But in retrospect she realizes the specialization proved invaluable training for her, heightening her individuality. She and Hampton had their disagreements. She would tell him to his face that she would rather be with a more modern band like Dizzy Gillespie's than Hamp's, which she considered a bit

old fashioned. He would fire her. And Hampton's wife, Gladys, would hire her right back. She was using the stage name "Lorraine Carter" when working with Hampton, but he chose to introduce her as Betty Bebop, which soon evolved into Betty Bebop Carter, and then just plain Betty Carter.

On her own as a single afterwards, Carter worked theaters and clubs and festivals, recording sporadically. She's made surprisingly few albums in a career that's spanned more than 40 years — only 15 as of this writing. Known for her refusal to compromise, she didn't try to do rock or soul or funk or disco, or sing in a more accessible pop-oriented style. (Even her own brother urged her to try and sing more like Frank Sinatra, she once told me.) When the bottom fell out of the jazz market in the late 1960s and early '70s, she produced her own albums. They weren't always easy to find, but she preserved her self-respect. She wasn't shy about knocking others, such as Miles Davis and Donald Byrd, who, she felt, were turning their

backs on jazz to go for the money in more pop/ rock oriented music. She knows that if you are not loyal to your muse, it may desert you.

Carter's stature has steadily grown in the past decade. In fact, since the deaths of Sarah Vaughan and Carmen McRae, and the retirement of Ella Fitzgerald, Carter is generally recognized as the pre-eminent female jazz singer working today.

She worries about the lack of good, original young jazz singers today. She doesn't like seeing copyists, and she doesn't like seeing people dabbling in jazz and then getting sucked into the commercial world, letting producers control them in the quest to make hits. She also doesn't like the fact that so many young black people today seem to know little about jazz and blues. She told Owen Cordle of the Raleigh *News and Observer* (April 8, 1988): "What I want to do is encourage young players to this black music. They don't even know what this music is about.... But Wynton Marsalis has had a lot of influence.

I think he's done a great deal for these black people, these young kids who come out and see him. I think this is the turnaround scene."

She has long been one of the best talent scouts in jazz. The musicians who accompany her often go on to make names for themselves. Carter also devotes considerable energy to finding and presenting new talent in showcases at the BAM Majestic Theater in Brooklyn and elsewhere. In fact, at Carter's April 9, 1994 BAM Majestic Theater concert (where Andreas Johnsen took the photograph of her with the young Reed Sisters), I spotted in the audience representatives from Verve and Blue Note Records, from George Wein's Festival Productions, top jazz musicians such as Roy Hargrove and Wallace Roney, and reviewers from the magazines *JazzTimes* and *Jazziz*. There's a lot of interest in seeing who her latest discoveries are.

The biggest hit with the crowd that night were the Reed Sisters of Milwaukee, Wisconsin (Brittany, 12, Tanya, 13, and Brandi, 16). "We love her," Brittany said to me of Carter after the show. Trumpeter Peven Everett, 18, of Harvey, Illinois, who had also made a good impression, had no comment except to shyly plant a kiss on Carter's cheek in gratitude. (As I write this, he has just gotten a booking into his first real New York jazz club, Iridium.) Pianist Xavier Davis, 22, whom Carter found in Grand Rapids, Michigan, told me: "If people like her weren't bringing young people into jazz, it wouldn't continue. Hopefully when we get older, we'll be doing the same thing. It's hard, sometimes, for a young performer to be heard. She's giving us a chance.

Jazz Veterans

JON HENDRICKS

Jon Hendricks always delivers a memorable show. But for his Christmas 1994 Blue Note engagement, he brought in an all-star line-up including trombonist Al Grey, tenor saxist Benny Golson, and former Duke Ellington vocalist, Milt Grayson. The highpoint, captured here by Andreas Johnsen, was when Hendricks (center) sang "Everybody's Boppin'" — joined by his daughter Michelle (who's been performing in Paris in recent years) and Clark Terry. Sheer magic, the way the three voices connected. Michelle Hendricks, incidentally, scats with a natural-ness that is all too rare. Growing up with one of the masters couldn't have hurt. Jon's daughter Aria has also proven, in engagements with him, that she is a singer of notable self-assurance and verve. Seeing the way his daughters perform (and the way audiences respond), he says, he has no worries about the future of jazz singing.

Much more could be said about the multi-talented Jon Hendricks but he's working on his own autobiography right now, and no one's likely to tell his story better than he will. Watch for it.

Jon Hendricks

BOBBY SHORT

Bobby Short is the quintessence of Manhattan sophistication. When he goes into one of those utterly adult Cole Porter numbers at the Cafe Carlyle (where he's reigned for some 30 years), you'd almost think Porter wrote them with Short in mind. His singing and playing on numbers by the likes of Porter, Noel Coward, the Gershwins, and Jerome Kern is elegant, imbued with both feeling and showmanship. But Short also knows (and revels in performing) a wealth of more obscure Tin Pan Alley, film, and show tunes — everything from "Laugh, Clown, Laugh" (popularized by Harry Richman) to "She's a Latin From Manhattan" (popularized by Al Jolson). And who else but Short can turn around after performing such numbers and carry off with great panache — and understanding — something as riproaringly lowdown as Bessie Smith's "Gimme a Pigfoot"?

What does he like best about his work? "It's the chance to express myself," he told me one afternoon at his Upper East side apartment. "Everyday people want to express themselves. They don't get the chance and become frustrated. Some become quite neurotic. I go out every night and give vent to some part of my own sensibility."

African statuary accented the 11-foot height of the living room's ceiling. His pet Dalmatian, Chili, wandered in from another room, giving the couch a try before settling for good on an oversized ottoman. "Pretty Chili, pretty Chili," Short told the pooch soothingly, rubbing his neck with affection.

Born September 15, 1926 in Danville, Illinois, Short taught himself to play piano. Blessed with a "marvelous ear," he never learned to read properly. "I still don't read well at all," he told me. Singing came easily to him. His family was poor, so if he could earn some extra money by singing on street corners or wherever, that was fine.

His big break came when an American Legion convention was booked nearby, when he was 11. There'd be plenty of people to sing for, people who could tip well, he figured. The convention would be good for the local economy. "Prostitutes, musicians, hot-dog vendors — all were out, trying to make some money off of all the people who had come in for the convention," Short recalled. Two promoters heard him singing, and told him they could manage him, and make him a child star. He'd be famous, like Shirley Temple and Bobby Breen and Deanna Durbin. "I was assured that my future was going to be all gold and platinum."

He soon hit the road, playing theaters from Kansas City to Harlem. Billed as "the miniature king of swing," he sang and played, dressed in white tails. Commercially, he never quite made it as big as his managers predicted. "I was in vaudeville, working four and five shows a day. But I learned things in the next two years in vaudeville that have stayed with me all my life, such as respect for other performers and for my audience, empathy for people who perform, and discipline. I

enjoyed it — there was a glamour about it — but at the same time, it was hard work. I worked with Fletcher Henderson and Bunny Berigan and Luis Russell and Louis Armstrong. I got to meet all the big people: John Hammond — I knew him when I was 12 — Mildred Bailey and Red Norvo, Art Tatum and Fats Waller, Earl Hines, Duke Ellington. They were the lights."

After a couple of years, he got off the road, returning home to finish high school before going out again. He found his own style. There were those who advised him to pattern himself on, say, Fats Waller, "but I've always been very stubborn about individuality." Others suggested he emphasize blues, barrelhouse, and boogie woogie, which were presumed more "natural" for a black performer than Cole Porter and Noel Coward. But he gradually gained a sure sense of where his own preferences and strengths really lay. "You go where your ear and sensibilities lead you."

It wasn't until the mid '50s that he broke through to great success, when he was "discovered" (after many years in show business) by New York's society crowd. His following has only broadened as he's grown older.

Andreas Johnsen's first informal shot captures Short signing an autograph for a fan after performing with the Alden-Barrett Quintet in one of producer Jack Kleinsinger's "Highlights in Jazz" concerts; the second shot shows him with Kleinsinger. Short has appeared many times in that jazz concert series, now the longest-running one in New York. (Tickets for Kleinsinger's concerts are reasonably priced; they give fans of Short who cannot afford the Carlyle's steep $45 cover charge a chance to enjoy his work.) Short also finds time to appear as a guest in concerts with

orchestras such as the Boston Pops, the Dallas Symphony, and the Sacramento Symphony; in occasional films, such as *Call Me Mister* and *Hannah and Her Sisters*; and in TV commercials, for products ranging from "Charley" perfume to *The New York Post*. In addition, he has hosted and headlined assorted concerts honoring bygone greats of jazz and the black musical theater. He doesn't want Florence Mills or Bert Williams or Adelaide Hall to be forgotten. And he has also spearheaded the fundraising campaign to erect a larger-than-life-size statue of Duke Ellington at the northeast corner of Central Park.

His base remains, as it has been since the late 1960s, the Carlyle; he could probably keep that gig for as long as he chooses. (The shot of Elliott with Short was taken in the lobby of the Carlyle.) What Short will play on a given night is generally thought-out ahead of time. "There's nothing like knowing what you're going to do in advance," he believes. But that doesn't mean he won't fulfill the occasional request, or offer something on the spot especially for a loyal admirer like George Wein (the world's busiest jazz-festival producer) or Susan Straub (wife of best-selling suspense novelist Peter Straub) or filmmaker Jean Bach ("Jean's just come in the room — we must do 'When Love Beckoned on 52nd Street' for her," he'll say).

He's generally recognized to have gotten better with age. "There were certain things I couldn't sing until I was old enough to sing them," he believes. "You have to be a little world-weary." He sometimes likes to affect that pose of weariness. Quite languorously, he told the fans who'd gathered for the opening of his 27th season at the Carlyle, in 1995: "I've dug up some old songs... because I'm too tired to learn any new ones." And then he dug into — with remarkable brio — "Guess Who's in Town."

His fingers flying across the keys of the Baldwin baby grand, his voice ringing out clear and high, he made the song — regardless of what its composers, James Johnson and Andy Razaf, may have intended back in 1922 — a celebration of the fact that Short, cafe singer *par excellence*, was back home. With scarcely a pause to catch his breath, he offered up evergreens with an air of ironic sophistication, then moved on, in a voice strangely knowing, to explore the mysteries of the blues: "Your eyes are lighted windows / there's a party going on inside...." Bassist Beverly Peer (Chick Webb's bassist in the '30s) added much to the blues with well-chosen figures.

Short never gives less than 100 percent. He offers big numbers with a flourish, a dash, a sense of grand style that none of his would-be competitors come close to duplicating. There's style even to the way he'll suddenly stand up at the end of particularly well-done number, raising his arms with a slight flick in acknowledgment of applause he knows is his due, then just as suddenly sit down again to resume playing. "There'll be no salacious songs tonight," he insisted midway through his generous opening-night show. "I'm feeling *much* too young and innocent."

Then, in a more serious voice, he remarked on how much he appreciated the elegance that Ginger Rogers (who had just died a few days before) always projected in her films with Fred Astaire. Honoring her memory with "Shall We Dance," he bore down unexpectedly on the line "life is short...," then ripped into a piano solo that bristled with defiance.

ELLIS LARKINS

Many jazz pianists dislike accompanying singers; they'd much rather play solo. Ellis Larkins, however, has quite often taken the accompanist's role. At one time or another, he has worked with such master singers as Joe Williams, Maxine Sullivan, Helen Humes, and Ella Fitzgerald, among others. In one of his infrequent interviews, he told Anthony Mancini of *The New York Post* (September 2, 1972): "I like the interplay of playing for people. I think I like it more than playing solo. If you're a good accompanist, you're going to be heard anyhow. I never had the urge to 'cut' anybody."

That may not be the temperament of the typical jazz player (and we'll be meeting an assortment of other jazz pianists in the pages that follow). But then again, Ellis Larkins didn't originally set out to become a jazz player. He was a child prodigy whose first preference was classical music.

Born in Baltimore in 1923, Larkins grew up listening to his father, a violinist in the City Colored Orchestra, practicing at home with fellow musicians. By age seven, he was playing Mozart in public. He studied with faculty members of the Peabody Conservatory (but not *at* the conservatory, which was segregated), and at age 17, in 1940, entered the Juilliard School to continue his classical studies. However, he didn't have the fi-

nances to complete his course of study. Playing jazz offered him a means of earning some money. In 1942, he made his club debut as a jazz pianist. He's remained in the field ever since. But even when he plays in the noisiest of joints — such as the club on New York's First Avenue where his bass player suggested they should use the trucks rumbling by to introduce their numbers — he carries a bit of the concert hall atmosphere with him. As perhaps comes through in Nancy Miller Elliott's portrait of him.

A man of few words, he has never sought publicity. He performs much less frequently than his admirers would like, and he does so with no fuss. He sits bolt upright at the piano, virtually motionless except for his hands, and simply plays the great standards — quietly, thoughtfully, and exquisitely, making wise use of the silences as well as the sounds in the music. His sets are unusually concise (he may play for a half hour — or decide to take a break after as few as three numbers), as are his performances of the individual numbers within those sets. He says, by way of explanation, that he likes short things.

I remember complimenting him after a particularly striking concert appearance; from the way he expressed his thanks, in that soft, modest voice of his, you would have thought he wasn't used to hearing praise. And yet when he does work, he invariably draws high accolades. Richard M. Sudhalter called Larkins "a living definition of taste, touch, subtlety and, in the occasional role of accompanist to singers, faultless discretion" (*The New York Post*, April 12, 1978). George T. Simon observed Larkins "plays some of the gentlest swinging jazz imaginable" (*The New York Post*, January 2, 1981). Don Nelsen of *The Daily News* noted (February 11, 1977): "I heard pianist Ellis Larkins for perhaps the 25th time the other night and, damn it, he was splendid again. This man plays so consistently well that one maliciously hopes for a clunker or two to prove that he's a flawed soul like the rest of us."

MARIAN McPARTLAND, JIMMY McPARTLAND

arian McPartland was through with her first set at Tavern on the Green, March 1, 1994 — or so she thought — when Tom Monetti, who runs the room, brought out a big cake topped with 15 candles and a miniature piano (a moment Andreas Johnsen captured on film).

The cake was to celebrate the 15th anniversary of McPartland's "Piano Jazz" public radio show, which has won the Peabody Award, the Armstrong Award, the ASCAP-Deems Taylor Award, the *JazzTimes* poll, and seemingly every other available honor.

But the mere presence of McPartland in a New York club was reason enough to celebrate. It had been a full decade — far too long — since she'd played a club, so busy had she been with radio and concerts.

The night was special — particularly the second set. By then, she'd gotten thoroughly relaxed; it felt like being in her living room.

The emphasis was on ballads: Benny Carter's "When Lights Are Low," her own "Twilight World," and (really exceptional — I got chills) "Singin' the Blues," in tribute to her late husband, cornetist Jimmy McPartland. She played

it with deep feeling, repeating a final passage softly to devastating effect.

Incidentally, she played that number unaccompanied. I wish she'd play one or two numbers in every set unaccompanied. Not that I have anything against her trio; but sometimes it's great to hear the beauty of her own work without distractions.

She also offered lilting Mary Lou Williams rarities, dug into Ornette Coleman's quirky "Ramblin'," and really evoked John Coltrane's spirit on "Red Planet." I don't know of many pianists who can get into as many different styles as sympathetically as McPartland.

Booking her was a coup for the Tavern. She projects exactly the right blend of elegance and informality the room wants for its image. Notables at the opening included pianist/vocalist Barbara Carroll (with whom she's standing in Andreas Johnsen's second photo of her) and filmmaker Jean Bach.

ting in a shot at the 1995 Lionel Hampton Jazz Festival) to Cecil Taylor, Harry Connick Jr., and Chick Corea.

When she first came on the scene, she had to overcome the narrow-minded prejudices of some who believed that because she was white, female, and British, she couldn't possibly play jazz well. In the early years of her career in the U.S., some also assumed she was getting work on the strength of the name of her husband, Jimmy McPartland, the noted Chicago cornetist. But she overcame all such doubts. Over time, in fact, her fame overshadowed that of her husband. They enjoyed successful careers, both together and apart, but he was viewed as somewhat of a symbol of the Jazz Age; her playing felt more contemporary.

She even accepted requests from patrons, provided they were numbers in her working repertoire. When one asked for "Melancholy Baby," she responded cordially: "We do that one in the third set." The Tavern offers two sets nightly.

Marian McPartland has become an institution. Thanks to her "Piano Jazz" radio show, she may well be the best-known jazz pianist in the nation today. Sooner or later, seemingly every fine jazz pianist appears on her show. She's probably played duets with pianists of more widely varied ages and styles than anyone else alive — everyone from Eubie Blake, Mary Lou Williams, and Hank Jones (with whom she's seen chat-

I was quite touched by the bond between Jimmy and Marian McPartland. When I was at Jimmy's house in 1985, he remarked that they had gotten divorced perhaps 10 or 15 years earlier; he couldn't remember the exact year. He said it bothered him that his memory was becoming increasingly unreliable; he supposed he might be getting Alzheimer's disease (although he was never actually diagnosed as having it).

But to me the date of their divorce hardly seemed worth remembering because — as he and Marian both liked to say — "the divorce didn't take." Their lives remained tightly intertwined. In fact, what brought my interview with him on that afternoon to an end was that he had to drive out to the airport to pick up Marian. (Periodically throughout our visit he'd remind himself out loud of when and where he had to pick her up, so concerned was he that he might forget.) Just two weeks' before Jimmy's death on March 13th, 1991, he and Marian married each other once again.

Although Jimmy complained about his memory regarding recent events, his memory was still terrific when it came to the early years. When he recalled for me, for example, doing work as a fishing guide on a lake in Wisconsin in his youth, he began reciting the names of all different types of fish *in Latin*: "*Percophylus San* is a perch; *Pomoxus Almoides* is a large-mouthed bass," and so on. There was no room for that incident in the profile of him I included in *Voices of the Jazz Age*, which focused on his career in music, but I was certainly impressed. And I liked

that I could ask him about anything in the teens, the twenties, the thirties, and the forties, and his answers came sure and strong. Who was the greatest trombonist he had ever heard? "Jack Teagarden — I would take him above anyone." He spoke at length about his original idol, Bix Beiderbecke (whom he had replaced in the Wolverines in the '20s). He spoke warmly, too, of Louis Armstrong, recalling good pot — not just good music — they'd shared back in the old days. His appreciation for good pot, I might add, didn't end with his youth. You'll note that in Nancy Miller Elliott's photo of Marian McPartland, Buck Clayton, and Jimmy McPartland, taken near the close of Jimmy's life, Jimmy has got a big bag of pot. (A few minutes later, he and Buck would be enjoying some of it.) I don't know of another jazz photographer, aside from Nancy, who'd have the nerve to shoot a photo like this. But she took it and the musicians got a kick out of it. Why not?

I liked the life-affirming confidence that Jimmy McPartland always seemed to exude. So did many others. At the memorial service for Jimmy at St. Peter's Church, trumpeter Richard Sudhalter quoted remarks Jimmy had once made to Studs Terkel concerning the Crash of 1929, remarks that seemed to capture his essence: "So many guys were jumping out of windows, you know, because they lost their money. Goodness gracious, what for? The important thing is life and enjoying life. So these guys lose all their money, what the hell's the difference? We used to say, '*You're still livin', aren't ya?*'"

Marian McPartland, Jimmy McPartland

JOHN BUNCH

Some performers' success seems to have hinged upon their having gotten "lucky breaks" in their youth. But John Bunch, whose deft, light piano playing has graced the big bands and small groups of Woody Herman, Benny Goodman, Gene Krupa, Buddy Rich, and Scott Hamilton, received anything *but* lucky breaks.

"It was the Depression when I was starting to play the piano, out in Tipton, Indiana," he recalls. "And the Depression just shattered our family. My father left us. My mother had to get a job and had never worked in her life. I just put myself into the music. I spent hours every day, just playing." By age 14, he was gigging regularly with local groups. "Then, in the late '30s, when I was still in high school, there was a radio program that Tommy Dorsey had, where they gave young musicians of high school age a chance to play with the band. They were coming to Cincinnati, and I won the right to go down there and audition to be on that show," Bunch recalls. "But we were so poor it was unbelievable. Cincinnati was 120 miles away from Tipton and I couldn't afford to go there. It just broke my heart. I really felt that I could have made it." Next, in his senior year in high school, he recalls, "a college band came through Indiana from Duke University, and I had a chance to join that band, but my mother wouldn't let me leave school. That bandleader turned out to be Les Brown, who became very famous."

Bunch's favorite pianists were Fats Waller and Teddy Wilson, and he mastered their approaches to the piano. With the advent of World War II, he was drafted, and wound up getting shot down on a mission over Germany. He became a prisoner of war.

After the liberation of Germany, Bunch returned to the U.S., ready to make his mark as a superb young jazz player in the Fats Waller-Teddy Wilson kind of tradition, only to find that such playing was now considered *passé*. In the U.S. of the late '40s, jazz musicians were idolizing beboppers such as Charlie Parker, Dizzy Gillespie, Thelonious Monk, and Bud Powell, whom Bunch had never heard of. Players who had been virtually unknown before the war were setting the pace in the post-war period. "Music had changed radically during the war. It was hard for me to make that adjustment." Eventually Bunch became an accomplished pianist in traditional and modern idioms, but it took time.

By the early '50s, Bunch recalls, "things were really rough. I played in a strip-tease joint for a whole year almost, a very depressing place. That was the low point." He was 33 before he finally made the big leagues. "In 1956, I got the job with Woody Herman, on the road. I'd always idolized Woody. I was with that band for a little over a year." He has worked with Herman repeatedly in intervening years. He then worked with Benny Goodman (for whom he also worked, off-and-on, into the 1980s), Gene Krupa, Maynard Ferguson, Buddy Rich, Al Cohn and Zoot Sims.

For six years (1966-72), he was Tony Bennett's pianist and orchestra leader. For a long while, he was Pearl Bailey's pianist of choice. He's currently one-fifth of the Scott Hamilton Quintet, recording regularly for Concord. He chooses other jobs carefully. Bunch has received invitations to conduct for performers ranging from Judy Collins and Lena Horne to Frank Sinatra. But he's turned them down, preferring to stick to piano playing. "I like to play jazz," he says simply. "It's much more fun."

ROMANO MUSSOLINI

"I never in my life thought I would be playing Moscow, Idaho," says the man sitting next to me in the car.

And I'm thinking: "I never in my life thought I'd be sitting next to the son of Benito Mussolini."

Romano Mussolini, 69, the youngest son of the notorious Italian dictator, has worked throughout Europe as a jazz pianist and composer for some 40 years, sharing stages with top musicians. He has never yet played a New York jazz club — although he mentions to me that he would like to. He's come to Moscow, Idaho, to play at the 10th annual Lionel Hampton Jazz Festival, a weeklong gathering in February 1995 of musicians from diverse regions.

I've been advised, prior to meeting him, that he doesn't like talking about politics, and that I shouldn't ask him about his father. This morning, we're riding together from our hotel to a classroom. He's agreed to answer students' questions. They ask him about almost everything in the world except his father. (How does he like American films? He tells them he's always been crazy about American films: "And I *loved* Greta Garbo.") I watch the pattern repeat when he gives a musical clinic for another group; he says he'll take any questions, but everyone avoids the obvious ones.

Finally, after a couple of days, we're having lunch and I feel comfortable enough to speak freely with him. I've been impressed by his warmth and gregariousness. I've watched him beam with approval, tap his foot, and clap along as other musicians have played things he's dug. I've seen him blush when a woman says something mildly flirtatious to him. I've enjoyed seeing him play and amiably grant every request for an autograph (as depicted in one of the shots taken at the festival; another shows him meeting noted jazz critic/historian Ira Gitler, while journalist Jan Holland looks on). So finally I asked him if he'd mind if we talked a bit about his father.

"You can ask me anything. I'm very open," he says. And that turns out to be true. "Everything good in me I got from my family. I loved my father. I got my sense of humor from my father. He loved his children very much, maybe too much."

It's hard for me to reconcile that description with the

brutal dictator we read about in history books. But he insists that much of what history has recorded is incorrect, or only a part of the truth.

"My father had two faces. What the public saw was acting. Who wore the pants at home? My mother," says Romano Mussolini.

Perhaps he notes a skeptical look on my face. I'm thinking of Benito Mussolini forming an alliance with Hitler and helping to plunge the world into the biggest war of all time.

"Ninety percent of what my father did was good. Oh, mistakes were made...but he drained swamplands, built roads, built buildings, made Italy a great nation, a modern nation. He was for the workers. He believed in workers' rights and social security.

"If you asked me, before the war broke out, what was my favorite nation, I would have told you — for I told everyone: 'I love America.' Everyone knew I loved America. And ever since I was four years old and I first heard Duke Ellington's 'Black Beauty' — and I still know every note of that — I loved American jazz."

An older brother and sister brought back many American jazz records from trips to America and England. "Every time I played Ellington's 'The Saddest Tale,' I would cry. The record still makes me cry, it is so beautiful. I remember my brother telling me: 'If I thought the record was going to make you cry, I would never have given it to you.'

"When my brother Vittorio went to America in 1938, he most wanted to see the Savoy Ballroom in Harlem. He was stunned to discover that Guy Lombardo's swing band was more popular with Americans

than the real jazz bands he loved, like Duke Ellington's. He met with Franklin and Eleanor Roosevelt — I remember him telling me how much he loved Eleanor. He brought my father secret messages from President Roosevelt.

"We all admired what President Roosevelt tried to do. I can remember how my whole family celebrated when Roosevelt was re-elected in 1936. And I remember, my father kept a picture of British Prime Minister Chamberlain in his office. My father didn't really want war." (And before people write me angry letters of contradiction, I should stress I'm merely reporting his views, not espousing them.)

"I remember my father telling us, right up until 1940, that he thought it would be possible to have peace. But he was forced into a position by circumstances beyond his control. And maybe there were other nations who didn't want Italy to be so strong."

What of persecution of the Jews? I ask him. His face clouds over. He suggests, with some awkwardness, that things were never as bad in Italy as in Germany, that being Jewish was not necessarily a death sentence. "You could stay in the country. Or you could change your religion. It was a transitory situation." (History records that nearly 9000 of Italy's 40,000 Jews were deported to Nazi concentration camps; most did not survive. And Benito Mussolini's government began treating Jews as second-class citizens even before the war began.)

Romano Mussolini's close friend and musical partner, multi-instrumentalist Oscar Klein, tries to help. He interjects: "The Italian concentration camps were humane by comparison with the

German camps. I know — I'm Jewish and I was interned in an Italian concentration camp. The Italians would not harm children. Had I been in Germany, I would have been turned into a lamp-shade." He takes a harmonica from his pocket, adding: "Do you know, the harmonica was invented in Germany? One of the few good things ever to come out of Germany."

Romano Mussolini believes his father and the West should have formed an alliance against Russia. "My father was strongly anti-Communist," he says. "And he was pure. He wasn't really interested in money. He could not be bribed — unlike many of the politicians of modern-day Italy. The people supported him. Today, my daughter [a member of Italy's parliament] is unifying the center-right parties of Italy. Look at all the votes she got! That shows the feeling people still have for the name 'Mussolini.' "

I could say something about how the way his father died (at the hands of enraged partisans in 1945) showed the feelings some Italians had. But I don't. He does not claim to be an objective historian. He is a son who, like many another loyal and loving son, wants to think kindly of his father, wants to remember him in the best possible light. I'm aware, too, that the recollec-

tions he has offered this afternoon are selective. He has not mentioned, for example, that after his father was killed, he had to live for a while in exile, in Ischia. Early in his career, he used the name Romano Full rather than the controversial "Mussolini." But such memories must be painful.

He makes it clear he no longer wants to discuss the old times. He'd rather talk about music; he enjoys such pianists as Oscar Peterson and George Shearing. And he asks me about New York's current jazz scene. He'd love to play a New York club. (He took part in a concert in New York once, over 20 years earlier, he recalls.) He and Klein, who's particularly good on trumpet, would probably go over well in New York today. Together, they work effectively in an enjoyable, older, hot-jazz style so rarely heard these days that it would be new to many listeners. As a solo pianist, Romano Mussolini's limitations may be evident, but he works well with others. And his partner Klein's facility on trumpet, guitar, clarinet, and harmonica would no doubt pique interest.

He reminisces happily about playing in Europe over the years, with everyone from Ellington to George Benson. Jamming with

Hampton at this festival, he assures me, is a high point of his life. (And Hampton, in turn comments: "That cat plays like he's from downtown Harlem.") It means much to Romano Mussolini to find acceptance from other members of the jazz community.

"They won't let you play with them unless you're good enough. It's not enough," he says, "just to have a famous last name."

JOHN LEWIS

Pianist John Lewis (shown in Nancy Miller Elliott's photo with jazz film-maker Bruce Frederickson) is best known as the guiding force behind the Modern Jazz Quartet (or MJQ). You can't quite call him the leader, since they chose to incorporate in 1954 as an officially leader-less cooperative ("Everybody would share in everything," he says), but he has been its artistic director, responsible for the group's unusually delicate touch and its borrowings from classical music traditions. The MJQ evolved from a quartet within the Dizzy Gillespie Big Band; Gillespie would periodically let a quartet play — both for variety's sake and to give the other members of the band a chance to rest their lips.

In the late 1980s and early '90s, Lewis also distinguished himself as the musical director of the American Jazz Orchestra (or AJO).

As I write this, the MJQ has been ensconced for a month at the chic Cafe Carlyle. From a listener's point of view, there's something quite special about being able to see the group play their subtle chamber jazz — they have the precision of a fine Swiss watch — in the intimacy of a club, rather than the concert halls they usually play. "We've always had good times together," Lewis says of the group, which is known for its unsurpassed rapport. And he likes the idea of being able to refine numbers by playing them night after night. The MJQ offers jazz that's about as refined as you'll find!

As for the American Jazz Orchestra, it was formed to offer concerts celebrating the music of distinguished jazz big-band leaders and composers. Someday, Lewis hopes to see similar jazz orchestras in most major cities — the way symphony orchestras may be found in most major cities. The idea is that great works of orchestral jazz deserve to be maintained in a regularly played repertory, no less than great works of so-called serious music.

The AJO was actually the brainchild of esteemed jazz critic Gary Giddins, who persuaded the authorities at Cooper Union to provide space for the proposed orchestra's rehearsals and performances, as well as some financial underwriting. As the orchestra's "artistic director," Giddins received a salary during the initial nine-month start-up period; afterwards he worked strictly on a volunteer basis. To hold costs down, Lewis, who conducted most AJO concerts and occasionally played piano as well, refused to take any salary at all. Giddins and Lewis put together an orchestra (supported by a mix of public and private funds — ticket receipts actually covered less than half of operating expenses) including such established musicians as Mel Lewis, Ron Carter, Jimmy Knepper, Bill Easeley, Jerry Dodgion, and Britt Woodman, along with impressive younger players, all of whom agreed to work for scale. Giddins and Lewis wanted an ongoing, organized band, because they knew that it takes time for musicians to develop a rapport and to play at their best as a unit.

Lewis liked the fact that the AJO was providing a way of passing along — to younger jazz musicians as well as to members of the audience — some of the jazz heritage he grew up with. The great band leaders were role models for him in his youth. He first made his mark as pianist, composer, and arranger in Dizzy Gillespie's big band, just after World War II. He enjoyed guiding the AJO as it brought to life once again the exhilarating music of the Gillespie band, as well as the bands of Jimmie Lunceford, Duke Ellington, Count Basie, Woody Herman, Tommy Dorsey, Benny Goodman, and so on, using original charts (or transcriptions made from the original recordings), but with fresh solos. Things didn't always click — sometimes the younger players had difficulty recapturing the old swing feel — but the band became an important addition to the jazz scene. Leading it for six years, Lewis said, was "a labor of love."

When the AJO was founded, both Lewis and Giddins said that they would consider it a success if it helped inspire the formation of other, similar jazz repertory orchestras. The subsequent establishment of such orchestras under the auspices of Lincoln Center and the Smithsonian Institution was viewed by Lewis and Giddins as a sign of the AJO's success in its mission.

Those better-funded orchestras have survived; unfortunately the AJO, which helped get today's jazz repertory orchestra movement going, has not. Cooper Union's financial support for the orchestra eventually ran its course. Giddins (who estimated he sacrificed $20,000 he could have made as a freelance writer during the time he donated to the orchestra) decided he could not afford to spend any more time filling out grant applications. The orchestra completed its sixth and final season of regularly scheduled concerts in December 1992.

RUBY BRAFF & DICK HYMAN

A portrait by Nancy Miller Elliott of the only ongoing cornet and piano duo in jazz: Ruby Braff and Dick Hyman. Sometimes they're billed in that order; sometimes they're billed as Dick Hyman and Ruby Braff. (Their album *Manhattan Jazz* gives Hyman's name first on the front, Braff's name first on the back.) They've been teaming for records and concerts, off-and-on (because both do myriad other things), since 1975.

The two make gorgeous music. Hyman, proceeding amiably in an often precise and rather straightforward fashion, keeps everything on an even keel; Braff provides the more surprising embellishments, descending at times abruptly and expressively — now tender, now moody — into the lower register, then rising up into jubilant little shouts, without ever fully losing sight of the melody.

Their musical roles seem to reflect their personal temperaments. Balding, bespectacled Hyman has a certain steadiness to his nature, along with a mild, playful humor; the more volatile Braff can give the impression of someone who's looking for an argument — although if you said that to him, he'd probably give you an argument.

198

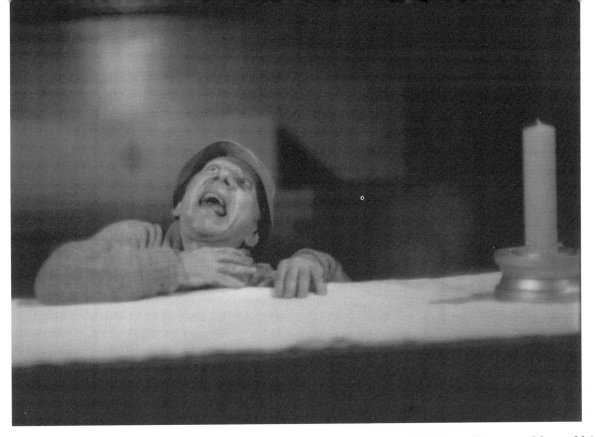

Braff is a bit gun-shy of critics, generally — and perhaps with good cause. He's received some stupid critiques from reviewers who, in a pejorative fashion, proclaimed that he was an "anachronism" or "reactionary" because his lyrical style was based in a pre-bebop tradition. The fact that his style was unique and immediately recognizable as his own (he was not a clone of Louis Armstrong or Bunny Berigan, although he's been influenced by them) didn't count; some simply knocked him for not conforming to the prevailing modern jazz trends. (Plenty of other critics, of course, appreciated his considerable gifts.)

Braff has always gone his own way. For him the main thing is (as he has put it) "the adoration of the melody." Born March 16, 1927 (Hyman was born eight days earlier), he practiced his horn in his youth by playing along to radio broadcasts of such melodic bands as Artie Shaw's, and Tommy and Jimmy Dorsey's, not by playing the usual scales and exercises. He went on to work professionally with Edmond Hall, Pee Wee Russell, Vic Dickenson, Buck Clayton, Urbie Green, Mel Powell, Bud Freeman, Benny Goodman, and George Wein's Newport All Stars. He formed a near-ideal association with George Barnes in the 1970s; the quartet they co-led played impeccable and highly musical chamber jazz. But personality differences ultimately drove them apart. Braff once insisted to me he couldn't stand "all that quiet," as he described the sound of Barnes' guitar. In a more serious vein, he said he resented having to do most of the work to get the group gigs. Elliott's portrait of him catches him in "hunchback of Notre Dame" mood.

Just listing Dick Hyman's credentials would take more space than we have here. Suffice it to say that this onetime student of Teddy Wilson has played on literally thousands of records. For he can play with a high degree of competence (and occasionally a welcome touch of humor) in seemingly any idiom, from ragtime (recording the complete piano works of Scott Joplin, for example), early jazz (salutes to Jelly Roll Morton and Clarence Williams), and early pop (Zez Confrey), to bebop (with Charlie Parker and Dizzy Gillespie), current jazz (with Roger Kellaway and Arnie Lawrence), and rock 'n' roll. He was one of the first to record on synthesizer. He's also done music for movies and Broadway shows, and produced engaging concerts at New York's 92nd Street Y that stress the accessible, joyful types of "hot jazz, ragtime, old time, and blues" that he prefers.

TOMMY FLANAGAN

If you appreciate graceful, bebop-based piano, you can't do too much better than Tommy Flanagan. Some listeners may prefer Hank Jones or a few other masters, but all would place Flanagan in rather select company. He usually ranks among the top two or three pianists in the *Down Beat* International Critics' Poll, for which 50-odd jazz critics vote each year — perhaps second only to Cecil Taylor (who plays so radically different a type of jazz that he really can't be considered a "competitor" in any sense). An impeccable artist, Flanagan is in high demand all over the world.

Born in Detroit in 1930, he performed there in his youth with Thad Jones, Elvin Jones, Milt Jackson, and others. He took inspiration from such pianists as Bud Powell, Art Tatum, Hank Jones, and Teddy Wilson — as well as (like so

many other musicians of his generation) saxist Charlie Parker. By his mid-20s Flanagan had moved to New York, where he was good enough to substitute, at times, for Bud Powell at Birdland. He soon found employment with such demanding artists as Miles Davis, J. J. Johnson, Coleman Hawkins, Tony Bennett, and — his longest and best-known association — Ella Fitzgerald. (Working with Ella was in many ways a satisfying experience, and certainly a prestigious one, he told me at his New York apartment one day — but financially it was never a very remunerative one.) Since 1978, he has worked primarily as a soloist or trio leader, touring widely.

But because this world-class pianist performs so frequently in New York, an appearance by him in that city — which would be an event for jazz fans anywhere else — may be taken for granted by some listeners. I remember going to hear Flanagan one night at the Fortune Garden Pavilion, a posh East Side Chinese restaurant he often played in the late '80s, and being appalled by the hubbub from diners who were acting as if he were just some local pianist hired to provide a musical background for their conversations. One woman rather audibly attempted in vain to shush the more talkative patrons, insisting they give this master jazz artist the respect he deserves. (That exasperated woman was none other than Mrs. Tommy Flanagan!)

That night, quite frustrating for me as a listener, heightened my appreciation for the Village Vanguard, another New York venue where I've repeatedly caught Flanagan. The audiences at the Vanguard, who've come strictly for the music, are almost invariably quiet. No one tells them to be quiet. They just are.

Nancy Miller Elliott took this close-up formal portrait of Flanagan in New York. Andreas Johnsen photographed Flanagan at a recording session held in conjunction with his winning the 1993 Jazzpar Prize. The Jazzpar Prize, presented each year in Copenhagen, is the biggest award for jazz excellence in the world. Winners receive a sculpture and a cash award of 200,000 Danish Kroner (approximately $30,000 in American money).

Tommy Flanagan

MAX & LORRAINE GORDON

"I opened the nightclub without any money. I don't think anybody could do it again," Max Gordon was telling me. It was 1988; he was 85, and he'd been running the nightclub in question — New York's oldest, the Village Vanguard — since 1934.

He recalled how he'd found laborers who worked with the understanding that he'd pay them when the club started making money. He found an electrician who connected him, ille-

gally, to a power line, since he didn't have the $75 deposit Con Edison required. And when the city cited him for offering entertainment at the Vanguard without a cabaret license, he convinced a sympathetic judge that the poets he was booking into the club could hardly be construed as "entertainment."

How, I wondered, had New York's club scene changed since Gordon first started in the business? "There's more of them now, and they're

more expensive," he noted. "We charged no admission in the early days. Even when we'd have Miles Davis back in the '60s, we'd have a $2.50 minimum, no cover charge; today it's a $12 admission. And people stayed out later then. We'd be open until 4 a.m. — we close at 2:30 now. People don't hang out like they used to. But in those days, they were all unemployed, and nobody wanted to go home."

Gordon wondered, in passing, if he had made the best possible use of his life. For he had come to New York from Portland, Oregon, in 1926 with fantasies of someday becoming a writer. (And he conceivably could have become quite an interesting one, judging from his memoir, *Live at the Village Vanguard*, published in 1980.) He suggested that what he had done really wasn't so much; he had simply booked artists that he liked — adding in a self-deprecating way that he had old-fashioned tastes.

Uncompromising tastes would have been more accurate. Jazz aficionados trusted Gordon's integrity; this was one club where you knew you wouldn't get schlock.

Initially, the Vanguard offered poets, comedians, and singers, before gravitating towards the jazz policy it has become famous for. Over the years, countless greats in various fields have appeared at Gordon's club. He remembered, for example, jazz pianist Eddie Heywood assuring him he'd made a big mistake in hiring one deep-voiced unknown, fresh out of Bennington College: Carol Channing. And he remembered Miles Davis refusing to go on with another unknown that he'd hired: Barbra Streisand.

He recalled the night at the Vanguard when Charles Mingus hit trombonist Jimmy Knepper in the stomach for not playing something just the way Mingus had written it, and the night Mingus ripped the front door off the club because he wasn't satisfied with his billing. He recalled Sonny Rollins once promising to be at the club the next day — and then showing up a year later. "He'd gone to India to play his horn in a cave," Gordon explained laconically, adding: "I'd like to see him again. He'd come in for

$2000 a night. Even if we don't make money, I'd like to see him play here again."

But Gordon died not long after that conversation (of "a glorious old age," as his widow, Lorraine, who's continued running the club since his death in 1989, put it). Admirers and associates, including some of the greatest of jazz musicians, packed the memorial service for him at St. Peter's Church. Mel Lewis' Jazz Orchestra played "Just Friends." And plenty of jazz players — who wouldn't speak highly about many other club operators — felt they had indeed lost a friend.

When Max died, a competing club's manager told me: "I give the Vanguard six months. Can Max's widow book the talent? And a jazz club's a cash business. Without a tough man in charge, your own employees can rob you blind. The smartest thing she could do would be to sell the business to the Japanese."

A half-dozen years have passed since then. The Vanguard remains as healthy as ever.

"There were many vultures swooping over the Vanguard when Max died," Lorraine Gordon acknowledges. Some would have loved to have bought the business. "And it's hard to say no to a million dollars. But what are you going to do with the money? Buy a house? A car? For that would you give up something vital, something you've given your whole life to?

"Some people suggested opening other clubs — franchising the Village Vanguard, like McDonalds, to make more money." (The New York Blue Note, for example, has opened foreign clone editions of the club.) "But this little Vanguard, on its own, has more going for it than 50 clubs all around the world."

It remains a place quite special. If I'm entertaining visitors from abroad — as I recently, for example, had an opportunity to help entertain versatile British saxist Nigel Scragg — the jazz club I most want them to see is the Vanguard. It's a landmark. The sound is terrific. And so, most nights, are the music and the audience. There's also a lot of history in the room. It's fun to point out things like the ceiling light fixture, up near the stage area, that Mingus once busted with his bass; it's been left unfixed ever since, in memory of him. I like the fact that Lorraine has an appreciation for the club's history, too.

She's been, of course, a lifelong jazz buff. She was active in the Hot Club of Newark in the late 1930s and early '40s. That's where she first got to know Jabbo Smith, who was to become one of her favorite musicians. Nancy Miller Elliott's tender photo on page 203, taken near the close of Smith's life, shows Lorraine Gordon polishing Smith's trumpet while he relaxes at her apartment. Elliott's photo on this page shows, from left to right, Smith, drummer Mel Lewis, Max Gordon, and Buck Clayton.

In the mid-1940s, Lorraine got Max Gordon, whom she would marry a few years later (her first marriage was to Blue Note Records head Alfred Lion) to listen to a pianist he'd never heard of: Thelonious Monk. She persuaded Max to give Monk bookings at the club, which Max did (even though he initially lost money on them), until Monk gradually acquired more of an audience. In the years that followed, she was never shy about giving Max suggestions.

Though she always deferred to her husband, as he got older Lorraine began assuming more responsibilities at the Vanguard. As Max's health began declining, Lorraine gradually took over more control; thus she was more ready to run things after his death than most onlookers might have supposed. She also gradually got her daughter Deborah, today the club's bookkeeper, more involved in the operation. Deborah says she hopes that the family can keep running the club indefinitely: "I like the continuity — especially in a city where everything changes so quickly."

MEL LEWIS & DENNIS MACKREL

The passing of the torch: Nancy Miller Elliott's photo shows Mel Lewis, one of the last of the great big band-era drummers, standing alongside Dennis Mackrel, a promising young big band drummer whom Lewis chose to take his place when he became terminally ill.

Although interest in big bands had crested by the late 1940s, plenty of leaders were still optimistically forming new big bands and experimenting with new sounds. In 1948, Lewis drummed in the big jazz band of Boyd Raeburn, whose progressive ideas were much admired by fellow musicians but didn't win a broad public

following. Over the next few years, Lewis drummed for other leaders whose big bands were less adventurous than Raeburn's but were more popular: Alvino Ray (1948-49), Ray Anthony (1949-50, 1953-54), and Tex Beneke (1950-53). From 1954-57, Lewis powered Stan Kenton's pace-setting post-Swing Era band, then enjoying a peak of popularity and winning one major poll after another (including the *Down Beat* readers' poll, 1954; the *Metronome* poll, 1954 and 1956; and the *Playboy* poll, 1957). Lewis went on to work with band leaders Terry Gibbs, Gerry Mulligan, and Benny Goodman, before co-founding in 1965 the Thad Jones-Mel Lewis Jazz Orchestra, which also went on to top numerous polls. Billed after Jones left it in 1979 as the Mel Lewis Jazz Orchestra (and since Lewis' death in 1990 as simply the Vanguard Jazz Orchestra), the 17-piece orchestra continues playing every Monday at New York's Village Vanguard — the city's longest continuing jazz gig.

Born 33 years after Lewis, in 1962, Mackrel began drumming along to his parents' jazz records when he was just two. "I never had any drum lessons. My mother took me to one lesson one time when I was five or six, but the teacher said the best thing would be to let it develop naturally."

The first band Mackrel heard live, when he reached New York from Las Vegas at age 18, was Mel Lewis'. He went on to play in Broadway shows and led a band of his own. At age 20, he became Count Basie's drummer. Basie, he says, was like a grandfather to him. (Thad Jones and Mel Lewis, he adds, were also like family to him.)

The fact that Mackrel was a young member of a very old tradition was brought home to him repeatedly. First, Basie died of cancer on April 26, 1984. Then Thad Jones, who had become the leader of the Basie Band, died of cancer on August 20, 1986.

Mackrel left the Basie Band to be with his mother when she, too, died of cancer. After rejoining the Basie Band, he wound up being at the hospital on March 1, 1987 when veteran guitarist Freddie Green was declared dead. Mackrel reflects quietly: "The education I've gotten from Basie and Thad and Freddie Green, you can't get anymore."

Mackrel went on to drum in Buck Clayton's Swing Band and in assorted small groups. Mackrel subbed for Mel Lewis on various occasions in the U.S. and Europe in 1988 and 1989 after Lewis became ill with cancer. Initially, he split concerts with Lewis when Lewis did not have enough strength to play entire programs; later he filled in for Lewis throughout entire nights. Lewis died February 2, 1990, and Mackrel assumed his chair in the band for a while. (He has since been replaced by John Riley.)

A devout Christian, Mackrel believes there is a reason that he has managed to work with so many jazz greats just before they died. "The Lord has really been blessing me, putting me with these people," he says. "God has really been giving me the knowledge I'm going to need for whatever's going to happen to me. Everything I've been learning is going to be called into service."

TOSHIKO AKIYOSHI

This stark, striking portrait of Toshiko Akiyoshi (taken by Nancy Miller Elliott in Nice, France, July 1988) captures well her resoluteness in the face of challenges. For about a quarter of a century, Akiyoshi has led or co-led one of the most respected jazz orchestras in the world. And the going has often been harder than admirers of her considerable talent would likely imagine.

I remember the wealth of good publicity she received when her band, then co-led by her hus-

band, saxist/flutist Lew Tabackin, first broke through in the mid-1970s. She did the composing and arranging for the band. And while not all critics went so far as those who called her the successor to Duke Ellington, all *did* take her seriously; they weighed the Akiyoshi-Tabackin Band against the very best big bands.

Akiyoshi had earned some recognition as a pianist/composer before forming the orchestra. (And she had made a name for herself in Japan even before moving to the U.S. in 1956.) The

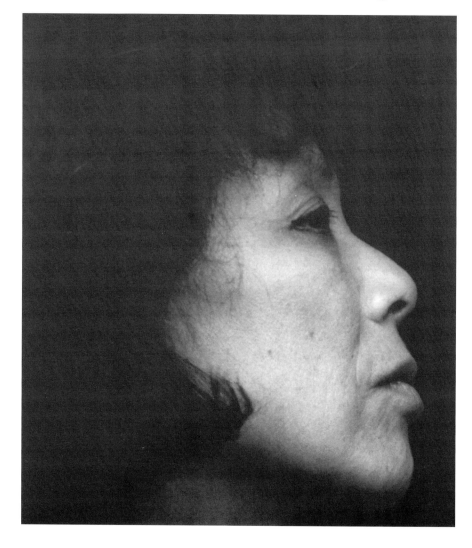

average jazz fan in the mid-'70s, seeing how often her name was cropping up in the press, might have assumed she was doing very well financially. But in the jazz world, great artistic success and great economic success do not always go together.

Although she made her debut as a composer/conductor at a well-received Town Hall concert in 1967, she was not able to establish an ongoing rehearsal band until after she and Tabackin moved from New York to California in 1972. Why? The cost of renting rehearsal space in New York — then about $30 a week — was beyond her means. It's hard to imagine that a sum so small (especially when measured against the enormous sums squandered by record companies on many quickly-forgotten rock musicians) could have prevented so gifted an artist from realizing her potential. But after paying for food, rent, and other essentials, there simply wasn't enough left to pay for rehearsal space.

In California, Akiyoshi and Tabackin lucked out. They found a place to rehearse for a token payment of just 50 cents (later upped to an even dollar) per session; the band remained based in L.A. for 11 years.

They were unable to obtain distribution in the U.S. for their band's first album. Only after the album became a jazz best-seller in Japan were they able to get a U.S. company interested in them. In 1978, the Akiyoshi-Tabackin band won its first *Down Beat* poll as the number-one jazz big band; it found sporadic work at colleges and festivals. (Akiyoshi saw a benefit in not working constantly: she had time to concentrate on her main work, composing and arranging for the band.)

Even in the late 1980s, with 10 Grammy nominations and an array of international poll victories to her credit, Akiyoshi was unable to find steady work for her band, by now known as Toshiko Akiyoshi's New York Jazz Orchestra (after she and Tabackin had moved back to New York in 1983, she had reorganized the band under her sole leadership, with Tabackin serving as the band's principal soloist when available). An attempt to establish the Akiyoshi orchestra as a permanent every-Monday-night attraction at New York's Indigo Blues did not work out.

But no one forms a jazz big band to get rich. (In fact, some jazz players will jest that the quickest way to become a millionaire is to start with ten million dollars and then form a big band.) You form one to express yourself musically, and maybe — as Akiyoshi will say — to make a contribution to our culture. And Akiyoshi, through writing that adds subtle Japanese influences to rich, modern, American jazz big band sounds, is doing just that.

STAN GETZ

When tenor sax great Stan Getz (photographed here by John Johnsen) first became popular in the '50s, some jazz aficionados wondered if a white man could *really* be a major jazz artist — or was he inevitably just a bland imitator of a black originator? Writer Roy Hemming has recalled Getz discussing the issue with him; Getz was well aware of such black/white talk, and profoundly an-

noyed by the suggestion that he was merely some kind of a copyist.

To writer Leonard Feather, Getz once declared explicitly: "I think jazz is mostly a black man's art, but there happen to be a few whites who can play it just as well, just as originally, as any black. Not many, but I know I'm one of them.... I would definitely say that Bill Evans is a creator; and Gerry Mulligan; and I could go all the way back to Jack Teagarden — my first master.... He was a giant of the trombone."

It ought to be unnecessary for Getz — or any other artist — to have to get so defensive. The supremely melodic, often languorous jazz that Getz produced for nearly 50 years was beautiful in its own special way; any serious jazz listener could identify Getz's work.

I can understand the controversy concerning race, though, for white artists have often enjoyed greater commercial success in jazz than black artists from whom they took inspiration, or copied, or hired to arrange for them — a reality of which musicians tend to be more aware than the general public. (Benny Goodman once berated sideman Paul Quinichette for upstaging him, admonishing Quinichette not to forget whose band it was. Quinichette then pointedly brought up the name of Fletcher Henderson — the black arranger who had created the style of the original Goodman band. Goodman never hired Quinichette again.)

What are the facts concerning Getz and the race issue? Getz started out as a disciple of Lester Young. Throughout his career, he favored, as Young did, a light tone, minimal use of vibrato, and a laid-back lyricism. Quite understandably, it bothered Young (and many who admired him) that Young did not reap the commercial rewards that disciples of his like Getz and Zoot Sims, who were white, did. Young knew that racism was a factor (which is not to imply that Getz or Sims were racists themselves; they were not).

But the black/white issue in jazz is not quite so "black and white" as some might imagine, either. The pattern is not always one of whites simply emulating blacks; influences can run in either direction. While it is true that Getz, who was white, took inspiration from Young, who was black, it is also true that Young named such white saxists as Frank Trumbauer and Jimmy Dorsey as having been inspirations to him. (And there are many cases like that.) Young, of course, found his own voice as a mature artist. So, too, did Getz. And Getz, in turn, went on to influence some younger musicians of all races.

Getz's abilities as a player manifested themselves early. Born in Philadelphia in 1927, by the time he was 16, Getz was working for (and recording with) legendary trombonist Jack Teagarden. Getz went on to work for Stan Kenton (1944-45) and Benny Goodman (1945-46). He broke through to fame when he joined Woody Herman's Herd in 1947. His masterly ballad performance of "Early Autumn" (1948), in particular, established him as a soloist of note. As a small-group leader in the early '50s, he enjoyed enormous appeal, his "cool" sound was widely admired, and he came to dominate jazz polls. He lost momentum in the mid-'50s, due to problems associated with drug addiction, but came back strong in the early '60s with well-received bossa nova recordings. When one interviewer asked him how he was weathering the general downturn of public interest in jazz in the '60s, he casually noted he had a recording contract guaranteeing him an income of at least a quarter of a million dollars over the next five years. Even if he never made a single club or concert appearance, he knew he would not have to worry about money. Getz continued creating gorgeous music right up until the last year of his life, as his acclaimed 1990 album, *Anniversary,* makes clear.

CHET BAKER

The sound of Chet Baker's horn was gorgeous, and somehow distant. He worked within constraints — never going too high or too low, never getting too loud. At his peak in the early 1950s, he played ballads laced with sadness about as well as anyone of his generation. In 1954, when he was just 24, he won the *Metronome* poll as best trumpeter. He won it again in 1955. He was being overpraised somewhat — he wasn't the best all-around jazz trumpeter (not as long as Louis Armstrong, Roy Eldridge, Dizzy Gillespie, and Miles Davis were on the scene) — but he was certainly the trumpeter of the hour. And unquestionably capable of deeply touching people.

In his early years, Baker was exceptionally good looking, which added to his public appeal. His lips were sensuous, with sometimes a hint of a pout. His dark hair was slicked back, but one errant forelock always seemed to be hanging down over his brow. A certain blankness in his eyes, which tended to be gazing off into space rather than looking at the camera, suggested vulnerability. One of his albums was titled *Let's Get Lost*. (The same title was later used for a film about him.) Looking at Baker, one often couldn't help feeling he somehow *was* lost.

He didn't have much to say to interviewers. People could read into his silences whatever they chose. Was he a man of great depths? A romantic hero with an air of mystery? Or just someone with little to say? Someone not fully comfortable with being considered, in his early 20s, the trumpeter to watch?

He worked with some of the best musicians around, including Charlie Parker and Gerry Mulligan, and made records rich with promise. The fragility one sensed in his playing was curiously affecting. He sometimes sang, too, which

helped him connect with audiences. Had Chet Baker's life been cut short in a mid-'50s car crash like James Dean's, he would have become a real jazz legend.

But a deepening involvement in drugs soon robbed him of his good looks and of his consistency as a trumpet player — and brought him frequent clashes with the law. He served jailtime in Italy on a narcotics charge in 1960 and '61. The next year, he was arrested again — in Germany — but charges were dropped and he was allowed to leave the country. He spent time in a sanitarium in an unsuccessful effort to free

himself from heroin. Somehow, between such problems, he still managed at times to make excellent recordings, although he had lost much of his following. Then in the late '60s, he gave up trumpeting altogether for a couple of years after an incident in San Francisco, in which he was beaten so badly he lost a number of his teeth.

He eventually pulled himself together as best he could. He got false teeth, entered a methadone treatment program, and worked hard to regain his abilities as a trumpeter. Reviewers found him playing more effectively than he had in years, and his career seemed to be regaining some momentum, although the long-time drug abuse had seriously weakened his health. (For more information on Baker's life, watch for James Gavin's forthcoming biography.) John Johnsen's portrait of Baker was taken in 1983; Andreas Johnsen's haunting photos were taken in 1988, the year that he died.

Wynton Marsalis never sounded more moving than in the New Orleans-style brass-band dirge he led at the memorial service for Dizzy Gillespie at the Cathedral of St. John the Divine, January 12, 1994. His searing horn, rising above muffled drums and answered by eery wails of clarinet, could be heard before it was seen, as he led a candle-lit processional from the rear of the great church to the front. Roberta Flack sustained the mood with an *a cappella* rendition of "Amazing Grace."

An extraordinary assemblage of talent gathered in the Cathedral, which was filled to overflowing, to pay final respects to the jazz community's patriarch. Some, such as Clark Terry, Tommy Flanagan, Donald Byrd, Jimmy Owens, Slide Hampton and a truly all-star big band, chose to remember Gillespie with music.

Others chose to remember him with words, which painted a remarkably consistent picture.

One great after another lauded Gillespie's unusual accessibility, and expressed gratitude for help Gillespie gave when they were young hopefuls. Master bassist Ray Brown recalled meeting Gillespie in a 52nd Street club the first day he arrived in New York, 47 years ago. Gillespie invited Brown to drop by his apartment the next night — where he met Charlie Parker, Max Roach and Bud Powell, and his career, he said, really began.

Trumpeter Jon Faddis recalled, as a 15-year-old, bringing 50 albums to Gillespie to sign. Gillespie patiently signed all 50 — marking the beginning of a musical mentor/disciple relationship that lasted until Gillespie's death. (Faddis was actually with Gillespie when he died.) Chuck Mangione said Gillespie invited him and his brother up onto the bandstand to jam the first night they met him, when they were in their mid teens.

Gillespie's attorney Elliott Hoffman recalled once asking Gillespie how old he felt he was; Gillespie answered, "You know, I can't tell you; I feel all ages" — which Hoffman felt symbolized Gillespie's ability to relate well to all different types of people, of all ages. Paquito D'Rivera offered his remembrances in Spanish, eliciting responses of "Si, si," from some in attendance.

Mayor David Dinkins praised Gillespie's ability to find unity in diversity, adding: "It is said that service to others is the rent we pay for space on Earth. Well, Dizzy Gillespie has departed 'paid in full.'"

Though I'd witnessed some unforgettable musical performances by Gillespie through the years, most of the images that played through my mind after his passing actually were not of him onstage, but offstage. I remembered first and foremost that irresistible smile of his — like a small boy trying not to give away that he'd eaten all the cookies in the jar. And the winning innocence of his voice.

In his later years, Gillespie was not only the most distinguished elder statesman in jazz, he was probably the most beloved. You could truly feel the good vibes around him. A member of the Baha'i religion — which stresses the one-ness of mankind — he lived his faith. He treated everyone, from street people he encountered to dictators, like brothers.

There was no one who could quite replace him as such a likable and human symbol of jazz. With Gillespie's passing, Wynton Marsalis became the spokesperson for the jazz community, but his personality was a bit more prickly than Gillespie's; he can sometimes antagonize people without intending to do so. Gillespie, with his big embrace for everyone, helped unify the often disparate factions of the jazz world.

He once mentioned to me, almost in passing, that he was descended from African royalty. Did he really believe that? I couldn't tell if he was putting me on when he said it; he didn't seem to be. That's an image — of Dizzy as royalty — that has stayed with me, too.

ART BLAKEY

rt Blakey's hands seemed to have a life of their own. He didn't look at them, or his drums, when he played. With his head thrown back, his jaw slack, and — when he was really into it — his eyes rolled skyward, Blakey appeared to be in another world. Those hands beat out incessant, explosive patterns on his two tom-toms, four snare drums, and six cymbals. Sometimes a vaguely ecstatic look would move across his deeply lined face. Sometimes he'd exclaim a seemingly involuntary "whoa!" after a sideman let rip a particularly good solo.

For more than three decades, Blakey's Jazz Messengers were among the hardest-hitting of jazz bands. Year after year, they were one of the highest ranked groups in the *Down Beat* Inter-national Critics' Poll, and Blakey was one of the highest ranked drummers.

𝄞

At Mikell's, an Upper West Side New York club where I've come to see Art Blakey's Jazz Messengers on this night in September of 1986, a standing-room-only crowd gathers in the club a half-hour before the first set begins. The Messengers mix intense uptempo originals by current members Kenny Garrett (alto sax) and Donald Brown (piano) with numbers by onetime member Wayne Shorter (tenor/soprano sax) and even, for a change of pace, Duke Ellington. Rounding out the group are trombonist Tim

Williams, bassist Peter Washington, and tenor saxist Jean Toussaint. Trumpeter Wallace Roney is unable to make it tonight; his surprise, unannounced substitute is none other than Terence Blanchard, who had graduated from the Messengers to greater fame on his own. His brilliant, stratospheric trumpeting knocks the crowd out. But no one — not even Blanchard — steals the show from the uninhibited Blakey.

Born in 1919, Blakey became part of the modern jazz scene during his years drumming in Billy Eckstine's big band (1944-47), which included such musicians as Miles Davis, Dexter Gordon, Gene Ammons, Fats Navarro, and others. After Eckstine gave up his big band in '47, Blakey formed a rehearsal big band of his own which he called the Seventeen Messengers, and recorded with an octet called the Jazz Messengers — a name he revived for a group organized on a permanent basis in 1955. His aggressive, blues-influenced, hard-bopping Jazz Messengers of the late 1950s set the pattern for all editions of the band since then. And its influence, through prominent alumni like Wynton Marsalis and Terence Blanchard, continues to be strongly felt today.

Being an orphan himself, Blakey used to say, made him aware of how important a father could be in a youth's life. Ultimately, Blakey became the father to fourteen children — seven by birth and seven by adoption. He also became, in a sense, the "musical father" to innumerable jazz players. Indeed, no jazz group leader nurtured the careers of a greater number of young jazz stars than he did. Noted former Jazz Messengers include, among others: Wynton and Branford Marsalis, Bobby Watson, Mulgrew Miller, Amina Claudine Myers, Walter Davis Jr., James Williams, John Hicks, Cedar Walton, Curtis Fuller, Woody Shaw, Freddie Hubbard, Lee Morgan, Donald Byrd, Kenny Dorham, Jackie McClean, and Clifford Brown. (Which is

not to say that his eye for spotting new talent was unerring, or that there were always promising unknowns available. He sometimes worried that the pool of talented young jazz musicians was shrinking. Not all members of the 1986 edition of the Jazz Messengers mentioned here, for example, went on to make names for themselves in jazz.)

Blakey impressed upon all who passed through his band the value of fairly concise, climactic solos, not the endless, self-indulgent blowing that became popular with some younger players after the rise of Ornette Coleman and Free Jazz. And while he sometimes appeared to be in a trance state when he played, he maintained careful control of dynamics for maximum dramatic effect, and responsiveness to the contributions of every member of the group.

Regardless of shifts in musical tastes (and occasional knocks from some critics for not getting with whatever the newest thing was), Blakey kept playing the same kind of uncompromising hard bop. Others could meander through endless pieces, exploring the wonders of polytonal post-structuralism. Blakey never gave up on such classic virtues as structure and pacing and communicating with an audience. "I wish more of the older guys from my generation would keep a group out there," he told *Down Beat*'s Kevin Whitehead in 1988. "That would help jazz so much. It would help the [younger] guys."

Blakey (photographed here by John Johnsen) left a tremendous void when he died in 1990. At his best, he seemed possessed by a force in a way that I've never seen duplicated by another drummer. (Tributes to him by other drummers are almost inevitably disappointing.) Freddie Hubbard is one of many ex-Blakey sidemen who appreciated the unique push and inspiration he got from Blakey. After Blakey, he'd say, all other drummers seemed like babies.

JEAN BACH

Producer/director Jean Bach may not be seen in her Academy Award-nominated film *A Great Day in Harlem*, but in a sense she's a star of it nonetheless. Her longtime friendship with, understanding of, and obvious affection for the jazz musicians she has interviewed has enabled her to capture them with a rare degree of naturalness. She brings us musicians as they are.

Such immortals as Art Blakey and Dizzy Gillespie, who could be quite curt with interviewers who didn't know the jazz scene, talk to her (and thus to the film's viewers) as an old friend. For Bach has been a dedicated follower

of jazz since the Swing Era. Her first husband, the late Shorty Sherock, was a jazz trumpeter.

Anyone who spends much time in New York jazz clubs soon meets "La Bach." And learns of her parties. For every jazz musician of note seems to eventually wind up at her townhouse. (Along with assorted other celebrities, we might add; Frank Sinatra, Ethel Merman, Soupy Sales have all graced her home.) She throws the kind of parties where the fellow playing piano for guests in the living room may well be — as was actually the case, the first time I walked into her home — none other than Tommy Flanagan.

Bach has put her knowledge of the jazz scene to good use. Ostensibly, her film *A Great Day in Harlem* is about a single day in 1958 in which musicians gathered to be photographed by Art Kane for *Esquire*. (In Nancy Miller Elliott's portrait, Bach stands before that famed photograph.) But Bach (assisted by writer Matthew Seig and editor Susan Peehl, who'd previously worked on some of the best jazz documentaries ever made, including *The Story of Jazz* and *The Many Faces of Lady Day*) has succeeded in conjuring up a whole era. The film is sweet, and also sad because so many of the boldly charismatic artists captured in the film are now gone

(and some of their young successors of today seem bland by comparison). New York remains, as it was in 1958, the world's jazz capital. But Bach's film — a valentine to so many greats who've passed on —leaves you feeling things ain't what they used to be.

Bach's film was given its world-premiere — even though it was not quite completed yet — at the 1994 Lionel Hampton Jazz Festival. The informal shot shows Bach at the 1995 Festival, where she'd gone to present the finished product, sitting with a notable assortment of friends. From left to right, we see: singer/songwriter Lorraine Feather (whose father was the late, highly respected jazz critic Leonard Feather), pianist Marian McPartland, Bach, her publicist Virginia Wicks (who's also worked for Peggy Lee, Dizzy Gillespie, Charlie Parker, and Oscar Peterson, among other greats), journalist Jan Holland (who was interviewing Bach for *Venice* magazine), and pianist Jane Jarvis (seemingly the only veteran musician from Indiana who claims *not* to have been a close personal friend of Hoagy Carmichael — although she was a friend of Hoagy's sister — she is also the first living female jazz musician to have a jazz festival named after her: the Jane Jarvis Invitational in Florida).

Jean Bach

TWO BROTHERS NAMED LEE

"**S**ome people might say this isn't a classy place. But the class is in the music," trumpeter Cliff Lee commented between sets at Brooklyn's Flamingo Lounge (where Andreas Johnsen took this evocative photograph), one blustery winter night in 1994. "The city used to be filled with neighborhood places like this, back in the '40s and '50s. Now this is almost unique. Where else can you just walk in — no cover charge, no minimum, a beer will set you back only $4 — and hear live music like this? Occasionally we'll see some white people in here, from Park Slope or somewhere. More people should come. It's safe. I've played here for 10 years and never seen an incident in the club or outside of it."

Entering the club is like entering a time warp. The decor and ambiance probably haven't changed in decades; nor has the music. There was nothing Cliff Lee played that night that a

young Miles Davis couldn't have played back in the '50s. But it's a great repertoire. Introspective, mood-setting numbers — slow, brooding, and heavy — like "Summertime" and "Bye Bye Blackbird," gave way to pieces that were slightly brighter but played with no less dignity, like "Star Eyes" and "There Will Never Be Another You."

As a trumpeter, Lee's intonation is inconsistent, and his range is limited. But the straight-ahead jazz his group plays is for real — heartfelt and direct — with moments (particularly in his codas) of unexpected grace.

"My family's into this music. This was in our house, when my brother and I were growing up in Snow Hill, Alabama. My brother's come by to see me, of course, along with some of his children. In fact, he's just arranged an album I've recorded, which we're hoping to get released."

The next night I went to hear the music of his brother, bassist/composer/arranger Bill Lee, whose children include noted filmmaker Spike Lee and actress Joie Lee. (Bill Lee is a bit older than the 65-year-old cutoff we've chosen for inclusion in this book; Cliff Lee is actually a bit younger, but we couldn't very well include one brother and not the other.)

Bill Lee (who's composed and conducted music for most of his son Spike's films) offers a more extroverted and uniquely personal music than his brother Cliff's, in which the jazz is richly seasoned with elements of gospel, blues, and R&B. Bill Lee's lyrics (and his occasional monologues) are drawn from his life. He'll periodically set down his bass to impersonate a curious character from his childhood (like "Mr. Tim," who had but one answer for every question) or muse on the wanderings of a "ghetto dollar." Even his manner of setting up numbers — as in telling a slave story that's part of his family's oral history — is absorbing.

Bill Lee's periodic concerts at the East Village's "University of the Streets" (where Andreas Johnsen photographed him) feature his "Family Tree Singers," a nine-member ensemble that deserves more exposure. He's found and nurtured a wealth of vocal jazz talent. An eight-year-old singing sax player (and son of his) named Arnold Lee adds life to the act. Like the multi-talented Marsalises, the Lees always seem to have another performing family member to introduce.

JOHNNY GRIFFIN

Though he was born in Chicago, tenor saxist Johnny Griffin notes he plays in a style with roots in Kansas City. Most of the saxists from whom he took inspiration — men like Ben Webster, Don Byas, Lester Young, and Charlie Parker — were either from Kansas City or made their marks in bands from Kansas City. He found his own sound within the tradition, and played faster than any of his predecessors had — some called him the fastest tenor who'd ever lived — but was very much aware he was part of a tradition.

His first important jobs, in the late '40s, were with Lionel Hampton and Joe Morris. But he really made a name for himself from around 1957, when he was featured in Art Blakey's Jazz Messengers, and 1958, when he held the tenor chair in Thelonious Monk's group. From 1960-62, he led an important bop group of his own, co-starring Eddie "Lockjaw" Davis, with whom he had impassioned sax battles.

He initially didn't get the amount of acclaim he should have because his playing — as daring, exciting, and hard-swinging as it was — was an extension of what had gone before. It was not a radical innovation like the Free Jazz of Ornette Coleman — which admirers felt mirrored contemporary feelings. "Change" was the byword of the day, whether in the fields of civil rights or jazz. And those who most strongly believed Free Jazz represented the future weren't much interested in seeing how well someone could work within an older style.

In 1963, for a variety of reasons, Griffin became an expatriate. The I.R.S. had presented him with a daunting bill for back taxes. He had family problems. The racism in the U.S. distressed him. And he was discouraged with the way the jazz scene in the U.S. was headed. He didn't have much interest in Free Jazz. He preferred hearing jazz with a more logical sense of construction.

In Paris he got to play with such brilliant American expatriates as Bud Powell, Kenny Drew, Art Taylor, and Kenny Clarke, as well as assorted Europeans whose competency at playing jazz came as a pleasant surprise to him. In the late '60s, he became the major soloist in the Kenny Clarke-Francy Boland Big Band. He was comfortable living in Europe, although he didn't believe Europeans really felt the music he played as deeply as Americans had.

In 1978, with the statute of limitations on his tax problems having expired, he began returning to the U.S. for periodic tours. He still found the racism in American society oppressive, but he welcomed the chance to play and hang out with many of his old American musician friends. He continued to make his home in the French countryside. (Andreas Johnsen photographed him, relaxing and sharing recollections with us, at his home in France; Johnsen took the other shots, in which Griffin has his sax, at a Danish jazz club).

Griffin found, too, that audiences seemed more receptive than ever to his playing (which had mellowed a bit). His style, which Free Jazz ideologues might have viewed as old-hat in the early '60s, was universally accepted as timeless. And with many of the older jazz saxists having died or retired, what he had to offer seemed rarer and more valuable. Today, he's a highly respected elder statesman of jazz, telling his stories on the sax with more authority than ever. Young musicians are glad to get opportunities to work with him; he has a way of bringing out the best in them (check out his team-up — as one of the "tenors of our time" — with young trumpet great Roy Hargrove on Verve). And none of the young cats are likely to cut him.

Johnny Griffin

ORNETTE COLEMAN

In 1961, crowds in Cincinnati protested when they found they would have to pay to gain admission to what had been advertised thusly: "Ornette Coleman — Free Jazz Concert." Unaware that the new form of jazz Coleman was developing was going by the name of "Free Jazz," they had assumed that the concert was being offered for free. It would not be the last time Coleman would find himself misunderstood.

If you have trouble appreciating or understanding recordings of Coleman's Free Jazz, which has been enthusiastically praised by certain critics and has won an enormously loyal following, fear not: you're in good company. After listening to Coleman's sax playing on *Embraceable You*, in a 1961 *Down Beat* magazine Blindfold Test conducted by Leonard Feather, Benny Carter responded: "I just can't figure it out. From the very first note it's miserably out of tune."

Coleman would consider the issue of whether he was "out of tune" irrelevant, a sign of a Western cultural bias. He told jazz writer Howard Mandel of *Down Beat* (August 1987): "Basically, all the music in the Western world that's tempered is played on the same notes; the solfeggio system is still used today to get people to say, 'Well you're flat or you're sharp....' Imagine what it was before they had that.... To me, lots of intellectual things have eliminated the naturalness in human beings. And it has really castrated lots of the pureness of people's hearts."

Besides playing alto and tenor saxophones, Coleman — as we see in John Johnsen's photographs — also plays violin and trumpet. His dictum has always been "play what you feel."

After listening to Coleman's trumpet playing on "Freeway Express" for a 1968 *Down Beat* Blindfold Test, trumpeter Freddie Hubbard (who had previously recorded with Coleman himself) commented: "I could have done what Ornette is doing when I was five.... Why should

a guy study for years — *study* trumpet — then see a guy come out on trumpet and he gets a lot of popularity, like this — it doesn't make sense."

But Coleman, who has avoided formal training on trumpet by choice, has nothing against primitivism. "I think 90% of what's called folk music and primitive music is probably the most advanced thing in melody today," he told Mandel.

Coleman wants his musicians to improvise as freely as possible. Different musicians in his group may be playing in different tempos. They are not basing their improvisations upon any

agreed-upon underlying chord structure (as they would in swing or bop), and they may choose to express their pain or elation or anything else. Each does his own thing, while trying to relate and respond to what others are contributing. Having like-minded sidemen helps keep things from descending into total chaos. (Coleman often benefited, for example, from having Don Cherry, with a strong sense for group feeling, as a fellow group member.) The musicians might play for a half-hour or more at a stretch, their meanderings theoretically reflecting the vagaries of life.

Pianist Andre Previn, upon hearing Coleman's *Focus on Sanity*, commented: "It is an unmitigated bore.... If someone is bent on broadening that which has come before...developing upon precedents, then I'm for it, but turning your back on any tradition is anarchy."

Most musicians who have worked with Coleman have dug his music. But not all. Bassist Jimmy Garrison grew so frustrated playing with Coleman that one night in 1961 he stopped mid-set at the Five Spot in New York City and began berating Coleman right in front of the audience. Coleman, almost invariably described by musicians as a notably warm and generous person, made clear to Garrison afterwards that he respected Garrison's opinions and sent him, with good wishes, to join John Coltrane's Quartet.

To admirers of Coleman's innovative music, he can seemingly do no wrong. In 1966, he began using as his drummer his son, Denardo — who was then only 10 years old! Critic John Litweiler wrote approvingly in *The Freedom Principal* that Denardo played "without style or more than rudimentary technique, but with a welcome spontaneity, a further step in the direction of indeterminacy." The authors of the *Harmony Illustrated Encyclopedia of Jazz* tried to be similarly sympathetic, writing: "Wayward, the youngster's playing certainly adds a random factor to the music." Of course, if Coleman had hired a three-year-old rather than a 10-year-old, the drumming could have been even more spontaneous and random.

In the liner notes to his 1958 album, *Something Else*, Coleman wrote: "I think one day music will be a lot freer. Then the pattern for a tune, for instance, will be forgotten and the tune itself will be the pattern, and it won't have to be forced into conventional patterns. The creation of music is just as natural as the air we breathe. I believe music a really free thing, and any way you can enjoy it you should." The question of whether one enjoys listening to Coleman's music as much the creators enjoy playing it is one that listeners must answer for themselves.

I must confess I've listened to some music by Coleman and his followers with feelings of utter bewilderment and discomfort. Yet all around me were fans of this music giving every indication of enjoying themselves enormously. Was I missing something? (The first time I heard the New Orleans polyphony of "Royal Garden Blues" as a boy, I can remember that it was hard to figure out, too, although I was hooked enough to keep listening until one day it all suddenly seemed remarkably clear.) Were the enthusiastic boosters of Coleman's music being taken in? Or was it simply a matter of taste? Responsible jazz critics whose tastes agree with mine in various other areas have found great beauty in some of Coleman's contributions.

There are some musicians (Don Cherry is a good example) who admire Coleman and have worked with him, whose playing I enjoy more than Coleman's own. Perhaps at some future date, I like to hope, I may understand Coleman's music better and gain more enjoyment from it. At present, it certainly does not speak to me as deeply and directly as, say, Ben Webster's playing does. And yet, even if I haven't gotten much pleasure from Coleman's camp myself, I'm still quite glad Coleman is a part of the jazz world (much as I'm glad for the thought-provoking contributions composer John Cage has made, even if I can't say I've much "enjoyed" what he has created). I just have a hunch that anyone who can shake up the established order the way Coleman does may be a catalyst for positive change. Certainly he has inspired others to take fresh approaches, which is important; experimentation needs to be encouraged. I agree with the melodic trumpeter Art Farmer, who once told Leonard Feather that although Coleman's style of playing was too extreme for his own tastes, "it does show that there is more freedom to be taken advantage of than is, as a rule."

SONNY ROLLINS

In his first few numbers at Carnegie Hall on May 19, 1989, Sonny Rollins proved so overwhelmingly vigorous, confident, and compelling a player as to make one wonder what role there was on the program for his special guest star, fellow tenor saxist Branford Marsalis. It was clearly Rollins' night, whether he was dancing exuberantly to the Calypso strains of "Duke of Iron," trading phrases with an unusually tentative Marsalis on "East of the Sun," or finding an emotional richness few would have imagined existed within the structure of "The Tennessee Waltz."

Rollins, one of the all-time masters of continuity in jazz solo construction — he's often been

called the world's greatest living improviser — attacked most of his material that night with a take-no-prisoners kind of zeal. His relentless, exhilarating work initially inspired unqualified awe, but before the night was over, there were moments when it seemed to me excessive, overwhelming. Rollins took one muscular chorus after another on "Three Little Words" and "O.T.Y.O.G." — the driving pace never letting up for an instant — until finally this critic began yearning for a bit of breathing room.

And, whether intended or not, that's the role Branford Marsalis wound up filling perfectly: taking the pressure off by playing a simple yet touching rendition of "Embraceable You" that refreshed and set the stage nicely for Rollins' now-welcome return to high energy: a boisterous "Don't Stop the Carnival," with some hall-shaking low-note work that won't soon be forgotten. Marsalis is an appealing, respected saxist in his own right. But his powers seemed altogether human alongside the near-godly Rollins.

Few instrumental concerts I've attended have had the overall impact of that one, which left me wondering why there aren't more saxists who play like Rollins — I mean who play *anywhere near* like Rollins. As a working critic making the rounds of the various clubs, I hear one saxist after another going through their paces quite competently, but so much less imaginatively, and so much less powerfully, than Rollins. (And they've come from the same general tradition Rollins has; they too are trying, to the best of their more limited abilities, to build upon what's been done by the likes of Coleman Hawkins and Charlie Parker and other past sax greats). Rollins' sheer *elan* is spirit-lifting in itself — even if, in large doses, occasionally he can be too intense for my nerves. Rollins holds back nothing. (It wasn't all that surprising to me when he collapsed from exhaustion in 1983, and had to take six months off to recuperate; to me, the wonder is that it doesn't happen more frequently.)

It seems entirely appropriate to me, too, that Rollins will sometimes dig into a classic Al Jolson number (not played by any other noted jazz musicians) such as "Toot Toot Tootsie, Goodbye" or "Rockabye Your Baby With A Dixie Melody" — for Rollins projects a boundless, warming bravado, a towering self-assurance much as Jolson did. Jolson, of course, was the quintessential one-man act; it never mattered who appeared with him in his many Broadway shows: *he* was the show. In a somewhat similar fashion, admirers of Rollins hardly care who he's got backing him up: an acoustic band, an electric matter, or even no band at all — and Rollins *has* made successful appearances in which he's played absolutely unaccompanied, a feat very few saxists could imagine risking. (Check out Robert Mugge's aptly named film *Saxophone Colossus*.)

Rollins doesn't perform that often anymore, which gives each performance a heightened importance. In New York, his rare concert appearances — he no longer bothers with little jazz clubs — sell out promptly. It is axiomatic among his fans that he must be seen live, that his studio recordings rarely capture him at his best. He digs into old tunes such as "I'm an Old Cowhand" and "It Could Happen to You" — tunes he loves, tunes that Rollins (who was born in New York in 1930) may have first heard at movie matinees in the 1930s and '40s, long before many of his current fans were born. Tunes that most other jazzmen today would probably dismiss as "not hip" — but which become hip very quickly when he starts messing with them. And he reminds us, in his concert appearances, of the particularly evanescent nature of jazz. Someone should be recording all of his major concerts, in the hopes of capturing some of the truly peak moments, of preserving for posterity how this giant of the current scene sounds when he is most inspired.

The photographs by John Johnsen (who has attended many Rollins performances over the years, both inspired and not-so-inspired) afford us a much closer look at Rollins than most of his fans these days can ever hope to get. The latest shots, capturing a clearly older, grayer Rollins as he appears today, were taken by Andreas Johnsen.

BUCK CLAYTON & WYNTON MARSALIS

Don't let the easy-going smiles give you the wrong idea: in the photo on the next page by Nancy Miller Elliott, you're looking at two *serious* musicians: Buck Clayton, a trumpet great of the Swing Era who upheld high musical standards for six decades, and Wynton Marsalis, a trumpet great of today.

In an interview with British jazz writer Max Jones, Clayton acknowledged, "I'm kind of serious myself. I mean, I take my music seriously — always do the best I'm capable of.... If I'm playing a date in an empty ballroom, then I play for myself, and I'm hard to please." One could easily imagine Marsalis (who is nothing if not serious) saying those same words. His own playing, of course, is technically superb. Some may criticize it as overly conservative for their tastes — I've occasionally wished he'd exhibit a bit more of the fire and fun that marked early jazz greats — but no one can deny his technical mastery of the horn. And his artistry is still expanding. In recent years his playing has grown richer — somewhat bluesier, more emotional, and more authoritative — as he seems to be getting more fully in touch with his New Orleans roots. At his best, in concert, he compels attention. He has that rare, indefinable something that forces you to sit up and take notice. (I say

"at his best" because I've also seen nights when he's played glibly, leaving me unmoved.) And he thinks big. I loved it when he premiered, in 1994, his first-ever extended work for large jazz ensemble, *Blood on the Fields* (which, incidentally, made brilliant use of the talents of veteran Jon Hendricks). Andreas Johnsen's photo of Marsalis playing plunger-muted trumpet was taken during *Blood on the Fields'* world-premiere at Alice Tully Hall.

Though the focus of this book has been veteran musicians, it seems appropriate to conclude with the multi-talented Marsalis. For he is the leading figure on today's jazz scene. And he quite proudly identifies himself as part of a long, noble tradition of uncompromising acoustic jazz, which he seeks to sustain. That he has posed over the years for portraits with Buck Clayton, Jabbo Smith, and many other jazz veterans is no fluke. He genuinely admires many of the gifted elders, both living and deceased, in the tradition. (If you haven't already done so, check out the tenth chapter of his warmly recommended book, *Sweet Swing Blues on the Road*. His comments on "the old oak tree" men of jazz are among the most touching in that book.)

While he, of course, works regularly with musicians of his own generation, we also see him recurrently reaching out to past generations, turning up in concerts with, for example, somewhat older musicians from his home city of New Orleans, or such senior mainstream jazz greats as Doc Cheatham and Harry "Sweets" Edison. He frequently takes leading roles in historical retrospective concerts (something we could not imagine a Miles Davis or a Henry Threadgill doing — indeed Threadgill believes: "To try to play like Louis Armstrong, or even to write a piece of music and infuse it with a bunch of stylistic things that came out of the idiom that Louis Armstrong was involved in, it's like being in a clown suit.").

By lending his prestige to historic retrospective concerts, Marsalis makes participation in such programs appear both natural and appropriate to novice musicians — which I applaud. He has encouraged aspiring younger musicians to try to become comfortable playing in various older styles. They don't always succeed, but there's value in making the effort to learn the rich language forged by our jazz elders. I liked the fact that drummer Jason Marsalis, Wynton's 17-year-old kid brother, mentioned in a brief meeting at the Village Vanguard in 1995 that he was checking out 1920s drum great Baby Dodds.

AFTERTHOUGHTS

I'd like to offer a few concluding remarks — afterthoughts, if you will — on Marsalis, the state of jazz today, and where it seems to be headed.

Marsalis is the best-known, most visible representative of the jazz community today. On balance, he has been good for jazz. By his words and actions, he promotes the idea that jazz is worthy of respect and that it must not be cheapened by commercial compromise. He came along at a time when all too many players were moving towards insipid forms of jazz/rock fusion in an attempt to win a mass audience. For a while in the '70s, it appeared as if uncompromising acoustic jazz was actually in danger of dying out. In the '70s, the biggest complaint you heard from older players about many of the young ones coming up was that they knew nothing about the past; it was not "relevant" to many aspiring younger players, who didn't see a need to learn standard tunes, much less check out vintage recordings. You don't hear such complaints quite

as frequently as you once did. For that, Marsalis deserves credit.

Major record companies got so strongly behind jazz/rock fusion in the '70s, many musicians concluded that was the only way to go unless they wished to be considered old fogeys. And not just aspiring young players, either. Even veterans like Woody Herman (who was always quite open-minded about trying new things) complained to me about feeling pressured to move too far in the direction of jazz/rock fusion.

When Marsalis emerged in the early '80s, he began turning things around. Columbia Records put its weight behind him, amplifying his opinions. Marsalis sharply criticized older players he felt had abandoned jazz in pursuit of bigger bucks, including two of the most gifted of all trumpet players, Miles Davis and Freddie Hubbard. Davis considered Marsalis disrespectful for saying that Davis had sold out. But it *was* a loss to jazz when talented players like Davis and Hubbard lowered their artistic standards in pursuit of bigger financial gains. By speaking out against such compromises, Marsalis was also trying to encourage aspiring younger players to follow his example and not Davis' or Hubbard's. (Columbia, I'm sure, had no objections to Marsalis' arguing that Davis was no longer playing the real jazz of his youth, Davis having "defected" from Columbia to rival Warner Bros. Records. Davis' leaving Columbia, incidentally, had created an opening for a trumpet star, which Marsalis filled.)

Marsalis has helped to discover, encourage, and nurture a whole cadre of younger players interested in "the tradition." His followers are expected to be somewhat conversant with the music of Jelly Roll Morton, King Oliver, Louis Armstrong, Coleman Hawkins, Dizzy Gillespie, Charlie Parker, and John Coltrane. In truth, they're not all nearly as familiar with the work of their jazz forebears as one might prefer (and many of them readily admit they did not grow up listening to jazz at home; they discovered it fairly late). But give Marsalis credit for encouraging respect for at least some of the tradition. It hasn't been an easy fight for him, consider-

ing the emphasis placed in our culture upon commercial pop, rock, and rap music of often ephemeral value. The older jazz greats are still dying off at a rate faster than equivalent younger talents are emerging to replace them, but Marsalis has worked hard to try and restock the talent pool, and to rebuild audiences for uncompromising acoustic jazz. He is making it easier for good young players to make a decent living today, without selling out, than it was in the 1970s or early '80s. Again, he deserves much credit.

If Marsalis can retain his artistic integrity, despite the temptations of commercialization — and so far (in contrast to his brother Branford) he's not wavered — we'll all be richer for it. Not just because we'll have Marsalis' own playing to enjoy, but because as reigning jazz king he strongly influences many other younger musicians. And he'll help to keep alive a part of the tradition represented by the veterans in this book. Much is being lost anyway as the older greats die off — much more would have been lost without Marsalis.

No one is perfect, of course, and there are apparent gaps in Marsalis' expertise concerning jazz history. He seems to have some blind spots regarding the contributions of certain respected past and present artists. (It would be unrealistic to expect him to be the greatest jazz historian as well as the greatest trumpeter.) But his encouragement of younger musicians to learn more about the history of the music is good.

I get enormous pleasure out of hearing Marsalis and the Lincoln Center Jazz Orchestra play classical jazz pieces by Duke Ellington, Louis Armstrong, and company. Those concerts (which I really miss when I'm away from the New York area) are important in keeping worthy music alive. I'm far from alone, though, in respectfully wishing that Marsalis would do a more thorough job of presenting historic jazz. Marsalis' Lincoln Center concerts have yet to celebrate the accomplishments of such notables as Bix Beiderbecke, Jack Teagarden, Benny Goodman, and Gil Evans. Most of the serious jazz critics (Whitney Balliett, W. Royal Stokes, Leonard Feather, Gene Seymour, George Kantzler, Gene Lees, and Peter Watrous, among many others) have raised valid questions about the narrowness of such programming. Young musicians should be encouraged to check out Bix Beiderbecke and Jack Teagarden, Artie Shaw and Gil Evans, no less than King Oliver, Jimmie Noone, and Jelly Roll Morton. They're all part of the jazz canon, their brilliance widely recognized by the musicians of their day. If Marsalis is not an expert in all areas of jazz history, he might be wise to augment his informal pool of advisors with others (such as, perhaps, Dan Morgenstern, Gunther Schuller, Dick Sudhalter, Ira Gitler, Stanley Dance — I could name many more) who could provide valuable help in programming different types of jazz retrospectives, and also in ensuring that the most capable musicians are used for such concerts (which isn't always the case now; too often, specialists in particular older styles have been overlooked).

Jazz at Lincoln Center exerts a considerable — and growing — influence. Via nationwide public radio and TV broadcasts, as well as concert tours, it brings jazz to far-flung audiences. If it is to introduce new listeners to jazz, if it is to help teach a new generation what jazz is, has been, and will be, I hope it will present jazz in all of its rich diversity. As artistic director of Jazz at Lincoln Center, Marsalis has an enormous responsibility to present a broad spectrum of high-quality jazz, to help see that the whole of the jazz tradition is passed along.

I have also heard *avant-garde* jazz musicians gripe that Lincoln Center is not open to *avant-garde* jazz because such music is not to Marsalis' own taste. They feel that Lincoln Center, as a quasi-public institution, should serve a broader interest than it now does. You're not likely to see, any time soon, concerts at Lincoln Center saluting a Lester Bowie or a Sun Ra or a Cecil Taylor or a Leroy Jenkins or a Roscoe Mitchell. Someone learning about jazz only from Lincoln Center's concerts or broadcasts would have no idea that such adventurous (and at times quite powerful) jazz musicians even existed, or that there are so many different ways of being a serious jazz musician today. I would welcome Lincoln Center finding more room for *avant-garde* musicians; it is too important an institution to

reflect only the preferences of one individual, no matter how talented. (Coming from an unusually large and diverse extended-family whose members are both white and black, Christian, Islamic, and Jewish, I've grown up believing that you must make a place at the table for everyone who wants to be there. I know *avant-garde* musicians who don't yet feel a place has been made for them, who would welcome Lincoln Center's acknowledgment that they're part of the jazz fold.) And experimentation in the arts is always to be encouraged.

♩

While this book has emphasized veteran players, we must always remember that jazz needs new players and listeners if it is to endure. Marsalis merits praise for his efforts to prod youths (whether players or just listeners) to explore jazz. He spends much time in schools, and musicians he has discovered and encouraged are becoming important factors on today's scene. He's helped spearhead a movement, reviving acoustic jazz.

I've been impressed by Marsalis' gift for communicating with youth. With an eye towards the future, I'd like to leave that as this book's concluding image. While controversies may swirl around various things Marsalis has or has not done, no one who has attended one of his "Jazz for Young People" concerts at Lincoln Center could be anything but highly pleased.

What are these concerts like? Well, let me share one recent memory. I was happy when I noticed audience members doing what Miss Charisma Jones was doing as she left Alice Tully Hall one Saturday morning: quietly singing to herself a blues number that Marsalis had made up and introduced at the concert she had just attended.

You see, Charisma Jones is just six. And while she was unable to articulate exactly what she had liked about Marsalis's "Jazz for Young People" concert when I put that question to her, it was obvious Marsalis had reached her. And not just her.

"He was funny," explained Tamara Leacock, age seven.

"Yeah, I liked it when his drummer picked up the trumpet and made it sound like a chicken," added nine-year-old Jesse Rhodes.

And even if children were the target audience, they weren't the only ones to benefit from that particular concert, whose subject was "the blues." One parent in attendance, Dr. Reed Pitts, acknowledged, "Although I've listened to Marsalis before, I've never understood the blues until today."

Considering the sorry state of music education in this country (and things have only gotten worse in recent years, as art and music programs have fallen victims to budget cutbacks), there's a real need for the children's concerts Marsalis periodically offers.

Occasionally that morning Marsalis was over the children's heads and you could see them growing fidgety, but for the most part he succeeded in making difficult concepts seem simple. He'd get one part of the audience to chant out a Charleston rhythm ("*Charles*-ton, *Charles*-ton, *Charles*-ton…") and then get the other half to superimpose a scatted melodic line, which changed (in classic blues pattern) after being repeated twice. He listened to their questions, and dropped names of bygone jazz greats that he felt they should be aware of. He was helping to acquaint kids, who might otherwise be exposed to little more than rap and rock, to a valuable part of their heritage.

He had children learning basic chords, which they sang as his band played. He had them count along with him as the chords changed (as caught in Andreas Johnsen's final photo). His first-rate septet, sounding more relaxed than it sometimes has in concerts for adults, demonstrated ways of "walking the blues," "swinging the blues," and "stomping the blues," while playing music by everyone from Jelly Roll Morton and King Oliver to John Coltrane. They were passing on a bit of the jazz canon to the next generation, sharing what had been passed down to them by the jazz veterans they'd learned from. And I was very glad to see that. Otherwise the contributions of the many veterans presented in this book would all simply die with them.

BIBLIOGRAPHY

Balliett, Whitney, *American Musicians: 56 Portraits in Jazz*. New York, Oxford University Press, 1986.

Balliett, Whitney, *American Singers: 27 Portraits in Song*. New York, Oxford University Press, 1988.

Balliett, Whitney, *Barney, Bradley, and Max: 16 Portraits in Jazz*. New York, Oxford University Press, 1989.

Basie, Count as told to Albert Murray, *Good Morning Blues: The Autobiography of Count Basie*. New York, Random House, 1985.

Berendt, Joachim-Ernst, ed., *The Story of Jazz*. Englewood Cliff, N.J., Prentice-Hall, 1978.

Berger, Morroe, Edward Berger, and James Patrick, *Benny Carter: A Life in American Music*. Metuchen, N.J., Scarecrow Press and the Institute of Jazz Studies, Rutgers University, 1982.

Bruyninckx, Walter, *Sixty Years of Recorded Jazz, 1917-1977*. Mechelen, Belgium, n.p., 1978.

Case, Brian and Stan Britt, revised and updated by Chrissie Murray, *The Harmony Illustrated Encyclopedia of Jazz*, third edition. New York, Harmony Books, 1986.

Charters, Samuel B. and Leonard Kunstadt, *Jazz: A History of the New York Scene*. New York, Da Capo Press, 1981.

Chilton, John, *The Song of the Hawk: The Life and Recordings of Coleman Hawkins*. Ann Arbor, University of Michigan Press, 1990.

Chilton, John, *Who's Who of Jazz*, fourth edition. New York, Da Capo Press, 1985.

Clayton, Buck, assisted by Nancy Miller Elliott, *Buck Clayton's Jazz World*. New York, Oxford University Press, 1987.

Collier, James Lincoln, *Duke Ellington*. New York, Oxford University Press, 1987.

Dahl, Linda, *Stormy Weather: The Music and Lives of a Century of Jazzwomen*. New York, Pantheon Books, 1984.

Dance, Stanley, *The World of Count Basie*. New York, Charles Scribner's Sons, 1980.

Dance, Stanley, *The World of Duke Ellington*. New York, Charles Scribner's Sons, 1970.

Dance, Stanley, *The World of Earl Hines*. New York, Charles Scribner's Sons, 1977.

Dance, Stanley, *The World of Swing*. New York, Charles Scribner's Sons, 1974.

Davis, Francis, *In the Moment: Jazz in the 1980s*. New York, Oxford University Press, 1986.

Davis, Miles, *Miles: The Autobiography*. New York, Simon and Schuster, 1989.

Deffaa, Chip, *In the Mainstream*. Metuchen, N.J., Scarecrow Press and the Institute of Jazz Studies, Rutgers University, 1992.

Deffaa, Chip, *Swing Legacy*. Metuchen, N.J., Scarecrow Press and the Institute of Jazz Studies, Rutgers University, 1989.

Deffaa, Chip, *Traditionalists and Revivalists in Jazz*. Metuchen, N.J., Scarecrow Press and the Institute of Jazz Studies, Rutgers University, 1993.

Deffaa, Chip, *Voices of the Jazz Age*. Urbana, University of Illinois Press, 1990.

Driggs, Frank and Harris Lewine, *Black Beauty, White Heat: A Pictorial History of Classic Jazz, 1920-1950*. New York, William Morrow and Company, 1982.

Ellington, Duke, *Music is My Mistress*. Garden City, N. Y., Doubleday, 1973.

Feather, Leonard, *The Encyclopedia of Jazz*. New York, Da Capo Press, 1985.

Feather, Leonard and Ira Gitler, *The Encyclopedia of Jazz in the '70s*. New York, Da Capo Press, 1987.

Feather, Leonard, *The Encyclopedia of Jazz in the '60s*. New York, Da Capo Press, 1986.

Feather, Leonard, *From Satchmo to Miles*. Briarcliff Manor, N. Y., Stein and Day, 1972.

Ferguson, Otis, *The Otis Ferguson Reader* (edited by Dorothy Chamberlain and Robert Wilson). Highland Park, Ill., December Press, 1983.

Friedwald, Will, *Jazz Singing*. New York, Charles Scribner's Sons, 1989.

Giddins, Gary, *Rhythm-a-ning: Jazz Traditions and Innovation in the '80s*. New York, Oxford University Press, 1985.

Giddins, Gary, *Riding on a Blue Note*. New York, Oxford University Press, 1981.

Giddins, Gary, *Satchmo*. New York, A Dolphin Book, Doubleday, 1988.

Gitler, Ira, *Jazz Masters of the Forties*. New York, Collier Books, 1966.

Gitler, Ira, *Swing to Bop*. New York, Oxford University Press, 1985.

Goodman, Benny, and Irving Kolodin, *The Kingdom of Swing*. New York, Frederick Ungar Publishing Company, 1961.

Gordon, Max, *Live at the Village Vanguard*. New York, Da Capo Press, 1982.

Gottlieb, William P., *The Golden Age of Jazz*. New York, Da Capo Press, 1985.

Gourse, Leslie, *Louis' Children: American Jazz Singers*. New York, Quill, 1984.

Gourse, Leslie, *Sassy: The Life of Sarah Vaughan*. New York, Charles Scribner's Sons, 1993.

Hadlock, Richard, *Jazz Masters of the Twenties*. New York, Macmillan, 1965.

Hemming, Roy, and David Hajdu, *Discovering Great Singers of Classic Pop*. New York, Newarket Press, 1991.

Holiday, Billie, with William Dufty, *Lady Sings the Blues*. New York, Lancer Books, 1969.

Johnsen, John R. (photos) and Erik Aschengreen, Niels-Jorgen Kaiser, and Ebbe Monk (texts), *Dance in Tivoli*. Copenhagen, Borgen Publishers, 1983.

Jones, Max, *Talking Jazz*. New York, W. W. Norton, 1987.

Keepnews, Orrin, *The View From Within: Jazz Writings, 1948-1987*. New York, Oxford University Press, 1988.

Keepnews, Orrin and Bill Grauer, Jr., *A Pictorial History of Jazz*. New York, Bonanza Books, 1966.

Kernfeld, Barry, ed., *The New Grove Dictionary of Jazz*. New York, Grove's Dictionaries of Music, 1988.

Lax, Roger and Frederick Smith, *The Great Song Thesaurus*. New York, Oxford University Press, 1984.

Lees, Gene, *Waiting for Dizzy*. New York, Oxford University Press, 1991.

Levey, Joseph, *The Jazz Experience*. Englewood Cliffs, N.J., Prenctice-Hall, 1983.

Litweiler, John, *The Freedom Principle, Jazz After 1958*. New York, William Morrow and Company, 1984.

McPartland, Marian, *All in Good Time*. New York, Oxford University Press, 1987.

Morgenstern, Dan (text) and Ole Brask (photographs), *Jazz People*. New York, Harry N. Abrams, Inc., 1976.

Pearson, Jr., Nathan W. *Goin' to Kansas City*. Urbana, University of Illinois Press, 1987.

Pleasants, Henry, *The Great American Popular Singers*. New York, Simon and Schuster, 1974.

Ramsey, Frederick, Jr. and Charles Edward Smith, editors, *Jazzmen*. New York, Limelight Editions, 1985.

Reisner, Robert George, *The Jazz Titans*. Garden City, N. Y., Doubleday, 1960.

Rust, Brian, *Jazz Records, 1897-1942*. Chigwell, England, Storyville Publications, 1982.

Sanford, Herb, *Tommy and Jimmy: The Dorsey Years*. New York, Da Capo Press, 1980.

Santoro, Gene, *Dancing in Your Head*. New York, Oxford University Press, 1984.

Schuller, Gunther, *Early Jazz*. New York, Oxford University Press, 1968.

Schuller, Gunther, *Musing*. New York, Oxford University Press, 1986.

Schuller, Gunther, *The Swing Era*. New York, Oxford University Press, 1989.

Shapiro, Nat and Nat Hentoff, editors, *Hear Me Talkin' to Ya*. New York, Dover Publications, 1966.

Shapiro, Nat and Nat Hentoff, editors, *The Jazz Makers*. New York, Rinehart, 1957.

Shaw, Arnold, *52nd Street: The Street of Jazz*. New York, DaCapo Press, 1977.

Simon, George T., *The Big Bands*. New York, Schirmer Books, 1981.

Simon, George T., *Simon Says: The Sights and Sounds of the Swing Era, 1935-1955*. New York, Galahad Books, 1971.

Stearns, Marshall, *The Story of Jazz*. New York, Mentor Books, 1958.

Stewart, Rex, *Jazz Masters of the Thirties*. New York, Macmillan, 1972.

Stratemann, Klaus, *Duke Ellington, Day by Day and Film by Film*. Copenhagen, JazzMedia ApS, 1992.

Sudhalter, Richard M. and Philip R. Evans, with William Dean-Myatt, *Bix, Man and Legend*. New Rochelle, New York, Arlington House, 1974.

Whitburn, Joel, *Pop Memories, 1890-1954: The History of American Popular Music*. Menomonee Falls, Wisconsin, Record Research, 1986.

Whitcomb, Ian, *After the Ball: Pop Music from Rag to Rock*. New York, Limelight Editions, 1986.

Williams, Martin, *Jazz Heritage*. New York, Oxford University Press, 1985.

Williams, Martin, ed., *The Art of Jazz*. New York, Oxford University Press, 1959.

Williams, Martin, *Jazz Heritage*. New York, Oxford University Press, 1985.

ACKNOWLEDGMENTS

This has been a complex project to carry off. The know-how, enthusiasm, and good will of editors John Fremont and Cynthia Frank, and their colleagues at Cypress House, who've invested many more hours in this undertaking than they originally planned on, are greatly appreciated. John and Cynthia — many thanks!

In writing this book, my primary sources have been the musicians themselves. I am deeply indebted to the many artists who have taken time to talk with me, whether in formal interviews or in casual chats at clubs and recording studios; they have provided invaluable first-hand information. To the dynamic Illinois Jacquet, the first jazz musician I ever saw "live" in a club and still a favorite; the ever-gracious and dignified Benny Carter, who made a profound and enduring impact upon me at Princeton some 25 years ago; and all the rest: thanks again. Without knowing it, Carter (whose photo I took at his Los Angeles home) planted the seed for this project.

In this book, I've written things at times from memory — things I've learned so long ago that in some cases I've forgotten just where I first learned them. I want to express gratitude to writers about jazz who've helped shape my understanding of it; facts and opinions they have provided have filtered into my work.

Such authorities as Dan Morgenstern, Stanley Dance, George T. Simon, John S. Wilson, and Leonard Feather qualify as "jazz veterans," no less than the musicians this book has focused on. They've spent decades chronicling the art form.

Dan Morgenstern (photographed by Andreas Johnsen), a former editor of *Down Beat* magazine and the ASCAP-Deems Taylor Award-winning author of *Jazz People*, is the Director of the Institute of Jazz Studies at Rutgers University in Newark, New Jersey. In my research on music, he and his associates, Ed Berger, Vincent Pelote, and Don Luck, have always been there for me, to answer questions or suggest avenues to explore. The Institute's renowned collection of jazz clippings, oral histories, records, and books has been an excellent source of background information for this book. (I don't know of another research facility that operates on quite the open-door policy of the Institute of Jazz Studies.) I've also been reading Morgenstern's liner notes all my life; he's one of the few annotators whose comments — kindly, judicious, and always well-informed — have stayed with me for decades. I can play certain albums and remember not just listening to them for the first time, but reading Morgenstern's notes as I listened in my Campbell Hall dorm room in college.

Grammy-winning writer Stanley Dance and his wife and occasional collaborator, Helen Oakley Dance (photographed here by Nancy Miller Elliott), have been part of the jazz scene since the 1930s. I've enjoyed their contributions to *Down Beat*, *Coda*, *Jazz Journal*, and books, appreciating that as eye-witnesses their commentary meant more than that of younger writers reconstructing jazz history from recordings and clippings. Anyone who attempts to deal with Duke Ellington, Count Basie, Earl Hines, or various other mainstream greats will be in Stanley Dance's debt; he did so many important interviews with now-deceased musicians that have been — and long will continue to be — repeatedly cited. (Mercer Ellington once told me humbly that Dance knew more about his own father's career and music than he did.) And Helen Oakley Dance, as one of the pioneering women working in the jazz world, has been a source of inspiration for Nancy Miller Elliott.

George T. Simon's joyously enthusiastic big-band reviews from the 1930s, '40s, and '50s are likewise invaluable primary sources, and his books, like Stanley Dance's, belong in any basic collection. He's also been exceptionally kind to me. *New Yorker* writer Whitney Balliett's profiles are perhaps the most elegantly written in jazz history. (Among the critics for daily newspapers, I often thought the erudite Dick Sudhalter, another important guide for me, had the most graceful style.) John S. Wilson had a subtle way of indicating artists' exact strengths and weaknesses without ever so much as a hint of meanness. Nat Hentoff's writings on jazz were so authoritative, I often wished he did more of it. (But I'll read and take seriously his writings on any almost any topic.)

If the late Leonard Feather had done nothing more than produce (with assistance from Ira Gitler) his esteemed *Encyclopedias of Jazz*, he'd have earned an honored spot in the pantheon of jazz chroniclers. Everyone who's written about jazz in the past 40 years has benefited from Feather's research. He maintained an extraordinarily high overall level of productivity from the 1930s into the 1990s, writing reviews, books, and songs, producing recordings, lecturing, and so on. (The

photo, courtesy of University of Idaho photo services, was taken when Feather, Gitler, and I shared a panel at the 1993 Lionel Hampton Jazz Festival.)

Growing up, I read and re-read everything I could find by Morgenstern, Dance, Simon, Balliett, Wilson, Hentoff, and Feather. I was reading them before Gary Giddins (perhaps the wisest and most knowledgeable of the reviewers writing today) came on the scene. Since Giddins began writing in the '70s, he's been essential reading for me, too. In more recent years, I've benefited, also, from the writings of Stanley Crouch, Gene Lees, Peter Watrous, Gene Santoro, Gene Seymour, Bill Milkowski, Josef Woodard, Jon Pareles, Bob Blumenthal, Ken Franckling, John McDonough, Stuart Troup, Becca Pulliam, Bill Quinn, John Diliberto, W. Patrick Hinely, Dave Burns, George Kanzler, Leslie Gourse, Scott Yanow, Kevin Whitehead, Jonathan Aig, David Hinkley, Loren Schoenberg, Will Friedwald, Lee Jeske, Sid Gribetz, and others. Their contributions to such publications as *Down Beat, JazzTimes, Coda, Cadence,* and *Crescendo* (all of which I read regularly), as well as liner notes, have become part of my store of knowledge and are in some way a part of this book. I'm indebted to Philip Elwood, longtime critic of *The San Francisco Examiner* for, among other things, supplying the quote from Friedenrich Hundertwasser which opens this book. (He found it inscribed at KunstHausWien, Vienna, Austria.)

I also feel a certain debt to George Wein, a "jazz veteran" whose contributions may too often be taken for granted. For more than 40 years, he's been producing or co-producing some of the most important presentations of live jazz in the world. Long before I became a professional critic and got to know Wein at all, I was buying tickets to his Newport Jazz Festival concerts, gaining my first exposure to Dizzy Gillespie, Cab Calloway, Ella Fitzgerald, and many other greats included in this book. His JVC Jazz Festival (a descendant of the original Newport Jazz Festival) remains a high point of the year for me. Wein (photographed by Roslyn Dickens) has done so much to keep jazz popular, he deserves a thank-you.

Billy Taylor deserves acknowledgment, too; his easy-going, informative TV and radio commentaries on jazz have long helped educate appreciative listeners (of which I'm one). He's helped spread the word about jazz far and wide. Andreas Johnsen's photo (below) catches Taylor relaxing backstage at a Highlights in Jazz concert with one of the greatest of all baritone sax players — a man who found previously undreamed-of suppleness on that instrument — the late Gerry Mulligan.

This book has benefited from input, suggestions, and contacts provided by many individuals. I appreciate the assistance in various ways that has been offered by Frank Reuter (the "first reader" of most of this book, as he was on my previous books), Gary Westby-Gibson (who's carefully vetted this book, along with others of mine), Harlem cultural historian Delilah Jackson, Geoffrey Vasile, Joe Franklin, David Hajdu, Roy Hemming, Bill Titone, Rich Conaty, Andy Rowan, Joe Boughton, Merilee Trost, Frank Driggs, Russ Dantzler, Marilyn Lipsius, Michael Bloom, and Didier Deutsch. My thanks, too, to

Wendell Echols, George Buck, C. A. Tripp, Jeff Nissim, Charles Bourgeois, Sherwin Dunner, Phoebe Jacobs, Marian McPartland, Jack Kleinsinger, Phil Leshin, Richard Sudhalter, Lloyd Rauch, Phil Evans, Ian Whitcomb, "Sister" Lynda Barry, Andrew Mytelka, Terry Lilly, David Gersten, Wil Wheaton, David Lotz, Frank Jolliffe, Rebecca Reitz, Peter Levinson, Helene Greece, and Abby Hoffer. I'm grateful to Lynn Skinner, Carolea Webb, Brenda Cain, Susan Erstine, Travis Quast, Chris Miller, and the staff of the Lionel Hampton Jazz Festival.

I'm grateful to the many young musicians I've met when I've given clinics and lectures. They inspire hope for the future of the artform. And they've directed some good jazz-history inquiries at me over the years—a number of which I've sought to answer in this book.

I appreciate also help received from Karl Emil Knudsen and the Danish Jazz Center, Vince Giordano, Howard Cruse, Bernice Doyle, Matthew Broderick, Sarah Jessica Parker, Sean Donahue, Lance Jonathan, Virginia Wicks, Deborah Grace Winer, Chuck Mann, James Gavin, Amy Kean, Wayman Wong, Orrin and Peter Keepnews, Wendel Trupstock, Steve Ridgeway, Andrea du Plessis, Tom Terrell, Jodi Petlin, Jane Dexter, A. Scott Berg, Anna Delyne, Michael Kerker of ASCAP, and Ellison Photos. Thanks to Danny Scott for devising the "basic typewriter mufflers" that made my work easier, and to Eric Orseck and Chris Burchfield for valuable help early on. By asking the right questions or supplying the right comments at the right time, some people have been more helpful than they realized. (Trombone-player David Broadbent fits in that category.) My gratitude — as always — to Princeton's ever-supportive Ferris Professor of Journalism Emeritus Irving Dilliard and his colleague Landon Y. Jones.

Thanks are due, too, to the editors of the various publications for which I have had opportunities, over the years, to write about the jazz musicians covered in this book: V. A. Musetto, Matthew Diebel, Steve Cuozzo, Jim Pratt, Cindy Killian, Clarence Fanto, and Sue Byrom of *The New York Post,* Mary Kaye Schilling, Dulcy Israel, and Ethan Smith of *Entertainment Weekly,* Mike Joyce, W. Royal Stokes, and Ira and Glenn Sabin of *JazzTimes,* Bill Smith and John Norris of *Coda,* Leslie Johnson of the *Mississippi Rag,* Rick Mattingly and Rick Van Horn of *Modern Drummer,* Ed Shanaphy of *Sheet Music Magazine,* Art Lange of *Down Beat,* Chuck Creesy and Jim Merritt of the *Princeton Alumni Weekly,* Bob Cannon of *Tutti,* Larry Marscheck of *New Jersey Monthly,* Warren Vaché Sr. of *Jersey Jazz,* and Dennis Matthews of *Crescendo.* I might add that my editors at *The Post* have shown most welcome support of jazz, and not just in print. V. A. Musetto is a Phil Schaap listener. I'll run into Steve Cuozzo at Illinois Jacquet opening nights. And Matt and Barbara Diebel even went so far as to hire the Flying Neutrinos jazz band to play at their wedding.

My deep gratitude to my family almost goes without saying.

Nancy Miller Elliott and I first began work on this project six years ago; John and Andreas Johnsen became involved a bit later on. It's been more of a pleasure and privilege to collaborate with them on this book than I can express. Here's hoping we might all have a chance to do it again sometime.

ABOUT THE COLLABORATORS

Chip Deffaa, the ASCAP-Deems Taylor Award-winning jazz critic of *The New York Post*, contributes regularly to such publications as *Entertainment Weekly*, *JazzTimes*, and *Crescendo and Jazz Music*. His books include *Swing Legacy*, Scarecrow Press; *Voices of the Jazz Age*, University of Illinois Press; *In the Mainstream*, Scarecrow Press; *Traditionalists and Revivalists in Jazz*, Scarecrow Press; *C'Mon Get Happy*, co-authored with David Cassidy, Warner Books; and *Blue Rhythms*, University of Illinois Press. He is a trustee of *The Princeton Tiger Magazine*. Further details about Deffaa may be found in *Who's Who in the World*, 12th edition, Marquis.

Nancy Miller Elliott's photographs have appeared in such publications as *The Village Voice*, *The New York Daily News*, *The New York Times*, and *Newsweek*, and in such books as *Jazz Giants, Talking Jazz, What Do They Want?, Swing Legacy, Wishing on the Moon, Voices of the Jazz Age, Homeless in America, Traditionalists and Revivalists in Jazz, Keeping Covenant with the Poor,* and *The New Grove Dictionary of Jazz*. Lauded in *Artforum International* for their "lucidity and strength," Elliott's photos have been exhibited in such cities as New York, Los Angeles, Chicago, Nashville, Portland, and Houston. Her work may be found in the permanent photo collections of the Library of the Performing Arts at Lincoln Center and the Institute of Jazz Studies at Rutgers. She is a member of the National Academy of Recording Arts and Sciences. She co-authored *Buck Clayton's Jazz World*, Oxford University Press.

Capturing artists at work is the forte of the widely traveled, Copenhagen-based father and son team of John and Andreas Johnsen. John R. Johnsen, who has distinguished himself as a photographer of dancers as well as of jazz musicians, has had his photographs exhibited at the Georges Pompidou Center in Paris, the Copenhagen Museum of Decorative Art, the Stockholm Opera, and the Kennedy Center for the Performing Arts in Washington, D.C., among many other venues. His work may be found in the permanent photo collection of the Schomburg Center for Research in Black Culture. His photo books include *Ballet Bogen*, Gyldendal; *Dance in Tivoli*, Borgen; and *Skandinavisk Ballet*, Bonniers. A tireless chronicler of both the international hip-hop and jazz scenes, Andreas Johnsen's photos have appeared on postcards and albums, and in such publications as *Politiken, Information, The Amsterdam News, Jazz Special, Jazz Ambassador, The Mississippi Rag, The New York Post,* and *JazzTimes*. He is a regular contributor to Europe's *Crescendo and Jazz Music*. He is now working on a full-color photo book about hip-hop for the Danish publishing firm of Tiderne Skifter.

The collaborators, who are available for lectures, clinics, and exhibits, may be contacted care of the publishers or at their own addresses: Chip Deffaa, *The New York Post* Entertainment Department, 1211 Avenue of the Americas, New York, NY 10036-8790 USA; Nancy Miller Elliott, Claytellio Music Inc., Suite 2-B, 508 E. 78th St., New York, NY 10021 USA: John and Andreas Johnsen, Rosforth and Rosforth, Box 1128, DK 1160, Copenhagen K, Denmark.

Pages 249 and 250 contain photo credits. On these pages, NME refers to photographer Nancy Miller Elliott, JRJ to John R. Johnsen, AJ to Andreas Johnsen, and CD to Chip Deffaa. The names of other photographers and contributors are spelled out.

CREDITS

111. Cootie Williams, photo by JRJ
112. Ben Webster, photo by JRJ
113. Ben Webster plays sax while Duke Ellington looks on, photo by JRJ
114. Upper right-hand corner: Ben Webster, photo by JRJ; bottom half of the page, from left to right: Paul Gonsalves, Harold Ashby, Ben Webster, Harry Carney, and Norris Turney, photo by JRJ
115. Paul Gonsalves, photo by JRJ
116. Harold Ashby, photo by NME
117. A three-shot sequence: Harold Ashby plays sax, urged on by Duke Ellington, photos by JRJ
118. Ella Fitzgerald and Duke Ellington, photo by JRJ
120. Louie Bellson, photo by JRJ
121. Mercer Ellington conducts the Duke Ellington Orchestra, photo by JRJ
123. Mercer Ellington, photo by NME
124. Clark Terry, photo by AJ
125. Clark Terry, photo by NME
126. Nancy Miller Elliott and Louis Armstrong, photo by Jack Bradley
128. Lower left-hand column: the entrance to Preservation Hall, New Orleans, photo by AJ; upper right-hand column: Willie Humphrey, standing in front of his home in New Orleans, photo by AJ
129. Two views of Percy and Willie Humphrey in Preservation Hall, photos by AJ
130. Evelyn Gorham and Percy Humphrey in front of their home in New Orleans, photo by AJ
131. Arvell Shaw, photo by NME
133. Archie Johnson, photo by NME
134. Roy Eldridge, photo by NME
135. Roy Eldridge, photo by JRJ
136. Dizzy Gillespie, photo by JRJ
138. Charlie Parker, archival photo courtesy of Fantasy Records
140. Doris Parker and CD, photo by AJ
142. Thelonious Monk, photo by JRJ
143. Thelonious Monk, photo by JRJ
144. Charlie Rouse playing sax, with Thelonious Monk at the piano, photo by JRJ
146. Tommy Potter, photo by NME
148. Kenny Kersey with Thomas Elliott, photo by NME
149. Kenny Kersey, photo by NME
152. Big Nick Nicholas, photo by NME
153. Max Roach, photo by JRJ
154. Max Roach, photo by JRJ
156. Tal Farlow, photo by NME
157. Tal Farlow, photo by NME
159. Miles Davis, photo by NME
160. Miles Davis, photo by NME
162. Buck Clayton, photo by NME
163. Miles Davis, photo by JRJ

164. Miles Davis, photo by JRJ
165. Upper right-hand corner: Miles Davis, photo by JRJ; bottom half of page: John Scofield and Miles Davis, photo by JRJ
166. Both shots of Miles Davis by JRJ
167. Duke Jordan, photo by AJ
168. All three shots of Duke Jordan by AJ
169: Sheila Jordan, photo by AJ
170. Sheila Jordan and Harvie Swartz, photo by AJ
171. Carmen McRae, photo by NME
172. Carmen McRae, photo by NME
174. Sarah Vaughan and Billy Eckstine, photo by JRJ
175. Sarah Vaughan, photo by JRJ
177. Billy Eckstine, Mercer Ellington, and Sarah Vaughan, photo by JRJ
179. Abbey Lincoln, photo by AJ
180. Betty Carter, photo by JRJ
181. Betty Carter, photo by JRJ
182. Betty Carter with the Reed Sisters (Brittany, Tanya, and Brandi), photo by AJ
183. From left to right: Michelle Hendricks, Jon Hendricks, and Clark Terry, photo by AJ
184. Bobby Short signing an autograph for an unidentified fan, photo by AJ
185. Jack Kleinsinger and Bobby Short, photo by AJ
186. Nancy Miller Elliott and Bobby Short, photo by CD
187. Ellis Larkins, photo by NME
189. Marian McPartland, photo by AJ
190. Midway down left-hand column: Marian McPartland and Hank Jones, photo by CD; at top of right-hand column: Marian McPartland and Barbara Carroll, photo by AJ
191. From left to right: Marian McPartland, Buck Clayton, and Jimmy McPartland, photo by NME
192. John Bunch, photo by NME
193. Romano Mussolini, photo by CD
194. Romano Mussolini signs autograph for an unidentified youth, photo by CD
195. From left to right: Ira Gitler, Jan Holland, and Romano Mussolini, photo by CD
196. Bruce Frederickson and John Lewis, photo by NME
198. Dick Hyman and Ruby Braff, photo by NME
199. Ruby Braff, photo by NME
200. Tommy Flanagan, photo by AJ
201. In upper right-hand corner: Tommy Flanagan, photo by NME; centered below: Tommy Flanagan, photo by AJ
202. Max Gordon, photo by NME
203. Jabbo Smith and Lorraine Gordon, photo by NME

205. From left to right: Jabbo Smith, Mel Lewis, Max Gordon, and Buck Clayton, photo by NME
206. Dennis Mackrel and Mel Lewis, photo by NME
208. Toshiko Akiyoshi, photo by NME
210. Stan Getz, photo by JRJ
211. Stan Getz, photo by JRJ
213. Chet Baker, photo by AJ
214. Upper left-hand column: Chet Baker, photo by AJ; upper right-hand column: Chet Baker, photo by JRJ; lower right-hand column: Chet Baker, photo by AJ
215. Dizzy Gillespie, photo by JRJ
216. Dizzy Gillespie and Bill Watrous, photo by JRJ
217. Dizzy Gillespie, publicity photo courtesy of Dizzy Gillespie
218. Dizzy Gillespie, publicity photo courtesy of Philip Caggiano
219. Art Blakey, photo by JRJ
220. Art Blakey, photo by JRJ
222. Jean Bach, photo by NME
223. From left to right: Lorraine Feather, Marian McPartland, Jean Bach, Virginia Wicks, Jan Holland, and Jane Jarvis, photo by CD
224. Cliff Lee (on trumpet) and his group, photo by AJ
225. Bill Lee, photo by AJ
226. Lower left-hand column: Chip Deffaa and Johnny Griffin, photo by AJ; upper right-hand column: Johnny Griffin, photo by AJ
227. Both shots of Johnny Griffin by AJ
228. Ornette Coleman, photo by JRJ
229. Ornette Coleman, photo by JRJ
231. Sonny Rollins, both photos by JRJ
232. Sonny Rollins, photo by AJ
233. Sonny Rollins, photo by JRJ
234. Sonny Rollins, both photos by AJ
235. Wynton Marsalis, both photos by AJ
236. Wynton Marsalis and Buck Clayton, photo by NME
237. Wynton Marsalis, photo by AJ
241. Saxophone on chair, photo by NME
244. Midway down left-hand column: Benny Carter, photo by CD; upper right-hand column: Dan Morgenstern, photo by AJ; lower right-hand column: Helen and Stanley Dance, photo by NME
245. Lower left-hand column: Leonard Feather, courtesy of University of Idaho photo services; lower right-hand column: George Wein, publicity photo by Roslyn Dickens, courtesy of the Jazz Ministry at St. Peters Church, New York City
246. Midway down left-hand column: Gerry Mulligan and Billy Taylor, photo by AJ; midway down right-hand column: Skyline High School Jazz Ensemble, Salt Lake City, photo by CD

INDEX

A

"A-tisket A-tasket," 33
Adderley, Cannonball, 161
"After You've Gone," 87
Ain't Misbehavin', 132
Akiyoshi, Toshiko, 208-209
Akiyoshi-Tabackin Band, 208, 209
Alden, Howard, 92, 93, 104
Alden-Barrett Quintet, 86, 104, 185
Alexander, Willard, 101-102
"All American Rhythm Section," 73
"All of Me," 178
Allen, Henry "Red," 8, 28, 150, 155
Allen, Steve, 59
"Amazing Grace," 217
American Jazz Orchestra, 99, 109, 197
Ammons, Gene, 168, 221
Anderson, Marian, 34
Andrews Sisters, 54
Andy Kirk Band, 112, 142, 150
Andy Kirk's Clouds of Joy Band, 150
Anniversary, 212
Anthony, Ray, 206-207
"Anthropology," 137
"Apollo Jump," 133
Apollo Theatre, 31, 37
Armstrong, Louis, 3, 4, 9, 14, 18, 20, 29, 34, 39, 43, 55, 57, 67, 78, 80, 88, 97, 99, 126-127, 128, 130, 131, 132, 135, 185, 191, 199, 213, 236, 238
Armstrong Legacy Band, 132
Art Blakey's Jazz Messengers, 219, 221, 226
Arthur Taylor's Wailers, 140
"As Time Goes By," 151
Ashby, Harold, 113, 116-117
"Ash's Cap," 117
Asmussen, Svend, 51, 76
Astaire, Fred, 53, 186
"At the Fat Man's," 58
Auld, Georgie, 59

B

Bach, Jean, 186, 222-223
Bachardy, Don, 49
Bagneris, Vernel, 4
Bailey, Buster, 18
Bailey, Mildred, 185
Bailey, Pearl, 119, 192
Baker, Chet, 213-214
Baker, Mickey, 8
Banks, Danny, 15
Banks, Nancie, 140
Barbarin, Paul, 128
Barefield, Eddie, 61-62
Barker, Blue Lu, 8
Barnes, George, 199
Barnet, Charlie, 71, 96, 125
Barrett, Dan, 104
Barron, Kenny, 145
"Basie," 89
Basie, Count, 5, 11, 14, 22, 27, 61-69, 87, 92-102, 115, 125, 145, 197, 207
Basie Alumni Band, 78
"Basie Talks," 89
"Baubles, Bangles, and Beads," 53
Bechet, Sidney, 8, 29, 59, 87
Bedford, Tommy, 3
"Begin the Beguine," 49
Beiderbecke, Bix, 7, 9, 49, 78, 191, 238, 239
Belle of the Nineties, 69
Bellson, Louie, 17, 48, 119-120
"Ben Webster, The Brute and the Beautiful," 114
Beneke, Tex, 207
Benford, Tommy, 27
Bennett, Tony, 192, 200
Bennie Moten Band, 63, 77, 112
Benny Carter: A Life in American Music, 24
Benny Carter Orchestra, 173
Benny Goodman Band, 41, 48
Benson, George, 101, 195
Berger, Edward, 24

Berger, Morroe, 24
Berigan, Bunny, 55, 58, 185, 199
Berlin, Irving, 33
Bernie, Banjo, 133
Best of Intentions, The, 50
Big Bands, The, 48
"Big Bands, The," 59
"Big Nick," 151
Big and Warm, 151
Bigard, Barney, 49
Billie Holiday — The Legacy, 69
Billy Eckstine's Big Band, 221
Bird, 141
"Bird Gets the Worm, The," 147
Birdland (club), 81
"Birth of the Cool," 155
Bitches Brew, 161
"Black Beauty," 194
Black and Blue, 37
"Black and Blue," 75
Blake, Eubie, 8, 190
Blakey, Art, 142, 151, 219-222, 226
Blanchard, Terence, 221
"Blanche Calloway and Her Joy Boys," 133
Blanton, Jimmy, 112
"Blanton/Webster Band," 112
Blood on the Fields, 235
"Blue Lou," 71
"Blue Minor," 29
Blue Note (club), 8, 72, 156, 173, 176, 177, 183, 204
"Blue and Sentimental," 78
"Blue Serge," 122
"Blues Backstage," 99
Bocage, Peter, 88
"Body and Soul," 21
"Bongo Bop," 147
"Boogie Woogie Blue Plate," 54
"Boogie Woogie Cocktail," 150
Booker, Bobby, 133
Boone, Pat, 118
"Bootsie," 89

Booze, Bea, 8
Boswell, Connie, 31
Bowles, Russell, 27
Boyd Raeburn Band, 206
Bracken, Jimmy, 47
Bradshaw, Tony, 151
Braff, Ruby, 26, 28, 101, 198-199
Braxton, Anthony, 155
Bregman, Buddy, 33
Brice, Percy, 26
Brown, Clifford, 155, 221
Brown, Donald, 219
Brown, James, 86
Brown, Laurence, 27
Brown, Lawrence, 119
Brown, Les, 192
Brown, Oscar, Jr., 155
Brown, Ray, 217
Brown, Ruth, 34, 176
Brunious, Wendell, 130
Bryant, Willie, 71
Bubbling Brown Sugar, 132
Buck Clayton Band, 86, 207
Buddy Rich's Band, 102
Bunch, John, 138, 192
Burkhardt, Jay, 90
Bush, Pres. George, 45
Bushkin, Joe, 54-55, 57
"But She's My Buddy's Chick," 58
Butler, Jack, 3
Byas, Don, 20, 226
"Bye, Bye Blackbird," 161, 225
Byler, Bob, 7
Byrd, Donald, 140, 181, 217, 221

C

Cab Calloway Band, 9, 38
"Cabbage Song, The," 129
Cafe Carlyle, 184
Cafe Society, 28
Cage, John, 230
Call Me Mister, 186
Calloway, Blanche, 87, 133
Calloway, Cab, 9, 14, 38, 48, 53, 61, 62
Campbell, Floyd, 14
Capp, Frank, 97
Carisi, Johnny, 138
Carlos 1 (club), 125
Carnegie Hall, 10, 34, 62, 71, 74, 79, 99, 174, 176, 231

Carney, Harry, 113, 122
Carroll, Barbara, 190
Carter, Benny, 10, 22-24, 25, 27, 49, 53, 87, 99, 101, 113, 133, 135, 138, 173, 189
Carter, Betty, 151, 173, 180-182
Carter, Ron, 161, 197
Casey, Al, 26
"Cash Box," 89
Castle, Lee, 66, 106
Cat Club, 37, 103-104, 105
Catlett, Sid, 8, 71
Celebrity Club, 83
"Centerpiece," 79
Central Plaza (club), 29
Challis, Bill, 22
Channing, Carol, 204
Charles, Ray, 93
Charlie Johnson Band, 22, 25
"Chasing Shadows," 135
Cheatham, Doc, 8, 9-13, 14, 29, 94, 236
"Cheatin' on Me," 57
"Cherokee," 26
Cherry, Don, 3, 106, 230,
Chicago Jazz Summit, 7
Chick Webb Band, 27, 29, 31
"Chocolate Beau Brummels," 133
Christian, Charlie, 101, 150, 156
Clark Terry's Spacemen, 125
Clarke, Kenny, 141, 142, 150, 155, 227
Clayton, Buck, 28, 65, 67, 68, 69-70, 77, 78, 80, 85, 86, 88, 101-104, 116, 147, 150, 161, 164, 191, 199, 205, 207, 235-236
Cockatoo, The (club), 71
Coda, 144
Cohen, Paulie, 104
Cohn, Al, 89, 192
Cohn, Sonny, 72
Coker, Henry, 94
Colax, King, 94
Cole, Nat King, 14, 75, 79, 83
Coleman, Ira, 180
Coleman, Kenny, 79
Coleman, Ornette, 190, 221, 226, 229-230
Collins, John, 79
Collins, Judy, 192
Coltrane, John, 21, 86, 97, 143, 151, 161, 179, 190, 230

Condon, Eddie, 7, 28, 59, 87
Confrey, Zez, 199
Connick, Harry, Jr., 190
"Constantly," 87
Continental Club, 105
Cootie Williams Band, 149-150
Corea, Chick, 190
Cotton Club, 42, 52
Cotton Club, The, 86
Count Basie Band, 38, 66, 72-80, 81, 85, 86, 88, 89, 90, 91, 92-93, 94, 97, 98, 99, 106, 107, 207
Countsmen, 81
Coward, Noel, 184, 185
Cox, Ida, 8
Crease, Robert, 105, 106
Creole Serenaders, 88
Crosby, Bing, 55, 178
"Crossing, The," 169
Crystal Cavern, 145
Cummings, Henry S., 47
Curtis, King, 8

D

Dameronia, 98
Dance, Stanley, 5, 74, 89, 108, 113
Dandridge, Putney, 71, 135
Daniels, Dee, 44
Dantzler, Russ, 26, 76
Dash, Julian, 27
Davidson, Mickey, 105-106
Davis, Eddie "Lockjaw," 89, 226
Davis, Jimmy, 71
Davis, Miles, 59, 147, 155, 158-166, 167, 168, 181, 200, 204, 213, 221, 225, 236, 238
Davis, Sammy, Jr., 94, 164
Davis, Troy, 180
Davis, Walter, Jr., 221
Davison, Wild Bill, 7, 28, 29, 87
Day at the Races, A, 38
Daylie, Daddy-O, 90
"D.B. Blues," 87
De Koenigswarter, Baroness Pannonica, 144-145
de Vries, John, 54
"Deep River," 57
Desmond, Paul, 86
Devil's Got Your Tongue, 179
Dexter, Baby Jane, 179

Diane Schuur and the Count Basie Orchestra, 72
Dickenson, Vic, 28, 87, 132, 199
Digital Duke, 119
"Diminuendo and Crescendo in Blue," 115
Dingo, 164
Dixon, Eric, 72
Dixon, Ivan, 179
Dizzy Gillespie Big Band, 196, 197
D'Lugoff, Art, 4
Dodds, Baby, 236
Dodds, Johnny, 50
Dodgion, Jerry, 197
"Doggin' Around," 83
Domber, Mat, 83
Don Redman Band, 27
Donahue, Sam, 59
Donegan, Dorothy, 131
"Donna Lee," 147
"Don't Be a Baby, Baby," 56
"Don't Blame Me," 147
"Don't Explain," 70
"Don't Stop the Carnival," 231
Dorham, Kenny, 221
Dorsey, Jimmy, 86, 199, 212
Dorsey, Tommy, 14, 22, 57, 58, 102, 119, 192, 197, 199
"Down for the Count," 99
"Down South Camp Meetin'," 19
Downbeat Club, 27
"Dream of Life," 173
Drew, Kenny, 227
du Plessis, Andrea, 10
Duchin, Eddie, 102
Duke Ellington Band, 38, 49, 69, 100, 102, 106, 110, 112, 116, 121, 122
"Duke of Iron," 231
Dukes of Dixieland, 62
Durham, Eddie, 78, 79, 80
Dylan, Bob, 101

E
Earl Hines' Band, 177, 178
"Early Autumn," 212
Easely, Bill, 197
"East of the Sun," 231
Eckstine, Billy, 145, 147, 161, 177-178
Eddie Condon's Club, 7, 8, 48, 87

Edegran, Lars, 4, 14
Edison, Harry "Sweets," 65, 77, 78, 79-80, 88, 91, 147, 236
Eldridge, Joe, 8, 133
Eldridge, Roy, 3, 14, 28, 93, 132, 133, 135, 137, 149, 150, 161, 213
Elite Seranaders, 133
Ella in Berlin, 34
Ellington, Duke, 5, 29, 38, 41, 42, 49, 63, 83, 99, 106, 108-109, 112, 115, 117, 118, 119, 124, 125, 145, 185, 186, 194, 197, 208, 219, 238
Ellington, Mercer, 99, 110, 121-123, 125, 173, 177
Elman, Ziggy, 57, 58
Embers (club), 53, 55
"Embraceable You," 147, 229, 231
"Epistrophy," 150
Erskine Hawkins Band, 27
Erwin, Pee Wee, 58
Esquire Silver Award, 58
Eureka Brass Band, 128
Evans, Bill, 212
Evans, Gil, 42, 147, 161, 238, 239
Evans, Herschel, 20, 65, 77, 81, 89, 98
Evans, "Stump," 20
"Evening with Friends of Charlie Parker," 140
"Every Day I Have the Blues," 90, 91
"Every Tub," 79
"Everybody's Boppin'," 183
"Extended Blues," 89

F
Fab 5 Freddy, 155
Fabulous Dorseys, The, 86
Faddis, Jon, 217
Faith, Percy, 7
"Family Tree Singers," 225
Famous Door (club), 55
Farlow, Tal, 156-157
Farmer, Art, 230
Fat Tuesday's (club), 41, 132, 180
Feather, Leonard, 47, 212, 223, 229, 230
Feather, Lorraine, 223
Fennimore, Linda, 75
Ferguson, Maynard, 59, 127, 192

Ferguson, Otis, 101
"Fine and Mellow," 67
Fitzgerald, Ella, 31-36, 38, 48, 61, 67, 71, 99, 118, 171, 173, 176, 181, 187, 200
Five Spot (club), 230
Flack, Roberta, 217
Flamingo Lounge, 224
Flanagan, Tommy, 140, 145, 200-202, 217, 223
Fletcher Henderson Band, 20, 21, 22, 27, 110, 112
"Fly Right," 150
"Flying Home," 45, 107, 135
Flying Neutrinos Band, 10
"For All We Know," 171
For the Love of Ivy, 179
"For You," 56
Forrest, Helen, 59
Fortune Garden Pavilion, 200
Forty Second Street, 86
Foster, Frank, 91, 93, 98-99, 100
"Four or Five Times," 57
'Four' and More, 161
Francis, Panama, 10, 83, 106, 133, 164
Franklin, Aretha, 101
Frederickson, Bruce, 196
Free Jazz, 221, 226, 227, 229-230
Freeman, Bud, 20, 199
"Freeway Express," 229
Fresh Air Taxi, 4
Friedwald, Will, 11
Fuller, Curtis, 221
Further Definitions, 22

G
Gale, Moe, 89
Gant, Willie, 5
Garrett, Kenny, 158, 219
Garrison, Jimmy, 230
Gavin, James, 214
"Gee Baby, Ain't I Good to You," 29
Gensel, Pastor John Garcia, 39-46
George Wein's All Stars, 87, 199
"Georgia on My Mind," 44
Gershwin, George, 71
Gershwins, The, 33
Getz, Stan, 11, 89, 168, 210-212
Gibbs, Terry, 58, 207
Gibson, Rob, 10

Gigliotti, Charlie, 93
Gillespie, Dizzy, 3, 14, 24, 33, 37, 52, 59, 88, 115, 133-155, 161, 178, 180, 192, 196-197, 199, 213, 215-218, 222, 223, 238
"Gimme a Pigfoot," 184
Giordano, Vince, 85
Gitler, Ira, 137, 143, 193
Glaser, Joe, 4
Glasser, David, 107
Golden Broom and the Green Apple, 119
"Golden Men of Jazz," 41
Goldkette, Jean, 18, 78
Golson, Benny, 46, 140, 183
Gonsalves, Paul, 113, 115
Good Morning Blues, 63
"Good Time Blues," 72
Goodman, Benny, 10, 15-17, 18, 22, 39, 48, 55, 57, 58, 85, 89, 98, 99, 101, 102, 110, 116, 119, 131, 132, 149, 156, 192, 197, 199, 207, 212, 238
Gordon, Dexter, 221
Gordon, Lorraine, 4, 143, 203-205
Gordon, Max, 143, 203-205
Grant, Darrell, 180
Granz, Norman, 33
Grappelli, Stephane, 76
Gray, Wardell, 147
Grayson, Milt, 183
Great Day in Harlem, A, 222-223
Green, Bennie, 138
Green, Charlie, 18, 27
Green, Freddie, 70, 72, 73, 76, 78, 80, 207
Green, Urbie, 199
Greer, Sonny, 119
Grey, Al, 41, 44, 83, 94, 140, 183
Griffin, Johnny, 226-227
"Groovin' High," 137
Grover Mitchell's Big Band, 140
"Guess Who's in Town," 186
Guys and Dolls, 28, 132

H
Hackett, Bobby, 87, 127
Haggart, Bob, 28, 87
"Hail, Hail, The Gang's All Here," 61
Haines, Connie, 54

Hall, Adelaide, 186
Hall, Edmund, 28, 150, 199
"Hallelujah," 33
Hallelujah, 70
Hamilton, Scott, 97, 192
Hammond, John, 101-102, 185
"Hamp's Boogie Woogie," 45
Hampton, Lionel, 19, 24, 39-46, 53, 88, 90, 94, 107, 180, 195, 226
Hampton, Slide, 217
Hancock, Herbie, 161
Hannah and Her Sisters, 186
"Happy Birthday," 46
Hardiman, Rebecca, 99
Hargrove, Roy, 182, 227
Harlem Blues and Jazz Band, 14, 62, 71
Harlem Opera House, 31
Harlem Suite, 123
Harmony Illustrated Encyclopedia of Jazz, 230
Harris, Barry, 145
Harris, Sharon, 99
Harrison, Jimmy, 18, 27
Harry Edison Quintet, 147
Harry James Band, 119
Hart, Clyde, 143
"Have Mercy," 34
Hawkins, Coleman, 18, 20-21, 22, 27, 29, 42, 59, 61, 66, 90, 93, 113, 135, 150, 155, 200, 232, 238
Hawkins, Erskine, 27
Hayes, Thamon, 78
Heath, Jimmy, 140
Hefti, Neal, 91, 98
Hello Dolly, 29
Hellzapoppin, 37
Henderson, Fletcher, 17-22, 24, 27, 29, 53, 57, 61, 66, 78, 101, 110, 112, 185
Henderson, Horace, 14, 29, 133
Hendricks, Jon, 33, 43, 183, 235
Hendrix, Jimi, 86
Henley, Clarrie, 7
Hentoff, Nat, 104, 166
"Here Comes Cookie," 135
"Here Comes the Man With the Jive," 51
Herman, Woody, 192, 197, 238

Herzog, Arthur, 70
Heywood, Eddie, 87, 204
"HFO," 89
Hicks, John, 221
Higginbotham, J.C., 27
"Highlights in Jazz," 185
Hill, Teddy, 137
Hines, Earl, 147, 177, 178
Hinton, Milt, 3, 46
Hinton, Mint, 83
Hinton, Mona, 46
Hite, Les, 61
Hodges, Johnny, 22, 27, 98-99, 100, 112, 113, 119, 122
Holder, T., 75
Holiday, Billie, 10, 43, 53, 55, 66, 67-70, 80, 89, 101, 135, 149, 171, 173, 176
"Honeysuckle Rose," 75
Hopkins, Claude, 29, 87, 133
Horne, Lena, 192
Hot Club of Newark, 205
"Hot Time in the Town of Berlin, A," 54
"House I Live In, The," 41
Hubbard, Freddie, 221, 229, 238
"Hucklebuck, The," 58
Hughes, Bill, 92
Humes, Helen, 187
Humphrey, Percy, 128-130
Humphrey, Willie, 128-130
"Hurry on Down to My House," 26
Hyman, Dick, 198-199

I
"I'm an Old Cowhand," 232
"I'm Be Boppin' Too," 137
"I'm Gonna Move to the Outskirts of Town," 178
"I Ain't Gonna Give Nobody None o' this Jelly Roll," 29
"I Can't Give You Anything but Love," 26, 35
"I Don't Want to Walk Without You," 52
"I Got it Bad and That Ain't Good," 117
"If Dreams Come True," 29, 71
"If My Friends Could See Me Now," 53
Illinois Jacquet Big Band, 62, 79

"I'm Up a Tree," 34
"I Hear Music," 135
Illinois Jacquet's Band, 62, 79, 83, 88
"In My Solitude," 117
"In a Sentimental Mood," 116
In a Silent Way, 161
Indigo Blues (club), 158, 209
"I'se a Muggin'," 51
"It Could Happen to You," 232
"It's Sand, Man," 78
"I've Got the World on a String," 9-10

J
"Jackass Blues," 27
Jackson, Milt, 93, 140, 200
Jacobs, Phoebe, 99, 122
Jacquet, Illinois, 62, 79, 83, 88, 107
Jamaica, 28
James, Harry, 96, 119
Jarvis, Jane, 44, 83, 223
Jay McShann's Band, 89, 139
Jazz Archives Records, 76
"Jazz at the Philharmonic," 150
Jazz Titans, The, 20
Jefferson, Hilton, 113
"Jelly, Jelly," 178
Jeske, Lee, 103
Jimmie Lunceford Band, 27, 56
Jimmy Ryan's Club, 29
Jimmy Walker's (club), 48
Jimmy Weston's Club, 53
"Jive at Five," 79
"Joe Franklin Show," 3
"Joe Temperley's Town," 104
John Coltrane's Quartet, 230
John Kirby Sextet, 58
"John's Idea," 102
Johnsen, John, 5
Johnson, Archie, 133-134
Johnson, Charlie, 22, 27
Johnson, James P., 5, 113, 186
Johnson, J.J., 179, 200
Jolson, Al, 184, 232
"Jonah Joins the Cab," 53
Jonah Jones Quintet, 59
Jones, Eddie, 78, 92-93
Jones, Elvin, 200
Jones, Hank, 44, 131, 190, 200

Jones, Jo, 11, 73-74, 78, 139
Jones, Jonah, 26, 51, 53
Jones, Quincy, 45, 100
Jones, Spike, 118
Jones, Thad, 93, 200, 207
Joplin, Scott, 199
Jordan, Duke, 167-168, 169
Jordan, Louis, 54, 155, 178
Jordan, Sheila, 169-170
Jordan, Taft, 29, 31
"Jordu," 168
"Joshua," 51
"Juggernaut," 97
"Jumpin' at the Woodside," 65, 83
"Jumpin' Punkins," 122
"Just Friends," 204
JVC Jazz Festival, 7, 10, 83

K
Katz, Richard Aaron, 11
Keepnews, Peter, 151
Kellaway, Roger, 199
Kellin, Orange, 4, 14
Kelly's Stable (club), 24
Kenny Clarke-Francy Boland Big Band, 227
Kenton, Stan, 96, 207, 212
Keppard, Freddie, 128
Kern, Jerome, 184
"Kerouac," 150
Kerr, Brooks, 89
Kersey, Kenny, 149-150
Keyes, Joe, 78
"Killing Time," 52
"Kind of Blue," 161
King, Wayne, 22, 102
"King Porter Stomp," 17, 18-19, 137
Kirby, John, 14, 52, 71
Kirk, Andy, 13, 75, 90, 105, 112, 142, 150
Kirk, Rahsaan Roland, 8
Klein, Oscar, 194
Kleinsinger, Jack, 185
Knepper, Jimmy, 197, 204
Kool Jazz Festival, 71
Krupa, Gene, 59, 73, 135, 192

L
Ladnier, Tommy, 18

Lady Sings the Blues, 67, 68, 100
Lambert, Donald, 113
Lambert, Hendrick, and Ross, 33, 44
Larkins, Ellis, 187-188
"Laugh, Clown, Laugh," 184
Lawrence, Arnie, 199
Lawrence, Doug, 38, 104
Lawrence, Yank, 58
Lawson, Yank, 28, 87
Lee, Bill, 224-225
Lee, Cliff, 224-225
Lee, Peggy, 223
Lend an Ear, 28
Lenox Lounge, 94
Leonard, Harlan, 78
Leshin, Phil, 45
"Let Me Off Uptown," 135
"Let My People Go," 91
Letman, Johnny, 14
"Let's Dance," 19
Let's Get Lost, 213
Levinsky, Walt, 98
Levy, Lou, 58
Lewis, Big Ed, 77-78, 80
Lewis, John, 196-197
Lewis, Mel, 197, 204, 205, 206-207
Lewis, Ted, 28
Liasons Dangereuses, Les, 168
Lieber, Les, 26
Lincoln, Abbey, 179
Lincoln Center Jazz, 10, 41, 50, 55, 109, 197, 238-240
Lind, Pastor Dale, 42
Lindy Hop, 37, 106
Linton, Charles, 31, 33
Lion, Alfred, 205
Lionel Hampton Band, 88, 107
Lionel Hampton Jazz Festival, 43, 193, 223
Little, Booker, 155
"Little Bit Later On, A," 31
"Little Liza Jane," 129
Litwak, Bob, 46
Live at the Roosevelt Grill, 87
Live at the Village Vanguard, 204
Locke, Eddie, 135
Lombardo, Guy, 102, 194
Londigan, Tod, 10
Louis Armstrong: Rare Items, 127

Louis Armstrong's Hot Five, 55
Louisiana Bar and Grill, 76
"Lover Man," 71
Lucky Millinder's Band, 133
"Lullaby for Ben," 117
Lunceford, Jimmie, 27, 56, 57, 197
Lutcher, Nellie, 26

M

McClean, Jackie, 221
"Mack the Knife," 35
McKinney, Nina Mae, 70
McKinney's Cotton Pickers, 61
Mackrel, Dennis, 206-207
McPartland, Jimmy, 86, 147, 189-191
McPartland, Marian, 43, 55, 86, 189-191, 223
McRae, Carmen, 171-173, 181
McShann, Jay, 75, 76, 78, 89, 139
Maher, James T., 99
Malachi, John, 145
Mallory, Eddie, 133
"Man I Love, The," 161
Man Called Adam, A, 94
Mance, Junior, 41, 46
Mangione, Chuck, 217
Manhattan Jazz, 198
Manning, Frankie, 37-38, 105-106
"Manteca," 151
Many Faces of Lady Day, The, 223
Marable, Fate, 88, 128, 131
"Marie," 58, 59
Marion, Percy, 115
Marsalis, Branford, 50, 221, 231, 238
Marsalis, Jason, 236
Marsalis, Wynton, 10, 41, 80, 127, 161, 166, 181-182, 217, 218, 221, 235-236, 237-240
Martin, Bobby, 71
May, Billy, 100
May, Earl, 26
"Me and Brother Bill Went Hunting," 127
Mel Lewis Jazz Orchestra, 204, 207
"Melancholy Baby," 190
Melody Maker, 142, 147
Mercer Ellington Orchestra, 173, 177

Merman, Ethel, 223
Metropolis (club), 25, 26, 94
Mezzrow, Mezz, 8
Michael's Pub, 41, 132
"Midgets, The," 98
Mikami, Kuni, 46
Mikell's (club), 219
Miles, The Autobiography, 160
Miley, Bubber, 110
Miller, Big, 117
Miller, Glenn, 48, 102
Miller, Laura, 105-106
Miller, Linda, 44
Miller, Mulgrew, 221
Miller, Norma, 37-38
Miller, Punch, 14
Millinder, Lucky, 14, 133
Mills, Florence, 186
Mingus, Charles, 204, 205
Minton's Playhouse (club), 142, 150, 155, 173
"Misunderstood Blues," 99
Mitchell, Grover, 100, 140
Mixed Bag, 50
Modern Jazz Quartet, 196
Mole, Miff, 27
Monk, Thelonious, 8, 42, 137, 141, 142-143, 144, 150, 151, 155, 179, 192, 226
Monroe, Clark, 70
Monroe, Jimmy, 69-70
Monroe's Uptown House, 70, 155, 161
"Moon Mist," 122
"Moonglow," 61, 62
Morgan, Lee, 221
Morris, Joe, 226
Morton, Benny, 18, 27-28, 68
Morton, Jelly Roll, 27, 199, 238, 239, 240
Moten, Bennie, 61, 63, 77, 77-78, 112
"Moten Swing," 61
"Mr. Tim," 225
Mugge, Robert, 232
Mulligan, Gerry, 48, 85, 207, 212, 213
Muranyi, Joe, 127
Mussolini, Romano, 193-195
"My Father's Island," 123
My Funny Valentine, 161

"My Romance," 124
Myers, Amina Claudine, 221

N

Nancie Banks' Jazz Orchestra, 140
Nanton, Tricky Sam, 27
Nat Towle's Band, 89
Navarro, Fats, 221
Nelson, Oliver, 100
New Orleans Jazz and Heritage Festival, 95
New World a Comin', 123
New York Jazz Quartet, 98
New York Jazz Repertory Company, 88
New York Swing Dance Society, 37, 105
Newman, Dwight, 88
Newman, Joe, 78, 88, 93, 104, 165
Newport All-Stars, 93, 116, 132
Newport Jazz Festival, 115, 161
Newton, Frankie, 71, 87
Nice Jazz Festival, 76
Nicholas, Big Nick, 151-152
Nichols, Red, 9, 78, 135
Nifty Cat, The, 135
Night in Havana, A: Dizzy Gillespie in Cuba, 216
"Night in Tunisia, A," 137
Noone, Jimmie, 90, 239
"Norma Miller Jazz Dancers," 38
Norvo, Red, 156, 185
Nothing But a Man, 179

O

O'Day, Anita, 34, 173, 176
"Oh! Look at Me Now," 54
Oliver, King, 9, 128, 238, 239, 240
Oliver, Sy, 28, 56-57, 133
"On a Clear Day," 176
"On the Street Where You Live," 53
"One I Love Belongs to Someone Else, The," 56
One Mo' Time, 4
"One O'Clock Jump," 65
Onyx Club, 51
"Oop Pop A Da," 137
"Opus One," 56
Orient Club, 147
Original Dixieland Jazz Band, 8
Osborne, Mary, 67

"O.T.Y.O.G.," 26, 231
"Out the Window," 81
Owens, Jimmy, 26, 217

P
Page, Hot Lips, 71
Page, Walter, 73
Palm Court (club), 130
Palmer, Robert, 151
Palomar Ballroom, 15, 19, 48
Panama Cafe, 14
Panico, Louis, 7
Paradise Club, 151
Parenti, Tony, 8
Parker, Charlie, 8, 10, 22, 24,
    33, 37, 86, 97, 137-161, 167,
    168, 170, 178, 192, 199, 200,
    213, 216, 223, 226, 232, 238
Parker, Doris, 140-141
"Passing Strangers," 177
"Passion Flower," 123
Patrick, James, 24
Payne, Cecil, 168
Payton, Nicholas, 9
Pearlman, Ingrid, 10
Peer, Beverly, 186
Peplowski, Ken, 80
"Perdido," 98
Peress, Maurice, 99
Persip, Charli, 26
Personal Best, 50
Peterson, Oscar, 89, 195, 223
Pettiford, Oscar, 137, 145, 147
Pettis, Jack, 20
Philharmonic Hall, 58, 119, 150
"Piano Jazz," 189, 190
"Picasso," 21
Pied Pipers, 54, 59
Pierce, Nat, 96-97
Pletcher, Stew, 71
Plugged Nickel Club, 161
Poitier, Sidney, 179
"Porgy and Bess," 53
Porgy and Bess, 161
Porter, Cole, 33, 184, 185
"Portrait of the Duke," 5
"Portrait of the Lion," 5
Potter, Tommy, 145, 147-148
Powell, Benny, 26, 94-95
Powell, Bud, 141, 147, 155, 192,
    200, 227

Powell, Mel, 48, 199
Pozo, Chano, 216
"Prelude to a Kiss," 123
Preservation Hall, 129-130
Presley, Elvis, 19, 89
Pretty Wild, 7
Previn, Andre, 230
Price, Sammy, 8, 89
"Prince of Wails," 61
Procope, Russell, 116
Puente, Tito, 46

Q
Quebec, Ike, 8
Queenie Pie, 121, 123
"Queen's Suite, The," 108
Quinichette, Paul, 89, 212

R
Radio City Music Hall
    Orchestra, 28
"Rain," 57
Rainbow Room (club), 57
Rainey, Ma, 9
"Ramblin'," 190
Ramirez, Ram, 71
Ray, Alvino, 206
Razaf, Andy, 186
Red Blazer Too (club), 48
"Red Planet," 190
Redman, Don, 18, 22, 27, 61
Reed Sisters, 182
Reeves, Dianne, 179
Reisner, Robert, 21
Reitz, Rebecca, 37
Rena, Kid, 128
"Rhapsody in Blue," 71
Rich, Buddy, 42, 57, 85, 102,
    119, 150, 192
Richards, Red, 26, 87
Richardson, Rodney, 92-93
Richman, Harry, 184
Riley, Ben, 145
Riley, John, 207
Ringling Brothers and Barnum
    & Bailey Circus, 62
Ritz, The, 99
Roach, Max, 46, 137, 140, 141,
    153-155
Roberts, Caughey, 78
Robinson, Jackie, 41

Robinson, Price, 20
Robinson, Prince, 11
"Rockabye Your Baby With a
    Dixie Melody," 233
"Rocky Comfort," 29
Rogers, Ginger, 186
Rollins, Sonny, 21, 147, 204,
    231-233
Roney, Wallace, 182, 221
"Rose Room," 53
Roseland Ballroom, 27
"Roseland Shuffle," 75-76
Ross, Annie, 33, 140
"'Round Midnight," 143, 161
Rouse, Charlie, 144-145
"Royal Garden Blues," 230
Royal Roost, 141
Royall, Marshall, 86
Rushing, Jimmy, 8
Russell, Luis, 185
Russell, Pee Wee, 199

S
"Saddest Tale, The," 194
"St. James Infirmary," 88
St. Louis Woman, 28
"Saints and Sinners," 87
Sales, Grover, 143
Sales, Soupy, 223
"Salt Peanuts," 137
Sanborn, David, 62
Sandke, Randy, 15
*Sassy, The Life of Sarah
    Vaughan*, 176
"Satin Doll," 117
Saunders, Red, 90
Savoy Ballroom, 29, 31, 33,
    37, 105, 106, 110, 194
Saxophone Colossus, 232
Schapp, Phil, 9-13, 83, 135
Schuller, Gunther, 20
Scott, Raymond, 110
Scott Hamilton Quintet, 192
Scragg, Nigel, 204
"Segue in C," 98
"Send in the Clowns," 176
"Sent for You Yesterday," 79
Seventeen Messengers, 221
"Shake, Rattle, and Roll," 91
"Shall We Dance," 186
Shank, Bud, 86

Shapko, Dmitry, 26

Shavers, Charlie, 14, 28, 58-59, 150

Shaw, Artie, 15, 18, 49-50, 68, 106, 147, 156, 199, 239

Shaw, Arvell, 131-132

Shaw, Woody, 221

Shearing, George, 195

"Sheila's Blues," 169

Shepp, Archie, 155

Sherman, Jimmy, 71

Sherock, Shorty, 223

"She's a Latin From Manhattan," 184

Shinbone Alley, 28

"Shiny Stockings," 37, 99

Shore, Dinah, 118

Short, Bobby, 184-186

Shorter, Wayne, 161, 219

Silk Stockings, 28

Silverman, Stephen, 4

Simon, Bill, 48

Simon, George T., 47-48, 71, 78, 101, 143, 188

Simon, Rogers, 83

Simon Says: the Sights and Sounds of the Swing Era, 48

Sims, Zoot, 89, 192

Sinatra, Frank, 41, 54, 59, 67, 178, 192, 223

"Since My Best Girl Turned Me Down," 57

"Sing Me a Sweet Song," 33

"Singin' the Blues," 189

Sketches of Spain, 161

Skinner, Dr. Lynn, 43, 45

"Skylark," 178

Slack, Freddie, 14

Smith, Bessie, 43, 67, 80, 184

Smith, Jabbo, 3-4, 9, 14, 205, 236

Smith, Joe, 18, 78

Smith, Russell "Pops," 112

Smith, Stuff, 51-52, 53

Smith, Trixie, 8

Smith, Willie "The Lion," 5-6, 113, 119, 125

Smithsonian Jazz Orchestra, 109, 197

"Smoke Gets in Your Eyes," 52

"Someone to Watch Over Me," 176

"Song of India," 58

Sophisticated Ladies, 121

"Sophisticated Lady," 123

"Sound of Jazz, The," 67

Speed Webb's Band, 133

Sphere, 145

Springsteen, Bruce, 101

Stafford, Gregg, 130

"Star Dust," 44, 49, 150

"Star Eyes," 225

"Statesmen of Jazz," 83

Staton, Dakota, 100

Stewart, Rex, 18, 21, 29, 71

Stitt, Sonny, 168

"Stompin' at the Savoy," 29, 34

"Stormy Monday Blues," 178

Story of Jazz, The, 223

Strayhorn, Billy, 122

Streisand, Barbra, 204

"Struttin' With Some Barbecue," 9, 53, 127

"Stuff Smith and his Onyx Club Boys," 51

Sullieman, Idries, 142-143

Sullivan, Joe, 27

Sullivan, Maxine, 31, 42, 51-52, 132, 187

"Summertime," 225

"Sunny Side of the Street," 45

Swartz, Harvie, 169

Sweet Basil, 9

Sweet Swing Blues on the Road, 236

"Swing, Brother, Swing," 69

Swing Era, The, 20

Swing Goes Dixie, 135

"Swing Legacy," 99

Swing to Bop, 137, 143

Swingin' Dream, A, 104

"Swinging at the Daisy Chain," 76

Sylvia's, 153

T

Tabackin, Lew, 208

"Tain't Nobody's Bizness," 35

"Tain't What You Do," 33

Talmadge Farlow, 156

Tate, Buddy, 78, 81-84, 86, 89, 131, 147

Tatum, Art, 113, 185, 200

Tavern on the Green, 41, 55, 79, 107, 189

Taylor, Art, 227

Taylor, Arthur, 140

Taylor, Cecil, 155, 190, 200

Teagarden, Jack, 27, 191, 212, 238, 239

Temperley, Joe, 10, 104

"Tennessee Waltz, The," 231

Terry, Clark, 3, 14, 46, 124-125, 131, 183, 217

Texas Blusicians, 8

Thad Jones-Mel Lewis Orchestra, 207

Tharpe, Sister Rosetta, 8

"That's-a-Plenty," 7

"Them There Eyes," 26

"There Will Never Be Another You," 225

"These Foolish Things," 50

"Things Ain't What They Used to Be," 122

Thompson, Sir Charles, 72

Threadgill, Henry, 236

Three Black Kings, 121

"Three Little Words," 26, 231

Titone, Bill, 45

Tizol, Juan, 119

"Toby," 61

Together — Maxine Sullivan Sings the Music of Jule Styne, 52

Tommy Dorsey Band, 54, 55, 56, 57, 59

Tommy Dorsey's Clambake Seven, 56

Tony Awards, 37

"Toot Toot Tootsie, Goodbye," 232

Tormé, Mel, 41, 50

Toshiko Akiyoshi's New York Jazz Orchestra, 209

Toussaint, Jean, 221

Towles, Nat, 89

Trent, Alphonso, 8

Tribute to Jack Johnson, A, 164

Triola, Lenny, 55

Troup, Stuart, 103

Trumbauer, Frankie, 22, 212

Turentine, Stanley, 100

Turney, Norris, 10, 86, 113

Twilight Jazz Band, 48

"Twilight World," 189

"Two Franks, The," 98

Tyner, McCoy, 11

U

Ulanov, Barry, 47
"Undecided," 58
University of Idaho Jazz Festival, 43

V

Vaché, Warren, 97
Van Der Zee, James, 38
Vanguard Jazz Orchestra, 207
Vaughan, Sarah, 99, 173, 174-176, 177, 178, 181
Village Gate, 4
Village Vanguard, 4, 117, 143, 145, 200, 203-205, 207, 236
Visiones (club), 169
Voices of the Jazz Age, 191

W

Walker, T-Bone, 71
Waller, Fats, 5, 26, 55, 97, 113, 185, 192
Walton, Cedar, 221
Warren, Earle, 77, 78, 80, 81-84, 85-86
Washington, Peter, 221
Waterloo Village, 15
Waters, Benny, 25-26, 83
Waters, Ethel, 28
Watrous, Bill, 216
Watrous, Peter, 125
Watson, Bobby, 106, 221
We Insist! Freedom Now!, 155
Webb, Chick, 27, 29, 31, 186
Webster, Ben, 5, 20, 93, 112-114, 115, 116, 117, 122, 226, 230
Wein, George, 87, 93, 116, 147, 182, 186, 199
Welk, Lawrence, 118
"Well, Git It," 57, 58

"Well You Needn't," 143
Wells, Dickie, 27
Wells, Dicky, 77
Wendt, Eric, 44
Wess, Frank, 86, 89, 92, 93, 98-99, 104
West, Mae, 57
Weston, Randy, 94, 179
Whaley, Tom, 108
"What Can I Say After I Say I'm Sorry?" 9
Wheatstraw, Peetie, 8
"When Cootie Left the Duke," 110
"When Lights Are Low," 189
"When Love Beckoned on 52nd Street," 186
When There is Love, 179
White, Freddie, 27
White, Herbert "Whitey," 37, 38
"White Christmas," 141
Whiteman, Paul, 78
Whitey's Lindy Hoppers, 37
"Who She Do," 91
Whyte, Zach, 61, 133
Wicks, Virginia, 223
Wiedoeft, Rudy, 61
Wilder, Joe, 83
Wilkins, Ernie, 91, 98, 125
Willard Alexander Agency, 102
William Morris Agency, 102
Williams, Bert, 186
Williams, Buster, 145
Williams, Clarence, 99
Williams, Claude "Fiddler," 75-76, 83
Williams, Cootie, 14, 110, 112, 113, 149-150
Williams, Fess, 27
Williams, J. Mayo, 8
Williams, James, 221

Williams, Joe, 90-91, 93, 187
Williams, John, Jr., 21
Williams, Mary Lou, 142, 190
Williams, Sandy, 27, 29-30, 31, 72
Williams, Tim, 220-221
Williams, Tony, 161
"Willow Weep for Me," 71
Wilson, Cassandra, 34
Wilson, Chuck, 85-86, 104
Wilson, Gerald, 125
Wilson, John S., 27, 71, 103, 151, 167-168
Wilson, Teddy, 19, 27, 39, 53, 67-68, 101, 131, 132, 192, 199, 200
Wolverines, The, 7
"Woman," 123
Wooding, Sam, 5, 9
Woodman, Brit, 197
Woodman, Britt, 108
Woodward, Aaron, 63
Woody Herman's Herds, 96, 212
World's Greatest Jazz Band, 28, 87
"Wrappin' It Up," 19
Wright, Gordon, 47
Wynters, Gail, 46

Y

Yaged, Sol, 150
Yellow Front Cafe, 8
"Yes, Indeed," 57
You Gotta Pay the Band, 179
Young, Lester, 8, 11, 20, 21, 65-70, 77, 80, 83, 87, 89, 98, 113, 150, 212, 226
Young, Snooky, 93
"You'se a Viper," 51